WineTrails OF WALLA WALLA

A guide for uncorking your memorable wine tour

Happy WineTrails!
Steve Roberts

BY STEVE ROBERTS.

WineTrails NW

WineTrails of Walla Walla

Published by
South Slope Productions
9311 SE 36th St., Suite 108, Mercer Island, WA 98040

Readers should also be aware that maps and directions as well as other tasting room details (e.g., hours of operation and tasting fees) may have changed since this book was printed. Readers are advised to contact the winery in advance to verify the information. Remember to drink responsibly, drive responsibly.

Note that no wineries, restaurants, hotels, motels, inns or transportation companies paid to be included in this book.

Library of Congress Cataloging-in-Publication Data available.

Original WineTrails Northwest logo by Beth Hayes, King Salmon Creative Designs; modified by Lisa J. Pettit, Lisa Pettit Designs

Edited by Sunny Parsons

Unless otherwise indicated, photos by Steve Roberts.

Contributing photographers: Alan Ayers, Sean Parsons, Kevin Ayers and Kathleen Roberts.

Cover and interior design by Lisa J. Pettit, Lisa Pettit Designs

Restaurant descriptions provided by Faye Tomlinson

Production by Seattle Publishing, Inc.

First Edition

ISBN 978-0-9792698-4-4

Printed in China by C&C Offset Printing Co. Ltd.

Acknowledgements & Dedication

Sometimes it takes a village to accomplish a task, but in the case of this guidebook, it took the collective soul of Walla Walla. In particular, I am indebted to the passionate workers associated with Walla Walla's wine industry, who have succeeded in making the area a new international wine destination. They poured more than wine; they poured a rich story infused with rural splendor. *WineTrails of Walla Walla* also benefits from the insights and care provided by a legion of gracious hosts at restaurants, hotels, and inns. All of these people welcomed us and showed us that small-town friendliness and charm still exist.

For the design of the book, from the outside cover to inside layout, I am forever grateful to the artistic talents of Lisa J. Pettit of Lisa Pettit Designs. It takes only a quick glance at this book's cover to appreciate her gift of storytelling through color, detail, and masterful art. She's amazing. Of equal importance is Sunny Parsons' editorial work. I really don't know how she does it, but I imagine her at a young age in grade school, grasping the split infinitive while the other kids were sounding out their choices on the school menu. The actual production of this book is the work of a very gifted team of professionals at Seattle Publishing. As with the other books in the WineTrails series, they have a singular focus during production to get it right. And speaking of getting it right, accuracy is vital for any guidebook, and I thank my assistant, Sarah Born, for the many hours she spent calling restaurants, country inns, and hotels to verify the data presented within this book.

To reflect the culinary scene of the Walla Walla Valley, Faye Tomlinson, a food and wine lover (who also happens to have a degree in food science) visited, dined at, and ultimately got to the essence of 11 fabulous Walla Walla-area restaurants. Her contributions to the book highlight an emerging cuisine relying on fresh local ingredients, sustainable agriculture, and a fusion of foods from around the world. To complement this great food, Walla Walla also offers another nice component: ultrapremium wine.

Photographer and graphic artist Alan Ayers joined Faye to capture images of the select restaurants that appear in this book. Other pictures of wineries and Walla Walla landmarks photographed by Alan appear throughout *WineTrails of Walla Walla* and reflect his ability to go beyond the two-dimensional image to tell the story behind the story. He does it with a strong aesthetic sense of natural light and composition — and a steady hand.

My wife, Kathleen Roberts, was involved in every step of the project, including accompanying me on numerous trips to Walla Walla. Her thoughtful suggestions are evident throughout this book, from its title to its price. Without her loving support, the creation of this book would have been a very lonely endeavor indeed.

In closing, I wish to dedicate *WineTrails of Walla Walla* to my parents, Paul and Betty Roberts. My dad gave the best bear hugs, and my mom possessed the most infectious laugh. I think of them daily and wish that I could be their personal guide around Walla Walla. We'd have had a good time.

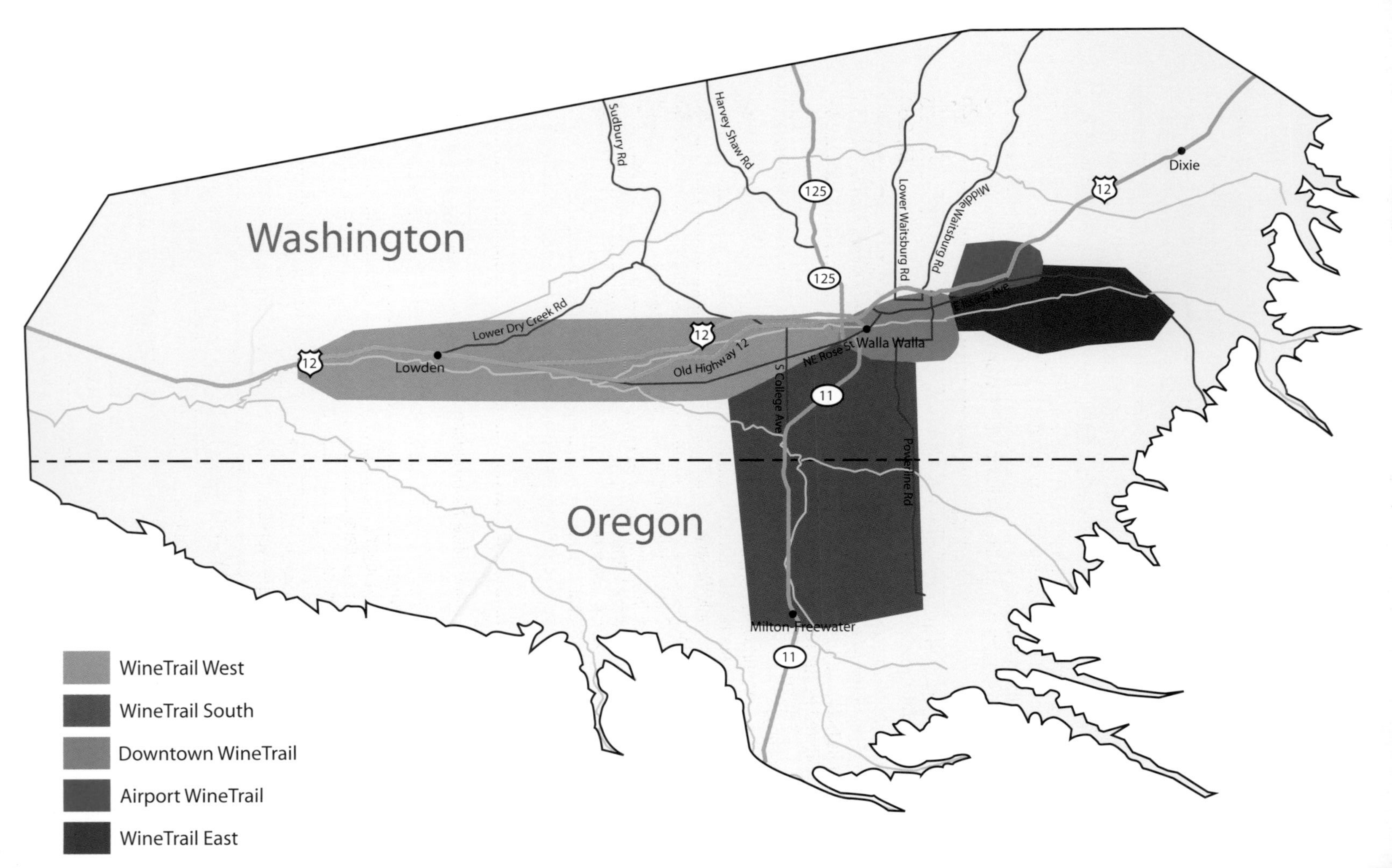
Washington
Oregon
Sudbury Rd
Harvey Shaw Rd
125
125
Lower Waitsburg Rd
Middle Waitsburg Rd
12
Dixie
Lower Dry Creek Rd
12
12
Lowden
Old Highway 12
NE Rose St
Walla Walla
S College Ave
11
Powerline Rd
Milton-Freewater
11
WineTrail West
WineTrail South
Downtown WineTrail
Airport WineTrail
WineTrail East

Table of Contents

Introduction

Practical Stuff – Planning Your Wine Tour Getaway

WineTrail West

Downtown WineTrail

Airport WineTrail

WineTrail East

WineTrail South

Tamarack Cellars

Voilà, Voilà! Walla Walla

So you're heading to Walla Walla, and it's been forever since you've been there — or perhaps you have never been. Get ready to have a good time! Despite the fact that I have been to Walla Walla numerous times, I'm a little jealous. I want to go! I want to go, because every time I visit this charming little city, I discover a part of its history that I never knew about, or an amazing restaurant, or a trail in the Blue Mountain foothills where I can soak in a view of the valley floor. Besides that, there are the wineries to sample. Ah yes, the wineries. Lots of them. More than 100 bonded wineries and growing.

In 2005, something amazing happened to this city, with its population of 32,000 (not all of which are winemakers). This heretofore rather sleepy burg in southeastern Washington took *Sunset* magazine's top honors for Wine Destination of the Year. Sure, wine lovers knew that Walla Walla was producing some amazing wines, from the likes of Leonetti Cellar, Cayuse Vineyards, Woodward Canyon Winery, and many others, but "Destination of the Year"? Criteria for receiving this award include the presence of luxury hotels, restaurants, tasting rooms, and what the magazine's editors feel is an exclusive winemaking experience. In other words, visitors to this fair city were seeking posh places to stay, topnotch cuisine, and a setting you simply won't find elsewhere.

One thing about Walla Wallans is that they know how to party. There seems to be a big event every month, and it doesn't matter what time of year it is. Whether sponsored by the chamber of commerce, the winery association, or one of the local colleges, event weekends fill the calendar. Visitors will stumble onto grape-stomping events, colorful hot-air balloons filling the sky, auctions for good causes, classic-car shows, and more. There is an event to satisfy nearly every passion. But plan ahead. Say you want to go to Walla

Walla the first weekend in May. The big "spring release" event may be taking place at that time, when wineries release their new vintages. Be sure to check the availability of accommodations before forging ahead. If you are thinking about a quiet retreat in December, you want to be sure that it's not planned for the weekend of the Holiday Barrel Tasting (always a crowd favorite). Be informed. Consult winetrailsnw.com for event information. And even if you're planning a visit for mid-March, it's still a good idea to book your hotel and restaurant reservations early.

Walla Walla Wine, Historically Speaking

When it comes to growing grapes and making wine, the Walla Walla Valley has a rich history. Early French fur trappers planted wine grapes in the area in the mid-1800s, and the Italian immigrants who followed them cultivated additional grape varieties. Along with wheat and sweet onions, the valley floor of yesteryear included acres of vines. However, a terrible cold snap in 1883 killed most of the grape vines and forced many grape growers to abandon their crops. In the early 1890s, the fledging wine industry was dealt another blow: The temperance movement eventually brought about the 18th amendment to the U.S. Constitution, which prohibited the manufacture and sale of alcohol beverages. From 1920 until the repeal of Prohibition (also known as the "Great Experiment") in 1933, America's wine industry essentially laid dormant (unless you count the wine for churches' communion services).

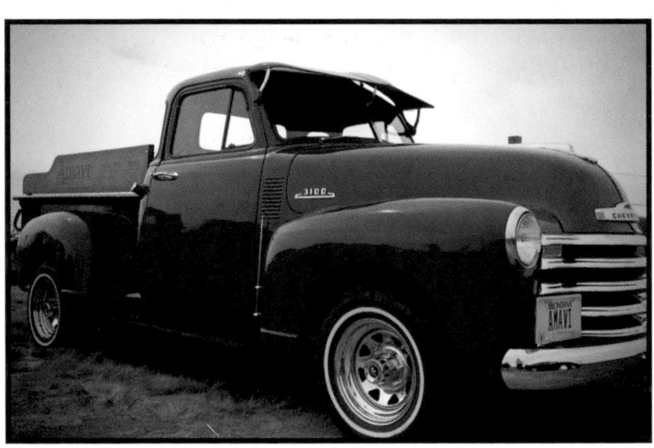

Amavi Cellars

But in 1977, a great thing happened in Walla Walla: Leonetti Cellar was born, and its first release, a cabernet sauvignon, created a cult following. The founders of Leonetti Cellar, Gary and Nancy Figgins, demonstrated to wine geeks everywhere that premium wine production could occur in southeast Washington. Today, Gary's son Chris Figgins also carries on the family tradition, with the continued nurturing of the family's winery through the Figgins Family Wine Estates.

After the success of Leonetti Cellar came the emergence of Woodward Canyon Winery in 1981 (thanks to Rick Small and Darcey Fugman-Small), and in 1983 the opening of the equally famous L'Ecole N° 41 (originally founded by Jean and Baker Ferguson, and now owned by their daughter and son-in-law, Megan and Martin Clubb). Other wineries followed soon thereafter. Fast-forward to 30 years later and now the valley abounds with more than 100 bonded wineries — and that number continues to grow.

Abeja

However, that is only part of the wine scene. In tandem with the emergence of the winemaking industry, the grape-growing industry grew as well. In 1984, the federal government designated the Walla Walla Valley basin (an area that covers parts of southeast Washington and spills into Oregon) as an American Viticultural Area, or AVA. Except for an occasional cold snap, the Walla Walla AVA, with its semi-arid climate, northern latitude (an extra two hours of sunlight during the summer relative to California), and loess soil, is ideal for growing *Vitis vinifera*.

However, in order to become a successful wine-tourist destination, two other important ingredients were needed: food and lodging. Walla Walla has filled those requirements, and not merely with the ubiquitous Red Roof Inn or McDonald's (although I recently paired a Big Mac with a Walla Walla merlot and I was lovin' it!). With more than a dozen exceptional restaurants relying extensively on local ingredients, along with numerous independent hotels, motels, bed-and-breakfasts, and quaint vineyard inns, Walla Walla has options aplenty for visitors.

Terroir is a French term generally defined as a combination of climate, soil type, topography, and viticultural practices that contribute to the unique taste profile of a region's wine, and Walla Walla's *terroir* is clearly working to its benefit. Geological events — some cataclysmic — have favorably shaped the topography of this valley, and the semi-arid climate creates the intense flavors of its grapes. However, the renowned wines of Walla Walla are more than the sum of their parts. They're a unique union of earth, vine, the elements, and human passion for the grape. You can taste the love.

How to Use This Guidebook

Winery touring is the focus of this book, that's true. However, your stay in Walla Walla also calls for lodging and eating choices (unless you are flying in and out, and just plan to hit the wineries and grab a burger on the run). Therefore, Chapter 2 of this guidebook, "Practical Stuff - Planning Your Walla Walla Getaway," profiles dozens of places throughout the Walla Walla Valley where you can stay or dine. What's more, threaded throughout the book are my favorite restaurant destinations sure to satisfy even the most world-weary culinary traveler. But at the heart of *WineTrails of Walla Walla* are the region's extraordinary wineries and their delectable wines. To that end, I have focused on the wineries that are open to the public, although this guide does include a section on wineries that accept visitors by appointment only.

Rulo Winery

It's in the tasting rooms of these public wineries that visitors can enjoy samples of wine and learn about the individual winery's wine varieties and style; gain insights into its owner's hopes and dreams; and get the answer to that elusive question on every visitor's mind, "How did the winery dog get its name?"

To make *WineTrails of Walla Walla* easy to digest, I divvied up the wineries into five distinct WineTrails:

1. **WineTrail West** — This trail includes those lovely wineries west of downtown along old Highway 12, including the historical wineries of Woodward Canyon Winery and L'Ecole Nº 41.

2. **Downtown WineTrail** — Twenty five tasting rooms await your palate's pleasure and, for most of it, you can ditch the family car in favor of your walking shoes.

3. **Airport WineTrail** — The old barracks of the World War II airport complex have been put to modern use as wineries. Such gems as Dunham Cellars, Tamarack Cellars, SYZYGY, and Five Star Cellars make this a mandatory stop.

4. **WineTrail East** — Situated near the airport complex are the fabulous wineries of College Cellars, K Vintners, Abeja, àMaurice Cellars, and Walla Walla Vintners. Please note: Abeja is open to the public, but only if you are a guest at the Abeja Inn or are on Abeja Winery's mailing list.

5. **WineTrail South** — Here are the elegant wineries of Walla Walla considered by many to be the heart and soul of appellation's terroir, with their great views of the Blue Mountain foothills provided at no extra charge.

Despite my pleas to the Walla Walla wine industry to stop evolving so quickly, it won't listen. Change occurs with great regularity: new wineries, new winemakers, new tasting room hours. A guidebook is only good if it is accurate, and the challenge that all guidebook publishers face is currency. However, I think I have come up with a neat solution. It's called the Internet, and I think it's here to stay. The WineTrails Northwest website provides current information about each winery in Walla Walla as well as other Northwest wineries. Simply go to winetrailsnw.com, do a search for the winery in question, and you'll have its most current information (at least as it has been provided to us).

The other piece of advice I must give is to call ahead to confirm that the wineries are open; also, you don't want to suffer the dreaded "sold out" phenomenon — good for the wineries, but disappointing for visitors. Please be aware that many tasting rooms are not open in the winter, and many are open only on the weekends. Plan ahead and call ahead is the best counsel I can give.

Ready, Set, Swirl!

It's a cardinal rule of mine to be flexible and open-minded, and I advise WineTrail trekkers to do the same. Don't rule out visiting a winery housed in a former army barracks, a winery featuring unusual varieties, or a winery that requires a few miles drive down a dusty road. Often, those places can be the most interesting and fun. If the tasting fee is a nominal amount, spring for it. You have traveled a great distance to get there, and the $5 tasting fee allows your taste buds to experience a full range of wines. Besides, the tasting fees are usually waived with the purchase of wine.

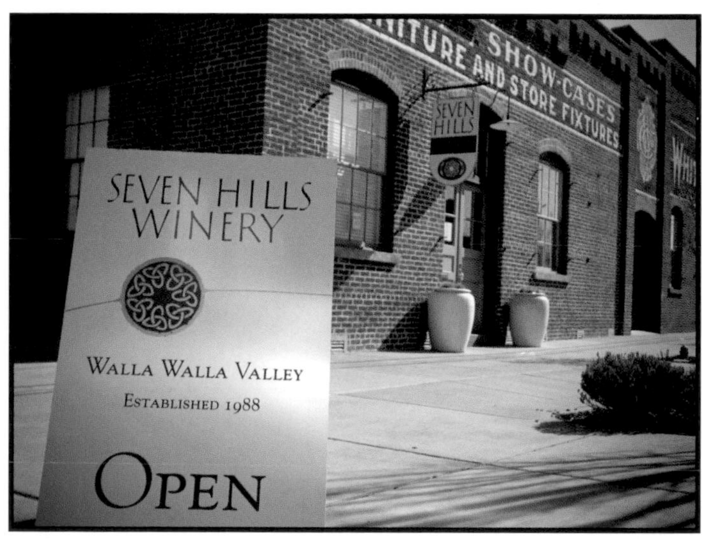

Be open to different styles of winemaking. There is no one right way to make wine, and over the course of a few thousand years, many winemaking styles have emerged. It is amazing how the same wine varietal can vary depending upon the winemaker's choice of oak barrels or how long the wine has aged. Again, jettison preconceived notions and allow yourself to experience something out of the ordinary. With just one sip, you may become a convert.

Besides the "call ahead" advice I've already given, my travels have reinforced four other key to-dos before venturing out on a wine tour:

1. Have cash on hand for tasting fees.

2. Keep a cooler in your vehicle to transport wine in hot weather.

3. Take drinking water.

4. Keep a local map or GPS device in your vehicle.

In **Appendix A — Touring and Tasting Tips**, I offer information for planning your wine tour, helpful hints for traveling with kids and pets, tips on bicycling in wine country, and advice for those who wish to get married at a winery. Phone numbers, along with website and email addresses, are given. Perhaps the most important advice I can give any winery tourist is to designate a driver before hitting the WineTrail, or at least go slow — those ounces add up. Know that it is fine to spit or dump after sampling. That's what those receptacles on top of the tasting-room bar are for. Drink responsibly. Drive responsibly.

Take along this guidebook and read aloud as you swirl and sip your way through wine country! It includes maps, driving directions, and tasting-room hours, with WineTrail tips sprinkled throughout. Oh, and make a point of asking the winemaker for his or her autograph. They get a big kick out of it and take great pleasure in signing their winery's page in this book.

Happy WineTrails!

Steve Roberts

Steve Roberts, the WineTrails Guy

Walla Faces Vineyard Inn

Practical Stuff — Planning Your Wine Tour Getaway

Travel Resources

WineTrails Northwest
Companion website to this guidebook; provides latest winery and event information
info@winetrailsnw.com
winetrailsnw.com

AAA
800-829-5448, aaa.com

Alaska Airlines — City Guides
800-ALASKAAIR (252-7522), alaskaair.com/Destinations

The Washington Lodging Association (WLA)
877-906-1001, stayinwashington.com

Tourism Walla Walla
877-WWVISIT (998-4748), wallawalla.org

Virtual Tourist
virtualtourist.com

Washington Wine Highway
washingtonwinehighway.com

Washington State Travel Counselor
800-544-1800, experiencewa.com

Washington Wine Commission
206-667-9463, washingtonwine.org

Wine Press Northwest — winery and event information
509-582-1564, winepressnw.com

Getting There

By Plane

Walla Walla Regional Airport
About 3 miles east of downtown Walla Walla, served by Horizon Air
509-522-3321 or 800-654-3131, wallawallaairport.com

Tri-Cities Airport (Pasco)
About a 50-minute drive southeast to Walla Walla, served by Delta, United Express, and Horizon Air
509-547-6352, portofpasco.org

By Car

From Seattle (about 4.75 hours):

- Take Interstate 90 East for about 110 miles.
- Take the I-82 East/U.S. 97 South exit.
- Follow Interstate 82 for approximately 100 miles.
- Take the I-182 East/U.S. 12 East exit.
- Follow Interstate 182 for approximately 10 miles.
- Interstate 182 becomes U.S. 12 East.
- Follow U.S. 12 East to Walla Walla.
- Take City Center Exit (N. Second Avenue).

From Portland (about 4.5 hours):

- Take Interstate 84 East for approximately 200 miles.
- Take Exit 210, the Oregon Route 11 (OR-11) exit toward Pendleton/ Milton-Freewater.

Getting There (Continued)

- Turn left onto Oregon-Washington Highway/OR 11.
- Turn right onto S.E. Court Ave./ OR-11/Oregon-Washington Highway/Pendleton Highway/ U.S. 30.
- Continue to follow OR-11/ Oregon-Washington Highway.
- OR-11 North becomes Washington State Route (S.R.) 125 North after approximately 33 miles.
- S.R. 125 North brings you into Walla Walla.
- S.R. 125 becomes Ninth Street.
- Turn right on Main Street toward Walla Walla city center.

From Spokane (about 3.5 hours):

- Take Interstate 90 West for approximately 60 miles.
- Take Exit 220 for U.S. Highway 395 toward Ritzville/ Pasco.
- Continue about 75 miles to U.S. Highway 12 East ramp to Walla Walla.
- Go 45 miles to City Center Exit (N. Second Avenue).

From Boise (about 4.15 hours):

- Take Interstate 84 West for approximately 215 miles.
- Take Exit 216 toward Walla Walla.
- Turn right off the exit ramp.
- Follow this road past Mission until you reach OR-11.
- Turn right on OR-11.
- OR-11 North becomes Washington State Route 125 North.
- S.R. 125 North brings you into Walla Walla.
- S.R. 125 becomes Ninth Street.
- Turn right on Main Street toward city center.

Car Rental

Budget
Walla Walla Regional Airport
45 Terminal Loop Road, Suite 5
509-525-8811 or 800-527-0700, budget.com

Enterprise Rent-a-Car
Off-site pick-up service only
629 W. Main St.
Walla Walla, WA 99362
509-529-1988 or 800-261-7331, enterprise.com

Hertz
Walla Walla Regional Airport
45 Terminal Loop Road, Suite 9
509-522-3321 or 800-654-3131, hertz.com

Tours and Limousine Service

4 Star Limos
509-521-7849, fourstarlimos.com

A+ Pacific Limousine Tours
509-585-7717, limo01.com/winetours.html

Black Tie Limousines
509-585-8585, blacktielimos.net

Sacco's Ultimate Vintage Wine Tours
509-783-7060, saccotours.com

Other Ground Transportation

Grape Line
Daily bus service between Walla Walla and Pasco
877-433-4775, grapeline.us

Taxis
ABC Taxi
509-529-7726

A-1 Taxi
509-529-2525

Road Conditions

For Washington
Go to wsdot.wa.gov/traffic or call 511 (inside Washington).

For Oregon
Go to tripcheck.com, or call 503-588-2941 (outside Oregon) or 800-977-6368 (inside Oregon).

For Idaho
Go to http://511.idaho.gov/ or call 888-432-7623 (outside Idaho) or dial 511 (inside Idaho).

Walla Walla Wine Events

Walla Walla rolls out the red carpet for several wine-related events each year. These are major events that have hotels filling up and restaurants scrambling to accommodate the masses. The bottom line is to book ahead. Also throughout the year, individual wineries host events, from winemaker dinners to live music. For information about those events, check out the event section at winetrailsnw.com. However, if you're partial to sampling this year's vintage from the barrel or carting away just released wines, the following are the key events to circle on your calendar.

Spring Release Weekend — First weekend in May
Here's your chance to purchase new vintage wines from Walla Walla wineries while enjoying culinary treats and admiring local artwork. Many wineries elect to sell these releases — freshly bottled and ready to be drunk (or cellared) — exclusively through their tasting rooms. With vines beginning to leaf out and winter's brown giving way to spring green, this is a favorite event for thousands of wine fans. Check out wallawallawine.com or winetrailsnw.com for event information.

Vintage Walla Walla — June
With proceeds benefiting Walla Walla Valley Wine Alliance and ArtWalla, Vintage Walla Walla is eagerly awaited by many a visitor, who look forward to tasting a variety of wines, visiting with winemakers, and giving to a good cause. But more than a chance to taste wines and bid on signed, large-format bottles of wine, this event is also an educational opportunity. In past years, Vintage Walla Walla has featured wine writer Paul Gregutt leading a panel discussion

with celebrated winemakers, or a winemaker discussing why a particular vintage turned out so special. A geologist might give a presentation about the soils of the valley, or perhaps you'll find yourself walking through a vineyard and learning about canopy management from a noted grape grower. Wine blends with education, art, and culture to create this special weekend. For event information, check out wallawallawine.com or winetrailsnw.com.

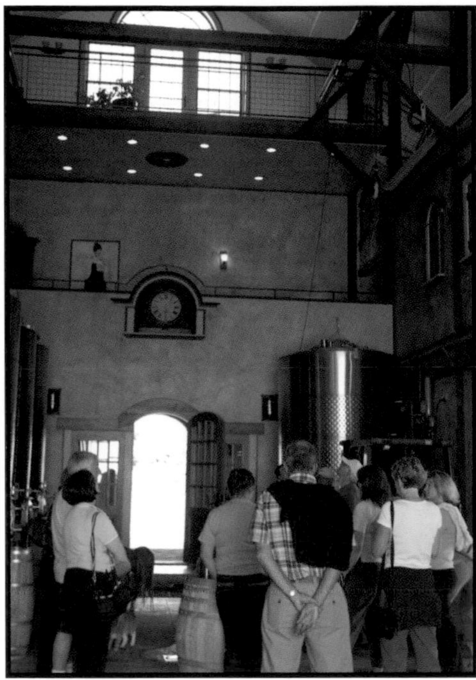

Abeja

Entwine — October

This is Walla Walla's annual signature benefit auction, hosted at the Marcus Whitman Hotel and Conference Center. Black tie is optional for this evening's dinner event, which benefits Walla Walla arts. Be sure to pack your Visa or American Express and prepare to experience more than 70 wineries, regional art, and tantalizing auction items, including some nicely packaged great escapes for the winning bidder. For tickets, call 509-527-4253.

Holiday Barrel Tasting — First weekend in December

Don't you agree that there's something special about tasting young wine right of the barrel? Well, that's just what the Holiday Barrel tasting event offers, and often with the winemaker doing the pouring honors. For this event, most valley wineries open their doors with freshly barreled wine to sample, and many offer discounts on wine purchases, along with delectable meats and cheese to nosh on while listening to live music. Come hungry and reserve plenty of space in your car's trunk to cart away some holiday treasures. For event information, go online to winetrailsnw.com or wallawallawines.com.

In addition to wine-related events, Walla Walla hosts a variety of other happenings throughout the year. In May, there's the annual Balloon Stampede weekend, which draws crowds to witness the spectacle of many brightly colored hot air balloons hovering over the valley (a very impressive sight). For car aficionados, early September brings the popular Wheelin' Walla Walla event, featuring hot rods and vintage vehicles. In mid-April, the Tour of Walla Walla bicycle race wheels in, attracting cycle fans from throughout the Northwest. For a snapshot of Walla Walla event times and places, see wwvchamber.com and click on the calendar icon.

Beyond the Tasting Room — 30 Things to Do in the Walla Walla Valley

Year around, Walla Walla offers a ton of things to do beyond its tasting rooms. Even the most ardent wine tourist needs a break now and then to clear the head and renew the spirit. Whether you are a history buff, an artsy type, a food lover, or just you want to get some exercise, "the biggest little city" offers a wide range of activities. I could easily fill up another guidebook with great things to do in Walla Walla, but for my money and time, I'd put the following 30 activities on my "must-do" list when visiting the valley.

Historic & Educational Sights

1. Fort Walla Walla Museum

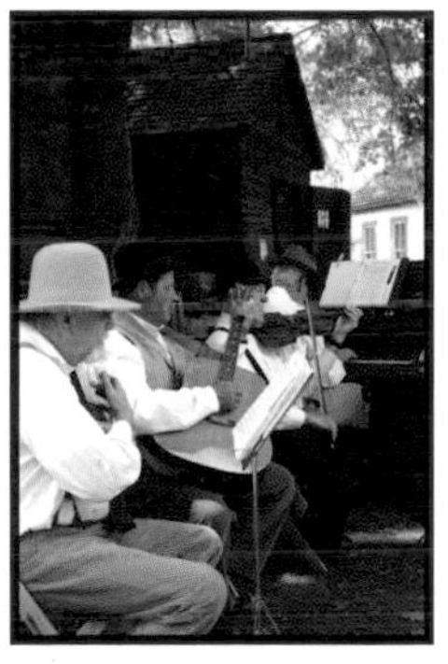

I admire people who take part in the normal workaday world and then don period costumes during their time off to play historical characters. Their enthusiasm and love of history doth spilleth over. Watch as they relive history at Fort Walla Walla Museum, which is located within a military reservation that served as Fort Walla Walla from the 1850s to the early 1900s. Here, in this kid-friendly museum, you can visit the fort's jail and barbershop, and view pioneer artifacts throughout the fort's exhibit halls. Who knows, the guy with the Union Calvary outfit might just be the winemaker you saw the day before. **Details:** Open daily 10 a.m.-5 p.m., April-October. Admission fee. 755 Myra Road, Walla Walla; fortwallawallamuseum.org, info@fortwallawallamuseum.org, 509-525-7703.

2. Whitman Mission National Historic Site

A statue of Marcus Whitman near the campus of Whitman College bears the inscription "My plans require time and distance." I love that line, but to truly appreciate its meaning, take time to visit to the nearby Whitman Mission National Historic Site located seven miles west of the city. Built in 1836, the mission was the dream of Dr. Marcus and Narcissa Whitman. After more than a decade of living and working with the Cayuse tribe, the mission's founders and others were massacred by a group of Cayuse and Umatilla Indians on November 29, 1847. There ensued the so-called Cayuse War. However, before you get up in arms and grab your musket, be aware that there are two sides to this story. Hence a visit to this solemn ground is required to appreciate the circumstances. **Details:** Open 8 a.m.-6 p.m. in

summer; 8 a.m.-4:30 p.m. for rest of the year; closed Thanksgiving, Christmas Day and New Year's Day. Admission fee. 328 Whitman Mission Road, Walla Walla; nps.gov/whmi/index.htm, 509-529-2761.

3. Children's Museum of Walla Walla

OK, you brought along the kids on your winery tour, and as payback for their patience, it's time to let them run around. To that end, the Children's Museum of Walla Walla (CMWW) is the perfect venue for "children playing to learn and adults learning to play." Located off Poplar on the Veterans Administration grounds, the CMWW provides hands-on experiences through ongoing exhibits, including the Wee Walla Walla Harvest Market, an Italian restaurant, and a Civil Service exhibit (who doesn't want to don a firefighter's outfit?). **Details:** Open Thursday-Sunday, 10 a.m.-5 p.m. Admission $4 (children younger than 1 admitted free). 77 Wainwright Drive, Walla Walla; cmww.org, 509-526-7529.

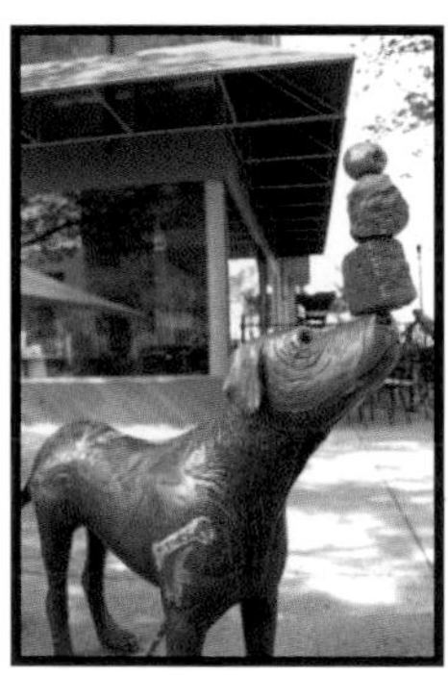

4. Downtown Walking Tour

Lace your sneakers and enjoy a walking tour through downtown Walla Walla's historic district. It's a terrific way to scope out the tasting rooms you will later visit while experiencing history via some wonderfully preserved architecture. Discover the Liberty Theatre, the Die Brücke Building, the Sayer Building (formerly the Bee Hive dry goods store) and more. If you are semi-geek like me and find yourself reading brass plaques, craning your neck to read the inscription on the building's façade, or imagining horse-drawn carriages (and their smells), this is the tour for you. **Details:** Visit the Downtown Walla Walla Foundation office, 33 E. Main St., Suite 213, or call 509-529-8755. For a printable map, go to wallawalla.org/downtown.cfm.

5. Historic Dayton

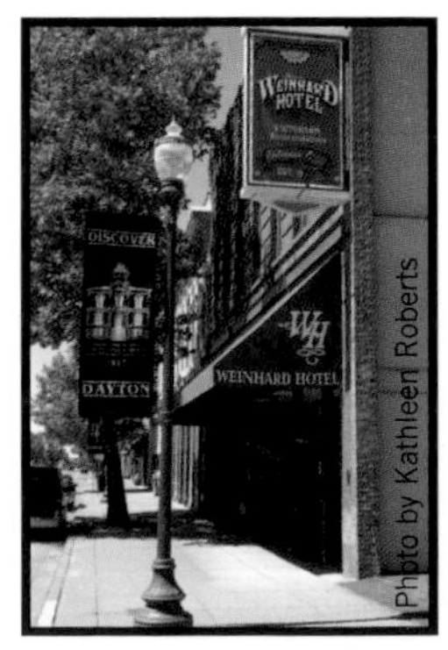

Photo by Kathleen Roberts

Located a short 30-minute drive from Walla Walla is the historic town of Dayton, an area Lewis and Clark explored in 1806 on their return from the Pacific. Chockfull of historic buildings, quaint shops — including Elk Drug, featuring an old-fashioned soda counter — nice restaurants, and friendly natives, Dayton is a fun day trip. Be sure to stroll through the historic Weinhard Hotel and perhaps grab lunch at the Weinhard Café. Reserve time and break out the camera for artisan cheesemaker Monteillet Fromagerie — located a few miles west of Dayton towards Waitsburg.

6. Kirkman House Museum

Listed on the National Register of Historic Places, the Kirkman House Museum is a Victorian home containing some of the original furnishings of the Kirkman family. We have William Kirkman of merry ol' England to thank for building the home on Colville Street. This is clearly a period structure, and it is easy to imagine what life was like in the 1800s with a visit to this thoughtfully maintained museum. **Details:** Open Wednesday-Saturday, 10 a.m.-4 p.m. 214 N. Colville St., Walla Walla; kirkmanhousemuseum.org, 509-529-4373.

7. Frazier Farmstead Museum

A short drive south of Walla Walla takes you to the relaxing hamlet of Milton Freewater. Here, visitors can ramp up on their historical knowledge of this community by visiting the Frazier Farmstead Museum in between visiting some delightful wineries. The drive to Milton-Freewater reminds us that the Walla Walla Valley viticultural area dips into Oregon. In fact, many of its renowned vineyards are on the Oregon side of the state line. The Frazier Farmstead Museum provides a quick dose of history, capturing the spirit and lifestyle of the early settlers. Listed on the National Register of Historic Places, the 6-acre complex features several farm buildings, an herb garden, a gift shop, and a historical research facility. **Details:** Open Thursday-Saturday, 11 a.m.-4 p.m.; closed January-March. Free admission, donations appreciated. 1403 Chestnut St., Milton-Freewater, Oregon; museum.bmi.net, 541-938-4636.

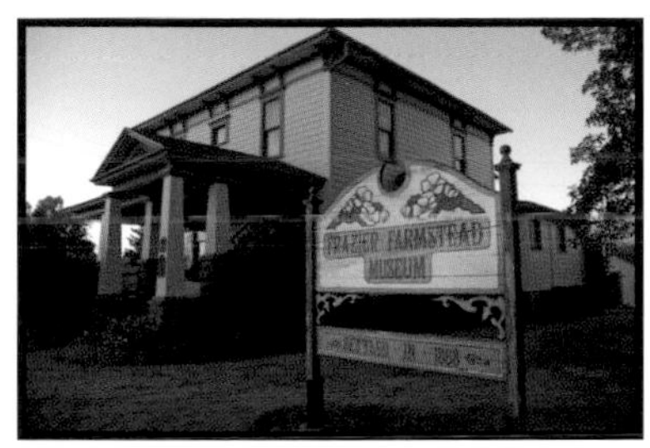

8. Whitman College

Located a few blocks east of downtown Walla Walla is the charming campus of Whitman College. It's a predilection of mine that whenever I visit Walla Walla (which is often), I walk through the campus. I marvel at the Deborah Butterfield sculpture of a horse, bearing the appropriate title of "Styx," on Ankeny Field; its stately trees and meandering, duck-populated stream; and the neoclassical architecture of the buildings, featuring the proverbial clock tower of the administrative office building. Founded in the 1850s, the liberal arts school is home to 1,500 students. **Details:** 345 Boyer Ave., Walla Walla; whitman.edu, 877-462-9448.

The Arts

9. Walla Walla Foundry

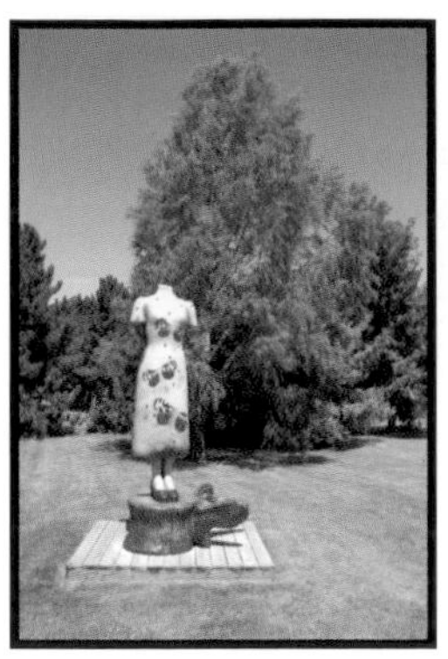

See where world-famous sculpture originates at the Walla Walla Foundry. Founded in 1980 by Walla Walla native Mark A. Anderson, the Walla Walla Foundry provides the space and equipment for artists who specialize in casting contemporary fine art in bronze, silver, and aluminum. Renowned artists such as Robert Arneson, Jim Dine, Deborah Butterfield, Ming Fay and many others rely on the foundry's facilities to give birth to their creations. **Details:** 405 Woodland Ave., Walla Walla; wallawallafoundry.com, 509-522-2114.

10. ArtWalk

The first Friday of each month from May through December, Walla Walla's art businesses open their doors (or more accurately, keep them open) from 5 to 8 p.m. It's a great way to discover Walla Walla's art galleries, museums, and artists' studios for free while sampling the valley's lively art scene. Artists from around the world exhibit their work, and there's plenty of wine to swirl and sip as you take in the fine art. What's more, you get some exercise while gathering some conversation starters for dinner. Grab a map at any of the participating locations and start your self-guided tour. **Details:** artwalkwallawalla.com, 509-529-8755.

11. Little Theatre of Walla Walla

Do you have a penchant for the live arts? Check out Little Theatre of Walla Walla, which produces "Good Plays, Done Well ... since 1944." Featuring volunteer actors from around the valley, the Little Theatre produces year-round entertainment to satisfy those of us who love to the experience of community theater. This is a venue where would-be Broadway artists come together to create sets, lighting, costumes, and characters. **Details:** 1130 Sumach, Walla Walla; ltww.org, 509-529-3683.

12. Walla Walla Symphony

"Walla Walla has a symphony?" you ask. Yep, and it is just one more reason why Walla Walla is the biggest little town in America. For more than 100 years, the Walla Walla Symphony has offered a full slate of concerts from October through June at Cordiner Hall on the Whitman College campus. Led by the creative genius of Yaacov Bergmann (is it a requirement that all conductors have names that sound Eastern European?), the Walla Walla Symphony spices up its programs with a mix of classical concerts, special concerts and unique performances that highlight music traditions from around the world. **Details:** 13 1/2 E. Main St., Suite 201, Walla Walla; wwsymphony.com, 509-529-8020.

Culinary Delights

13. Colville Street Patisserie

Located downtown is the delightful Colville Street Patisserie, where classic French pastries, cakes, desserts, gelato, and, in my humble opinion, the best espresso in town await you. It's the perfect setting for reading the morning newspaper while enjoying a double latte or sharing a delectable crème brûlée with a friend. The brainchild (born through tremendous sweat equity) of owners David Christensen and Tiffany Cain, the pastry shop fuses Parisian charm and Walla Walla hospitality. **Details:** Open Tuesday-Thursday, 9 a.m.-8 p.m.; Friday-Saturday, 9 a.m.-10 p.m.; Sunday, 9 a.m.-5 p.m. 40 S. Colville, Walla Walla; colvillestreetpatisserie.com, 509-301-7289.

14. Walla Walla Valley Farmers' Market

On Saturdays and Sundays, from the first weekend in May to the last weekend of October, Walla Walla visitors have the Farmers' Market to explore. From 9 a.m. to 1 p.m., immerse yourself in local produce, crafts, and art. Come hungry, too — there are plenty of edible delights to nosh as you wind your way through fresh corn, sweet onions, and savory bakery items. If you're in awe of the fresh fruits and vegetables, you're not alone. Walla Walla's finest restaurants rely on local producers for the ingredients in the summer salad and entrée you'll enjoy later in the evening. **Details:** Located at the corner of Fourth Avenue and Main Street (City Hall parking lot); gowallawallafarmersmarket.com/, info@gowallawallafarmersmarket.com, 509-520-3647.

15. Onion World: Home of the Walla Walla Sweet Onion Sausage

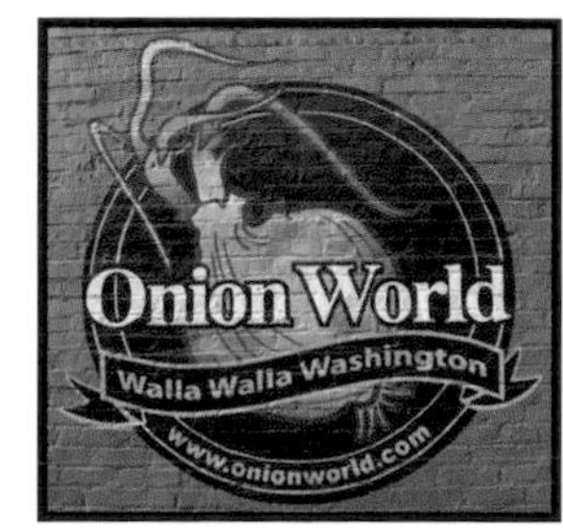

For me, no visit to Walla Walla is complete without a stop at the walk-up window of Onion World at First and Main in the historic Beehive building (Sayer Building). The Walsh family has been serving up their special sweet-onion sausage recipe since 1975, when founder Kelly Walsh, then a student at Whitman College, concocted this oh-so-yummy treat. The sausage itself is made from lean meats, a bonus for the health-conscious. However, I generally blow it with the addition of homemade chili and shredded cheese on top — heavenly! **Details:** Open daily for lunch, 11 a.m.-2 p.m.; extended hours Friday-Saturday, 11 a.m.-8 p.m. 2 S. First Ave., #100, Walla Walla; onionworld.com, 509-522-2541.

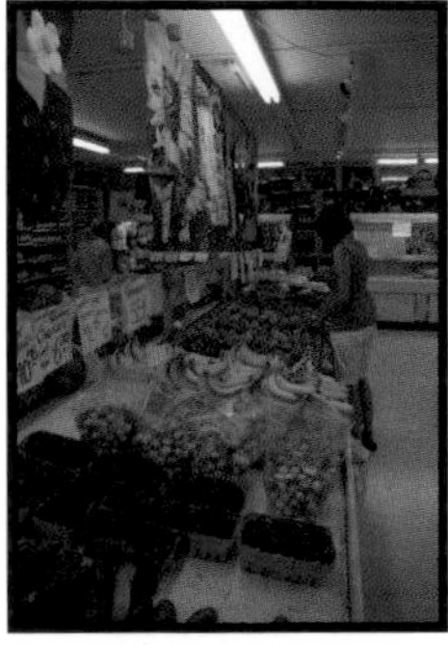

16. Klickers Berry Farm

Lucky visitors to Walla Walla in the late spring or early summer may want to get their fingers stained eating just-ripe strawberries at Klickers Berry Farm. With an antique shop on site and acres of strawberries to forage through, budget plenty of time at this fruitful oasis. And you thought Walla Walla just grew Walla Walla sweet onions and cabernet! Other produce is also offered at the Klickers store. **Details:** 3300 E. Isaacs Ave., Walla Walla; klickerstrawberry.com, 509-525-8650.

17. Monteillet Fromagerie

Located a quick half-hour drive from Walla Walla is Dayton's Monteillet Fromagerie. Monteillet Fromagerie is the place to experience for cheese lovers of all ages — especially if you like fresh goat and sheep cheeses paired alongside palate-cleansing wines. Expect a canine greeting committee composed of Great Pyrenees and a Border collie, in addition to plenty of assorted farm animals to ogle and photograph: chickens, ducks, lambs, goats, and elephants (just kidding about the pachyderms). Another treat is the town of Dayton itself, with its historical architecture, antique stores and gift shops, and hunger-satisfying restaurants. **Details:** 109 Ward Road, Dayton; monteilletcheese.com, 509-382-1917.

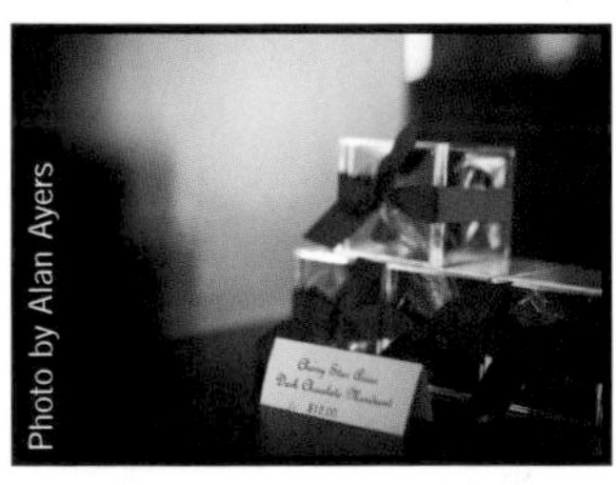

Photo by Alan Ayers

18. Petits Noirs Chocolatier

For those among you who love chocolate as much as you love wine, there's a mandatory stop to make on your winery-touring getaway. Take the quick drive to Milton-Freewater, in Oregon, and find the purple house on Main Street — the home of Petits Noirs. Created by New York City transplants Lan Wong and James Boulanger, Petits Noirs is a boutique chocolatier that embodies Lan and James' love of food and wine. Made with pure ingredients, including large doses of cacao, Petits Noirs chocolates are crafted to pair with premium wines, such as cabernet sauvignon and syrah. Temptation also takes the form of fresh, handmade truffles in exotic flavors, European-style hot chocolate, textured leather gift boxes, chocolate marmalades, and more. **Details:** Open Thursday-Sunday, 11 a.m.-5 p.m. 622 S. Main St., Milton-Freewater, Oregon; petitsnoirs.com, 541-938-7118.

WineTrails Note: Can't make it to Milton-Freewater and still have a hankering for something sweet? Bright's Candies in downtown Walla Walla is a venerable institution of confectionery that has been crafting sweets since 1934. **Details:** Monday-Friday, 9:30 a.m.-8 p.m.; Saturday, 10 a.m.-8 p.m.; Sunday, noon-6 p.m. 11 E. Main St., Walla Walla; brightscandies.com, 509-525-5533 or 1-800-350-5533.

19. Someone's In The Kitchen

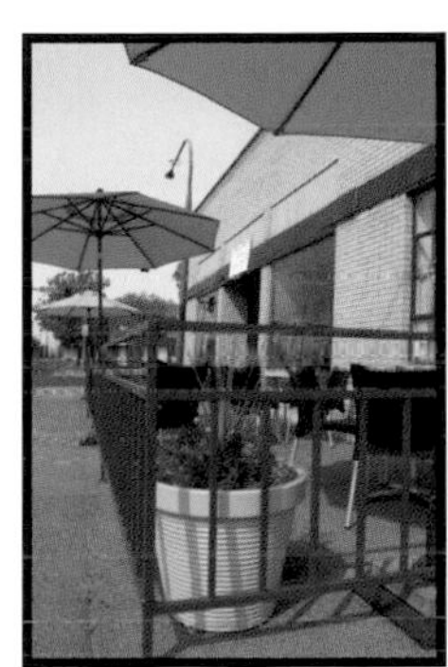

Join chef Gene Soto at Walla Walla's Someone's In The Kitchen (SITK) and learn to cook culinary delights while having fun. It's perfect for friends and couples who would like to master a variety of dishes. Go online to the website and see what's on the menu at SITK. Who knows, your next home-cooked meal might be a Gruyère fondue dish or a curry-spiced Indian dish, courtesy of Chef Gene's instruction. Bon appetit! **Details:** 132 W. Rose St., Walla Walla; sitkwallawalla.com, 509-240-6388.

Spa and Ahhh/Shopping Therapy

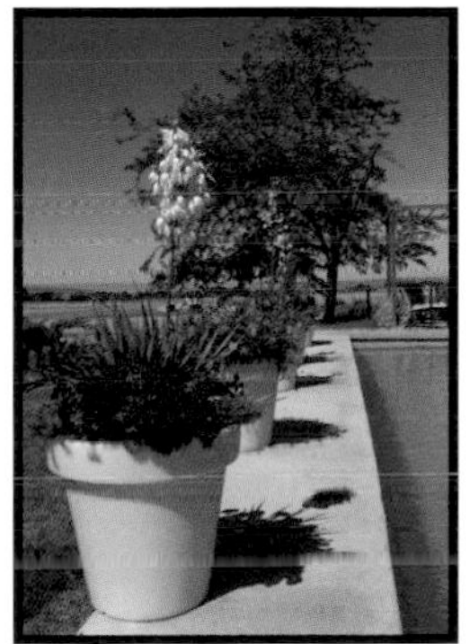

20. A Day at the Spa - Yoga, too

Imagine gazing at rolling wheatfields and vineyards while immersed in an ofuro (Japanese bath), followed by complimentary tea, massage, power yoga, and a cedar dry sauna. You can experience all these pleasures (and more) at Areus Inn and Spa, located east of Walla Walla off Highway 12. Giancarlo Solimano, whose extensive background includes stints with yoga gurus in India and New York, leads the yoga classes. Call ahead for the power yoga class schedule. **Details:** 1903 Smith Road, Walla Walla; areusyoga.com, 509-200-9931.

If, however, you're looking to be pampered in downtown Walla Walla, you're in luck. For nail and skin care, and some serious relaxation, check out Misbehaven Spa & Salon, 115 W. Alder St., 509-526-4585; City Slicker's Salon & Spa, 14 W. Main St., Walla Walla, 509-529-2108; or Impress Salon, 1423 Plaza Way, #B, Walla Walla, 509-529-3534.

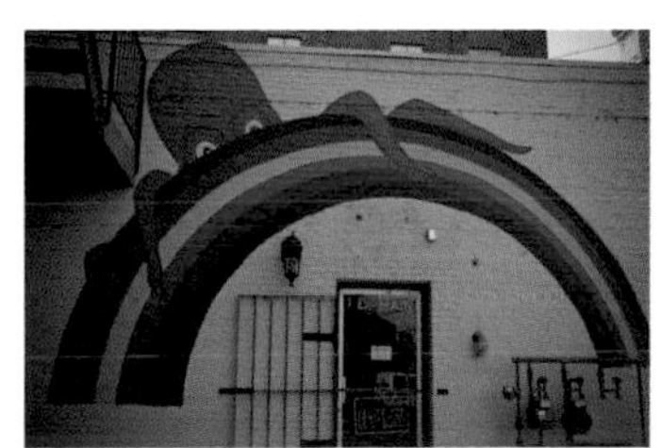

21. Inland Octopus

If the little tykes (and you) still have some energy, check out the best toy store in Walla

Walla Valley Inland Octopus toy shop. Find the best puppets, toys, and sundries at this store, and release your inner child. **Details:** Open daily, 10 a.m.-6 p.m. 7 E. Main St., Walla Walla; inlandoctopus.com, 509-526-0115.

22. Antiques

It may not be true that Walla Walla has more antique shops per square inch than other hamlets, but you'd be hard pressed to convince me otherwise. Those settlers of the valley left behind more than just pioneer stories and recipes for apple strudel; they left behind a lot of heirloom stuff, be it made of porcelain, glass, metal or wood. (Don't you just love the smell of antique shops?) Here's some marvelous places to check out:

- Antique Mall of Walla Walla, 315 S. Ninth Ave., Walla Walla; 509-529-0677
- Diettrich House Antiques, 625 W. Alder St., Walla Walla; 509-529-8707
- Empire Antiques, 1975 Walla Walla Ave., Walla Walla; 509-525-5137
- Maxine's, 15 Boyer Ave., Walla Walla; 509-526-3141
- Nothing New Lodging & Antiques, 214 Main St., Waitsburg; 509-337-6393
- Shady Lawn Antiques, 711 N. Rose St., Walla Walla; 509-529-2123
- Skylite Gallery, 7 N. Second Ave., Walla Walla; 509-525-4222
- The Clock Shop and Antique Co., 41 S. Palouse St., Walla Walla; 509-525-4589

Photo by Alan Ayers

23. Hot Poop

Featuring vinyl records, posters, and a heck of a lot more, Hot Poop, on Main Street, is a mecca for music lovers of all ages. Hot Poop is Washington's oldest independent record store- think Sgt. Pepper, eight-track tapes and tie-dyed T-shirts mixing it up with contemporary CDs of all music genres. Can't think of the name of a particular blues singer from Chicago? No worries. The staff likely knows the artist and has the record to boot. See if you can stump the experts! **Details:** Open Monday-Saturday, 10 a.m.-6 p.m. 210 E. Main St., Walla Walla; hotpoop.com, 509-525-9080.

Outdoorsy / Recreation

24. Bennington Lake Recreation Areas

Located about three miles northeast of Walla Walla near the Walla Walla Community College Campus is my favorite spot in the valley, Bennington Lake Recreation Areas (Bennington Lake, Rooks Park, and the Mill Creek Recreation Trail), which are part of the larger 612-acre Mill Creek area managed by the

Army Corps of Engineers. If you enjoy hiking, jogging, mountain biking, horseback riding, fishing, picnicking, and swimming, you'll be all over this place. (If you don't enjoy any of those activities, you might just want to invest in a defibrillator.) Throughout the year, visitors to Bennington Lake hike the paved and unpaved trails that thread throughout the recreation area, surrounded by bucolic splendor. The paved Mill Creek Recreation Trail follows Mill Creek from the city of Walla Walla to Rooks Park, forming part of a network of more than 20 miles of multipurpose trails. Parking, as well as access to these trails, is located at Rooks Park, Bennington Lake, and the Mill Creek office. **Details:** 3211 Reservoir Road, Walla Walla; 509-527-7160.

WineTrails Note: Hiking trails abound in the nearby Blue Mountains. Oregon Butte and Diamond Peak are but two examples of great day hikes. See trails.com for trail maps of the area.

25. Bicycling

With plenty of level terrain as well as heart-pumping hills, Walla Walla offers a treasure trove of on-road and off-road bicycle adventures. The website MapMyRide.com provides more than 200 bike routes to traverse in Walla Walla (see mapmyride.com/find-ride/united-states/wa/walla-walla). Or, you can contact local bike shops — Bicycle Barn, 509-529-7860, or Allegro Cyclery, 509-525-4949 — for their advice on where to ride. Some folks combine wine sipping and cycling, but caution is the operative word here. Cycle smartly.

26. Pioneer Park

Walla Walla is home to 18 different city parks and recreational facilities, including my personal favorite: 58-acre Pioneer Park, located near downtown at Alder and Division. Considered the city's most historic park, Pioneer Park was conceived by none other than John C. Olmstead, the creator of New York City's Central Park, who actually designed Walla Walla's original system of parks at the beginning of the 20th century. With its sheltered picnic tables, way-cool gazebo, rose garden, and sports area, along with two large duck ponds and an aviary for bird lovers, Pioneer Park has it all. It also is home to some of the state's oldest trees, which were here long before you and I arrived. Tuck the camera and a Frisbee into your picnic basket, and thoroughly enjoy this parcel of heaven on earth. **Details:** For further information, contact

the city's Parks and Recreation Department, 509-527-4527, or visit its website at ci.walla-walla.wa.us.

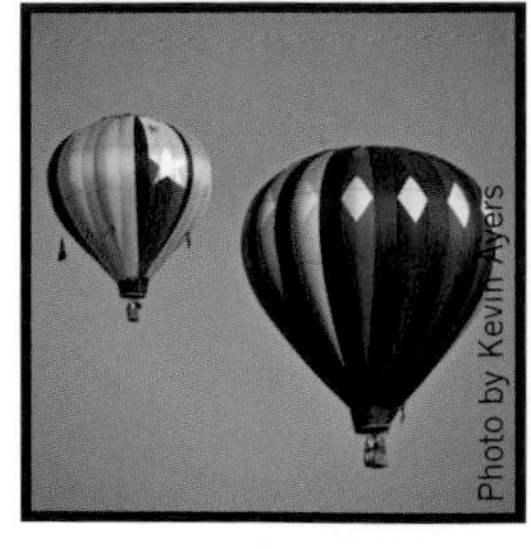
Photo by Kevin Ayers

27. Walla Walla Balloon Stampede

If the weather permits, look to the sky on the second weekend in May (Friday through Sunday) and see a sky filled with colorful hot air balloons. It's beyond cool - it's spectacular! But you're going to have to get up pretty early (6:30 a.m.) to see the balloons head skyward from any one of a dozen different schoolyards and parks throughout Walla Walla. This annual event, sponsored by the Walla Walla Valley Chamber of Commerce, includes a pancake feed, a classic-car show, live music, dance, and a whole lot more, all taking place at the Walla Walla County Fairgrounds (Ninth and Orchard). **Details:** For event information and tickets, call the chamber at 509-525-0850 or go online to wwvchamber.com.

28. Ski Bluewood

After a day of sampling Walla Walla's premium wines, it's downhill from there ... downhill skiing, that is. Located 52 miles southeast of Walla Walla in the Blue Mountains near Dayton is Bluewood Ski Resort. Its facilities include two triple chairlifts, a cafeteria, an après-ski pub, retail shop (someone always forgets their gloves), and a ski and snowboard rental and repair shop. If you are a beginner, no problem: Affordable lessons are easily arranged. With 21 runs and a half-pipe for snowboarders, Bluewood Ski Resort packs a full day of well-groomed joy. **Details:** bluewood.com, info@bluewood.com, 509-382-4725.

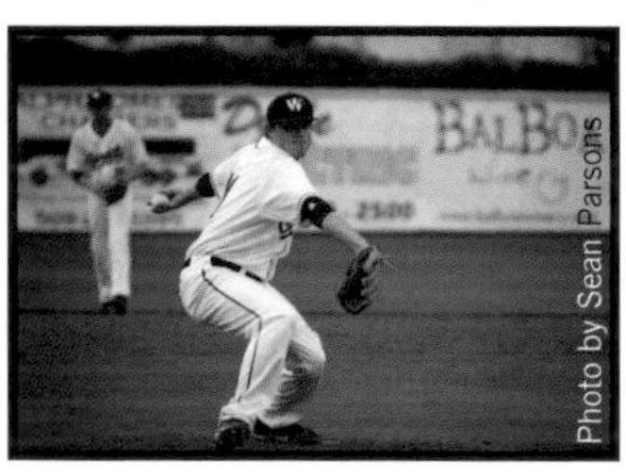

Photo by Sean Parsons

29. Walla Walla Sweets Baseball

All-American traditions of baseball, hot dogs, and apple pie (but alas, no cabernet) come together at Whitman College's Borleske Stadium, where the Walla Walla Sweets baseball team plays. Watch the Sweets do battle against the likes of the Wenatchee AppleSox and the Kelowna Falcons. **Details:** Borleske Stadium, 409 E. Rees Ave., Walla Walla. For schedule and ticketing information, call 509-522-BALL or go online to wallawallasweets.com.

30. Wine Valley Golf Club

Named by *Golf Magazine* as one of America's top new golf courses in 2009, Wine Valley Golf Club's course is the newest (and most spectacular) in the valley. Here's some of what *Golf Magazine* had to say about architect Dan Hixson's grand design: "massive bunkers that melt into the terrain dominate the design, but the endless vistas of the Blue Mountains and swaying wheatgrass rough will linger long after you've returned to civilization." **Details:** Green fees: $45-$90. 176 Wine Valley Road, Walla Walla; winevalleygolfclub.com, 877-333-9842.

WineTrails Note: There are other area golf courses that also await your mulligans, including Walla Walla Country Club, 509-525-1780 (members only); Veterans Memorial Golf Course, Walla Walla, 509-527-4507; Milton-Freewater Golf Course, Milton-Freewater, 541-938-7284; or Pheasant Creek Golf Course, Touchet, 509-394-4653.

Places to Stay

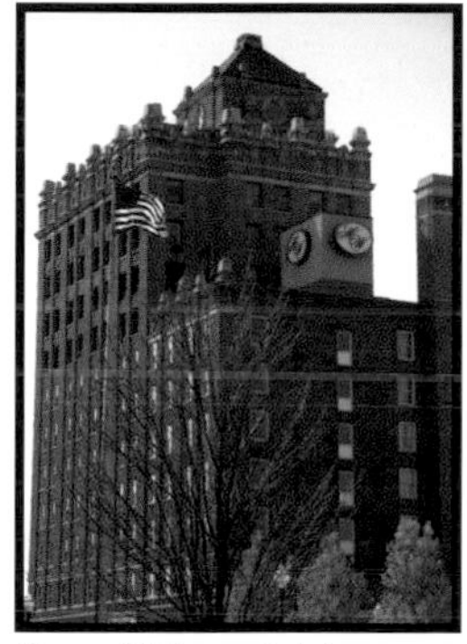

Marcus Whitman Hotel

With historic hotels, motels, charming B&Bs, and RV parks aplenty, lodging opportunities abound in the Walla Walla Valley. To find the accommodation of your choice, read on.

When many visitors to Walla Walla contemplate a place to stay, the iconic Marcus Whitman Hotel springs to mind — and for good reason. With more than 10 floors, it is clearly the tallest structure in the Walla Walla Valley. Renovated, with new wings to accommodate still more thirsty travelers and a jaw-droppingly elegant lobby, this grand hotel must be seen. With art galleries to explore, fine dining to experience (including clearly the best brunch spread in eastern Washington), and a cocktail lounge offering a host of local wines, the Marcus Whitman Hotel attracts repeat customers year after year. And its location is very convenient to downtown restaurants, shops, and, of course, winery tasting rooms.

Abeja

If, however, you desire a romantic getaway (or just a quick trip to renew your soul), the Inn at Abeja is a mere few miles east of downtown. Here you can experience signature Abeja wines created by winemaker and co-owner John Abbott. As the owners point out, Abeja's primary focus is the production of ultrapremium wines; and the overnight lodging and other amenities come second. But don't tell that to the inn's guests, who seem so firmly ensconced in their rooms that they appear not to want to leave. Of special note is the fact that the Abeja tasting room is not open to the public. That is, the only surefire way to gain entry to this exclusive tasting room is to be a guest of the Inn at Abeja. Upon arrival, the inn's guests are treated to a private wine tasting, which often leads to a stroll around the manicured grounds or a butt-plant in a nearby Adirondack chair. Life does have its challenges!

Walla Faces Wines provide another winery/inn combination. Owners Rick and Debbie Johnson provide two completely different locations (and experiences) for visitors: a downtown location (Walla Walla Inns Historic Downtown) and a vineyard setting (Walla Walla Inns at the Vineyard) just a few miles east of town, past the airport. If you seek a place where you can sip wine by the pool, surrounded by rows of cabernet sauvignon grapevines, then their vineyard location fits the bill. If you desire instead the convenience of being downtown on Main Street, within walking distance of urban amenities, then their downtown location is the solution. And this lodging just happens to be located above the Walla Faces Wines tasting room.

Walla Walla Inns at the Vineyard

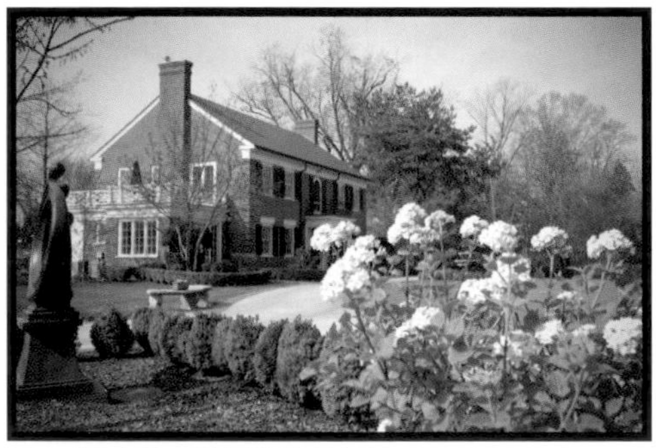

Stone Creek Manor Bed & Breakfast

Near downtown is the amazing Stone Creek Manor Bed & Breakfast, where George and Christine Bieto have lovingly restored a historic property to offer world-class accommodations and delightful amenities. Frankly, the words "lovingly restored" don't begin to describe this little slice of heaven. Attention to detail defines this property. You're made to feel welcome; it doesn't matter if you are the king of Siam or a janitor from Boise, you are the Bietos' special guest. The guesthouses come fully furnished, including a complete kitchen, soft-pillowed beds that are the definition of comfort, and an outside patio and furniture complete with an industrial-strength barbecue grill. This is a one-of-a-kind retreat.

A note of caution is in order. Walla Walla likes to celebrate, and throughout the year, hotels and other overnight lodges fill with guests in town for spring break, the holiday barrel tasting, the balloon stampede, college graduation, and other goings-on. For these event weekends, in-the-know visitors book their stays well in advance. So, for example, if you are thinking of going to Walla Walla for spring release (first weekend in May), select a place and go online or call early to book your stay. *Bonne chance!*

Places to Stay

Hotel/ Motel	Address	Contact	Price from*	Services
Best Western Walla Walla Suites Inn	7 East Oak Walla Walla, WA 99362	509-525-4700 bestwestern.com	$89	Complimentary breakfast
Blue Mountain Motel	414 W. Main Dayton, WA 99328	509-382-3040 bluemountainmotel.net info@bluemountainmotel.net	$44 to $90	
Budget Inn	305 North 2nd Walla Walla, WA 99362	509-529-4410 wallawallabudgetinn.com	$32-$70	Continental breakfast
Capri Motel	2003 Melrose, Walla Walla, WA 99362	800-451-1139 wallawallamotel.com	$32 to $65	Additional fee for pets
City Center Motel	627 West Main St Walla Walla, WA 99362	509-529- 2660 citycentermotel.net	$49	
Colonial Motel	2279 East Isaacs Walla Walla, WA 99362	509-529-1220 colonial-motel.com info@colonial-motel.com	$59 to $80	Bike friendly
Comfort Inn & Suites	1419 Pine St Walla Walla, WA 99362	509-522-3500 choicehotels.com gm.wa184@choicehotels.com	$89.95 to $99.95	Continental breakfast
Dayton Motel	110 South Pine Dayton, WA 99328	509-382-4503 daytonmotel.tripod.com daytonmotel@hotmail.com	$39	
Hampton Inn and Suites	1531 Kelly Place Walla Walla, WA 99362	509-525 1398 wallawallasuites.hamptoninn.com	$109 to $169	Romance package, Complimentary breakfast
Holiday Inn Express	1433 West Pine Walla Walla, WA 99362	509-525-6200 wwhie.com	$89 - $169	Complimentary breakfast
La Quinta Inn	520 N Second Ave Walla Walla, WA 99362	509-525-2522 wallawallalaquinta.com lq0469gm@lq.com	$59-$149	Complimentary breakfast
Marcus Whitman Hotel & Conference Center	Six West Rose Street Walla Walla, WA 99362	509-525-2200 marcuswhitmanhotel.com reservations@ marcuswhitmanhotel.com	Call for rates	Four pet rooms available
Mill House Lodging & Events	504 N 1st Dayton, WA 99328	509-382-2393, 425-327-9870 millhouselodging.com	$125 (subject to change)	Pets welcome; Wedding and event planning services available
Morgan Inn	104 N. Columbia Milton-Freewater, OR 97862	541-938-5547, 866-938-6369 morganinn.net marqhotel@hotmail.com	$64	
Out West Hotel	84040 Highway 11 Milton-Freewater, OR 97862	541-938-6647 outwestmotel.net	$42-$55	

* Rates vary by season and availability

Hotel/ Motel	Address	Contact	Price from*	Services
Super 8 Motel	2315 Eastgate St N Walla Walla, WA 99362	509-525-8800 super8.com	$69 to $113	Pets welcome
Travelodge	421 East Main Walla Walla, WA 99362	509-529-4940 travelodge.com	$44-$77	
Waitsburg Inn	731 Preston Ave. Waitsburg, WA 99361	800-718-9025	$40	
Walla Walla Inns -- Historic Downtown	214 Main St Walla Walla, WA 99362	877-301-1181 wallawallainns.com info@wallawallainns.com	$115 - $375	
Walla Walla Inns -- at the Vineyard	254 Wheat Ridge Ln Walla Walla, WA 99362	877-301-1181 wallawallainns.com info@wallawallainns.com	$115 - $375	
Walla Walla Vineyard Inn	325 East Main Walla Walla, WA 99362	509-529-4360 thewallawallavineyardinn.com	$49	Continental breakfast
Weinhard Hotel	235 E. Main Street Dayton, WA 99328	509-382-4032 weinhard.com	$125 to $180	

Bed & Breakfast Inns	Address	Contact	Price*
A Room With a View	28 Roland Court Walla Walla, WA 99362	509-529-1194 aroomwithaview.us Eileen.arroomwithaview@gmail.com	$125- $160
Cameo Heights Mansion	1072 Oasis Road Touchet, WA 99360	509-394-0211 cameoheightsmansion.com	$179 - $249
Fat Duck Inn	527 Catherine St Walla Walla, WA 99362	888-526-8718 fatduckinn.com info@fatduckinn.com	$160 - $185; Off /Peak season rates. Pets OK
Girasol Vineyard & Inn	504 Basel Walla Walla, WA 99362	509-956-9743 casagirasol.com innkeeper@casagirasol.com	$150-$198
Green Gables Inn	922 Bonsella Walla Walla, WA 99362	509-525-5501, 888-525-5501 greengablesinn.com innkeeper@greengablesinn.com	$195 - $225
Inn at Abeja	2014 Mill Creek Rd Walla Walla, WA 99362	509-522-1234 abeja.net molly@abeja.net	$215 - $450
Inn at Blackberry Creek	1126 Pleasant Walla Walla, WA 99362	509-522- 5233, 877-522-5233 innatblackberrycreek.com innkeeper@innatblackberrycreek.com	$139 - $209
Mcann Manor	212 S Second St. Dayton, WA 99328	509-382-8967 mccannmanor.com innkeeper@mccannmanor.com	$135-$240
Nothing New Lodging	214 Main St Waitsburg, WA 99361	509-337-6393 nothingnewlodging.net ltorres6299@charter.net	$80 - $125

* Rates vary by season and availability

Bed & Breakfast Inns	Address	Contact	Price*
Purple House Bed & Breakfast	415 E. Clay Dayton, WA 99328	509-382-3159 800-486-2574 purplehousebnb.com info@purplehousebnb.com	$95 - $135. Pets OK
Stone Creek Manor	756 Bryant Ave. Walla Walla, WA 99362	509-593-477 stonecreekmanor.com info@stonecreekmanor.com	$195 - $235
The Inn at Woodhaven Farm	1341 Walla Walla Ave. Walla Walla, WA 99362	509-529-4746 inn-woodhavenfarm.com jill@inn-woodhavenfarm.com	$140 - $165
The Maxwell House Bed & Breakfast Inn	701 Boyer Ave Walla Walla, WA 99362	509-529-4283, 866-377-0700 themaxwellhouse.com inn@themaxwellhouse.com	$160 -$165
Whispering Winds of Walla Walla	454 Van Donge Lane Walla Walla, WA 99362	509-525-4923 whisperingwindsbandb.com whisperingwindsbandb@charter.net	$119 - $189
Wine Country Inn	915 Alvarado Terrace Walla Walla, WA 99362	509-386-3592 wallawallawinecountry.net winecountryinn@charter.net	$150 - $275
Vines and Roses	516 S. Division Street Walla Walla, WA 99362	509-876-2213, 877-821-8363 vineandroses.com info@vineandroses.com	$199 - $239

Guest Houses	Address	Contact	Rates*
A VUE of Downtown	215 W. Sumach Walla Walla, WA 99362	509-526-7368 vrbo.com/210312	see website
AGK Cottage	610 E Sumach St. Walla Walla, WA 99362	888-526-8718 info@fatduckinn.com vrbo.com/293884	$275
A. K. Dice Guest House	524 Catherine St. Walla Walla, WA 99362	888-526-8718 info@akdiceguesthouse.com akdiceguesthouse.com	$395+
Barton Cottage	620 E. Sumach Walla Walla, WA 99362	425-765-3918 vrbo.com/218763	Call
Beit Nur Home	1221 Portland St. Walla Walla, WA 99362	509-301-4188 vrbo.com/220317	$150-$200
Bella Vida	404 E. Cherry Walla Walla, WA 99362	425-328-8898, 425-339-2683 marilynnc@gmail.com vrbo.com/133575	$200-$400/ Night
Bennington Bungalow	811 Whitman St. Walla Walla, WA 99362	509-525-0222 vrbo.com/175585	$150
Blanc De Blanc Guesthouse	1036 Boyer Ave. Walla Walla, WA 99362	888-526-8718 inquiries@blancdeblancguesthouse. com vrbo.com/152409	$325
Blue 32	College Place, WA 99324	509-540-2876 judithrich@charter.net www.myblue32.com	Call

* Rates vary by season and availability

Guest Houses	Address	Contact	Rates*
Bryant Creek Condominiums	17 Eagon St. Walla Walla, WA 99362	509-301-9300 info@bryantcreek.com bryantcreek.com	$150
B's Bungalow	1205 Portland Ave Walla Walla, WA 99362	888-526-8718 info@fatduckinn.com vrbo.com/300105	$250
Casa Del Sol Vacation Suite	Walla Walla, WA 99362	509-522-1484 vrbo.com/157515	$200+
Catnap Cottage	413 South Palouse Walla Walla, WA 99362	509-240-2402 catnap-cottage.net	$185
Clara's Cottage	735 Washington St. Walla Walla, WA 99362	253-886-2528 info@clarascottage.com clarascottage.com	$125-$250
Cottage Gardens	1455 SE Valley View Terrace College Place, WA 99324	888-249-8359 cottagegardens.info	Call
Cottonwood Vineyard Inn	2 Hill Rd. Walla Walla, WA 99362	509-301-0852 vrbo.com/144780	see website
Creekside Cottage	Walla Walla, WA 99362	909-985-7025, (909) 996-5071 vrbo.com/140995	$200
Di Nonna	1744 Old Milton Highway Walla Walla, WA 99362	509-520-2889, (509) 525-1330 reservations@dinonna.com dinonna.com	Call
Eden's Gate Guest Home	330 Cemetary Rd. Dixie, WA 99329	509-240-4401 atomsportraits.com/edensgate.html	Call
Eagan St. Townhouse	17 Eagan St. Walla Walla, WA 99362	888-526-8718 fatduckinn.com	$250
Farmstay Gite at the Monteillet Fromagerie	109 Ward Rd. Dayton, WA 98328	509-382-1917 509-876-1429 monteilletcheese@gmail.com monteilletcheese.com	Call
Fat Duck Guest House	615 Whitman St. Walla Walla, WA 99362	509-526-DUCK 509-526-3825 info@fatduckinn.com fatduckinn.com	$250
Fischer House On Eagan	128 Eagan Avenue Walla Walla, WA 99362	509-540-9518 509-876-2260 lorifischer@ymail.com thefischerhouse.net	$130-$155 per night
Grant House	Grant St. Walla Walla, WA 99362	888-526-8718 info@fatduckinn.com granthousewallawalla.com	$200-$300
Hence Room	Hence Cellars Winery 4122 Powerline Rd. Walla Walla, WA 99362	509-529-4010 hencecellars.com	$200
Juniper Guest House	Walla Walla, WA 99362	206-650-6077 vrbo.com/111648	$225+
Lewis Peak Estates	26 Lewis Peak Rd. Waitsburg, WA 99361	509-200-2131 lewispeakestates.com	$395-$425

* Rates vary by season and availability

Guest Houses	Address	Contact	Rates*
Lily of the Valley	605 Boyer Ave. Walla Walla, WA 99362	509-529-2745 lilyofthevalleyww.com	Call
Loma Loft	531 Catherine St. Walla Walla, WA 99362	509-529-4307 lomaloft.com	$95+
Lucky W Ranch	50 Frenchtown Rd. Walla Walla, WA 99362	509-529-4307 wallawallagrapehavens.com/ vacation-rental-home.asp	$325
Many Waters Guest House	709 Washington St. Walla Walla, WA 99362	206-323-7800 manywatersguesthouse.com	$265-$350
Melrose Place	Walla Walla, WA 99362	253-886-1259 509-301-4929 vrbo.com/188393	$124-$149
Osterman Guest House	421 Lincoln St. Walla Walla, WA 99362	888-526-8718 509-526-3825 info@fatduckInn.com vrbo.com/143852	$385
PJ's Vacation Rental	238 W. 5th Waitsburg, WA 99361	509-337-8876 pj@pjsvacationrentals.com pjsvacationrentals.com	see website
Red Door Cottage	647 1/2 Locust St. Walla Walla, WA 99362	888 526 8718 info@fatduckinn.com vrbo.com/282342	$95
Russell Creek Ranch	2426 Kendall Rd. Walla Walla, WA 99362	888-526-8718 509-540-9513 info@fatduckinn.com russellcreekranch.com	$395-495
Stone Compass Guest House	62 S. Madison St. Walla Walla, WA 99362	509-301-4188 vrbo.com/180085	$250-$275
Stone Creek Manor	756 Bryant Ave. Walla Walla, WA 99362	509-593-4770 info@stonecreekmanor.com stonecreekmanor.com	$165-215
Strawberry Canyon Lodge	9052 Mill Creek Road Walla Walla, WA 99362	509-529-5288 scox@bmi.net mountainretreats.com	$175
The Boyer House	741 Boyer Ave. Walla Walla, WA 99362	509-200-9931 email_info@theboyerhouse.com theboyerhouse.com	$180
The Bumble Abode	2 South First Avenue Walla Walla, WA 99362	509-526-0402 bumbleabode.com	Call
The Chestnut House	125 Chestnut St. Walla Walla, WA 99362	206-405-0957 info@escapetochestnut.com EscapeToChestnut.com	$225-325
The Evergreen Inn	1719 Evergreen Walla Walla, WA 99362	509-301-1651, 509-520-5461 vrbo.com/189356	$195-$275
The Haven	633 Pearson St. Walla Walla, WA 99362	509-529-7400, 818-438-7832 info@havenwallawalla.com havenwallawalla.com	$300+
The Inn at Willowhaven	1187 Taumarson Rd. Walla Walla, WA 99362	509-529-2755	Call

* Rates vary by season and availability

Guest Houses	Address	Contact	Rates*
The Painted Place	344 E. Chestnut St. Walla Walla, WA 99362	253-255-2987 painted-place.com	$300-$350
The Vue off Main	Rose St. Walla Walla, WA 99362	509-540-9513 vueoffmain.homestead.com	$199
Tucker Inn	1134 S. Howard Walla Walla, WA 99362	509-301-1068 stay@tuckerinnww.com tuckerinnww.com	$250-$435
TukanInn Guest House	310 North Tukanon Walla Walla, WA 99362	800-662-1961 x2157 vrbo.com/124034	$250-$425
Walla Walla Cottage	Walla Walla, WA 99362	509-529-2417, 877-243-2532 Info@wallawallacottage.com wallawallacottage.com	$125-$150
Walla Walla Inns at the Vineyard	254 Wheat Ridge Lane Walla Walla, WA 99362	877-301-1181 info@wallawallainns.com wallawallainns.com	see website
Walla Walla Retreats	601 Village Way #23 Walla Walla, WA 99362	509-200-1802	Call
Webster House	Walla Walla, WA 99362	509-540-9513 websterhouse.homestead.com	$140-$195

RV Parks	Address	Contact	Notes
Cameron Court RV Park	522 Cameron St. Walla Walla, WA 99362	509-382-4411	Full hook-ups, showers, pet OK
Blue Valley RV Park	50 W. George St. Walla Walla, WA 99362	1-866.855.8282 bluevalleyrv.com stay@bluevalleyrv.com	Full hook-ups, check-in lodge, 24-hour attendant, cable TV, showers, laundry, exchange library, pets OK
RV Resort Four Seasons	1440 Dalles Military Rd. Walla Walla, WA 99362	509-529-6072 travelingusa.com/rvfourseasonswa rvresort@gohighspeed.com	Full hook-ups, cable TV, showers, wireless internet. Pets OK with restrictions
Harris Park	78689 South Fork Walla Walla River Milton-Freewater, OR 97862	541-938-5330 harrisparkmf.com	27 sites, restrooms, no showers, picnic area, playground, covered shelter with electricity and hot water, pets OK. $20.00 per day
Last Resort RV Campground & Park	2005 Tucannon Rd. Dayton, OR 97862	509-843-1556, (800) 562-3417 thelastresortrv.com thelastresort@columbiaenergyllc.com	Located bettween Dayton and Pomeroy. Full hook-up sites, camp store, picnic tables, laundry, showers, pets OK.
Trails West RV Park & Campground	1420 S. Main St. Milton-Freewater, OR 97862	509-525-8450, 509-301-2400	RV hook-ups, pets OK, cable TV, hot showers, tent sites, laundry.
Tucannon River RV Park	511 HWY 261 Dayton, WA 99328	509-339-2056, 888-399-2056 trrvpark.com	28 spaces, full hook-up, all pull - through, spacious & quiet. RR/showers, HC accessible.
Villadom Mobile Home & RV Park	HWY 11 and Crockett Rd. Milton-Freewater, OR 97862	541-938-7247 villadmmhp@gmail.com	Full hook-ups, cable TV, garbage, showers, laundry, pets OK.

* Rates vary by season and availability

Places to Eat

Whether you are a gourmand or just have a craving for a juicy burger, Walla Walla wine country offers an eclectic assortment of eating establishments sure to fit all budgets and appetites. Walla Walla cuisine reflects the Pacific Northwest's evolving culinary scene, emphasizing sustainably grown and locally produced agricultural products. It embodies the slow-food movement, relying on good, fresh, organic food to counteract the fast-food movement. Walla Walla chefs have an abundance of wonderful ingredients to choose from, such as fresh seafood, just-ripened fruit and vegetables, and naturally raised beef. Ethnic diversity abounds in this region, and this rich mixture of cultural heritages — Italian, French, Mediterranean, Creole, and regional American — finds its way onto the menus of local restaurants.

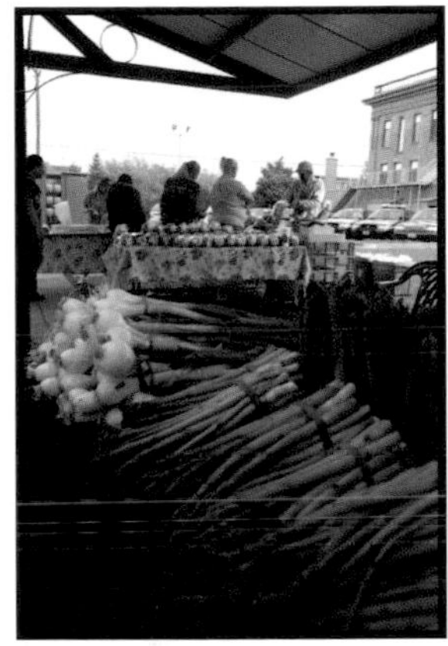

WineTrails of Walla Walla celebrates this unique gastronomic scene by highlighting select restaurants throughout this book. Restaurants such as The Marc, T. Maccarrone's, and Brasserie Four come alive through the insights of food writer Faye Tomlinson and the stunning photography of Alan Ayers. But for every restaurant noted in this guidebook, there are many more we didn't feature, simply because of limited space. So many places to eat, so little time!

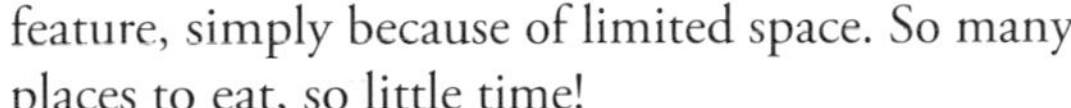

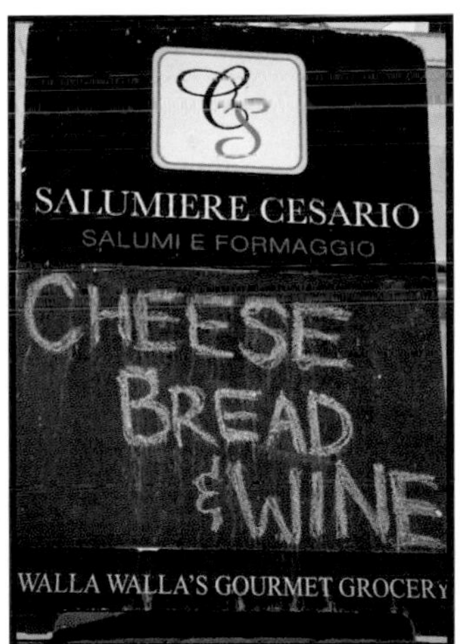

If your visit occurs during the fair-weather season — typically from May to October — make a point of packing a picnic basket and blanket. Choices abound in and around Walla Walla for enjoying an afternoon picnic, including many parks and wineries with picnic areas. Of course, you can always find a vineyard and toss your blanket next to a row of Walla Walla's finest vines for an afternoon respite. Check out Salumiere Cesario, on South Second Avenue, or Olive Marketplace & Café, on Main Street, for fresh meats, cheeses, breads, produce and other picnic fixings.

A list of suggested restaurants, offering a range of price points and types of cuisine, is given below. Admittedly, this is a partial list; there are many other restaurants in the Walla Walla Valley, and the culinary scene is forever changing. However, most of the eateries are unique to Walla Walla and sure to satisfy those pangs of hunger.

Places to Eat

Restaurant	Address	Contact	Hours
Aloha Sushi Sushi $$ - $$$	7 1/2 South 1st Avenue Walla Walla, WA 99362	509-527-8744 alohasushi.net	Mon - Fri 11am - 2pm, Dinner Mon - Thurs 5pm - 8pm, Fri - Sat 5pm - 9pm
Backstage Bistro American $$$	230 East Main Walla Walla, WA 99362	09-526-0690 backstage-bistro.com info@backstage-bistro.com	Lunch Mon - Sat 11am - 3pm, Dinner Mon - Sat 5pm - 9pm, Sun 5pm - 8pm
Bangkok 103 Cafe Thai $$	44 North College Avenue Walla Walla, WA 99362	509-522-3007	Mon - Thurs 5:30pm - 9pm, Fri - Sat 5pm - 8pm,
Brasserie Four French bistro $$ - $$$	4 East Main Street Walla Walla, WA 99362	509-529-2011	Tues 5pm - 10pm, Wed - Sat 12pm to 10pm, Sun 11am - 3pm
Coffee Connection Café American $$	57 East Main Street Walla Walla, WA 99362	509-529-9999 coffeeconnectioncafe.com	Tues - Fri 6am - 3pm, Sat - Sun 7am - 3pm
Colville Street Patisserie Dessert $ - $$	40 South Colville Street Walla Walla, WA 99362	509-301-7289 colvillestreetpatisserie.com	Mon - Tues Closed, Wed - Thurs 9am - 8pm, Fri - Sat 9am - 10pm, Sun 9am - 5pm
CrossRoads Steakhouse and Lounge Steakhouse $$	203 East Rees Avenue Walla Walla, WA 99362	509-522-1200	Sun - Thurs 7am – 11pm, Open until 1 a.m. Fri - Sat, Closed Mondays Oct 1 - May 1
Cugini Italian Import Market Italian/Picnic Supplies $$	960 Wallula Avenue Walla Walla, WA 99362	509-526-0809 cuginiimportfoods.com	Tues - Fri 10am - 6pm, Sat 9am - 5pm
Graze - A Place to Eat Italian sandwiches $ - $$	5 South Colville Street Walla Walla, WA 99362	509-522-9991 grazeevents.com info@grazeevents.com	6 days a week
Jimgermanbar Etruscan snacks/New Orlean cocktails $$	119 Main Street Waitsburg, WA 99361	509-337-6001 jimgermanbar.com	
Manilla Bay Café Asian fusion $$	311 East Main Street Dayton, WA 99328	509-382-2520 manilabaycafe.com	Daily 11:30am - 7:30pm
Mill Creek Brewpub American $$	11 South Palouse Street Walla Walla, WA 99362	509-522-2440 millcreek-brewpub.com gdjbrandy@gmail.com	Mon - Sat 11am - 11pm, Sun 12pm - 9pm
Olive Marketplace & Café Delicattessen, French $$	21 E Main Street Walla Walla, WA 99362	509-526-0200 tmaccarones.com	Daily 7am - 9pm
Onion World - Sweet Onion Sausage Walk-up window sausage and onions $	2 South First #100 Walla Walla, WA 99362	509-522-2541 onionworld.com	Daily 11am - 2pm Extended Hours Fri & Sat 11am - 7pm
Patit Creek Restaurant French $$$	725 Dayton Avenue Dayton, WA 99328	509-382-2625	Wed - Fri 11:30am-2pm & 4:30pm - 8pm or 9pm; Sat 4:30pm - 8pm or 9pm
Pho Sho Vietnamese $	123 West Alder Street Walla Walla, WA 99362	509-525-9794 phoshowallawalla.com	Tues - Sat 11am - 9pm

$ - less than $10 $$ - $10 to $20 $$$ - $20+

Restaurant	Address	Contact	Hours
Raphael's Restaurant & Catering American $$$	233 SE 4th Street Pendleton, OR 97801	541-276-8500 888-944-2433 raphaelsrestaurant.com	June 1st - Sept 15: Tues - Sat 5pm - 9pm, Sept 16 - May 31: Tues - Thurs 5pm -8pm, Fri & Sat 5pm - 9pm
Saffron Mediterranean Kitchen Mediterranean $$$	125 West Alder Street Walla Walla, WA 99362	509-525-2112 saffronmediterraneankitchen.com	May - Oct: Tues - Thurs 2pm - 10pm, Fri & Sat 2pm - 11pm & Sun 2pm - 10pm
Salumiere Cesario Gourmet grocery/ picnic $$	20 North 2nd Avenue Walla Walla, WA 99362	509-529-5620 salumierecesario.com	Mon, Thurs - Sat 11am - 6pm, Sun 11am - 4pm Closed Tues & Wed
Stone Soup Café Soups, salads & sandwiches $$	105 East Alder Walla Walla, WA 99362	509-525-5008 stonesoupcafe.net	Mon - Fri 8am to 8pm
Sweet Basil Pizzeria Pizza $$	5 South First Avenue Walla Walla, WA 99362	509-529-1950 sweetbasilpizzeria.com	Mon - Thurs 11am - 8pm, Fri - Sat 11am - 9pm
T Maccarone's $$$	4 North Colville Street Walla Walla, WA 99362	509-522-4776 tmaccarones.com	Dinner: 7 Days 4pm - 9pm Lunch: Mon - Fri 11am - 2pm Brunch: Sat & Sun 9am - 2pm
The Marc Restaurant Pacific Northwest $$$	Six West Rose Marcus Whitman Hotel Walla Walla, WA 99362	509-525-2200 marcuswhitmanhotel.com	Lunch: Mon - Fri 11:30am - 1:30pm, Dinner: Daily 6pm - 9pm Sun - Thurs 6pm - 9:30pm Friday & Saturday
The Oasis at Stateline American- steak and seafood $$	85698 Old Milton-Freewater Milton-Freewater, OR 97862	541-938-4776	Open 9am Wed - Sun
The Vine American $$$	1072 Oasis Road Touchet, WA 99360	509.394.0211 cameoheightsmansion.com info@cameoheights.com	Tues - Sat 5pm - 9pm, Lunch served on Friday
Tony's Sub Shop Subs $	1068 E Isaacs Ave Walla Walla, WA 99362	509- 529-5516	Open daily
Vineyard Lounge & Winebar Burgers, sandwiches & salads $$	Six West Rose Walla Walla, WA 99362	509-525-2200 marcuswhitmanhotel.com	Open daily at 5pm
Vintage Cellars Wine Bar Wine bar/Bistro fare $$	10 North 2nd Avenue Walla Walla, WA 99362	509-529-9340 vintagewinebar.org	Tues - Thurs 10am - 10pm, Mon 4pm - 10pm
Weinhard Café American $$$	258 East Main Dayton, WA 99328	509-382-1681 weinhard-cafe.com info@weinhard-cafe.com	11am - 2pm Dinner Starts 5pm
Whitehouse-Crawford Restaurant Pacific Northwest $$$	55 West Cherry Street Walla Walla, WA 99362	509-525-2222 whitehousecrawford.com	Wed - Mon 5pm - 9pm Drinks and Appetizers 4pm - 10pm
Whoopemup Hollow Café Cajun/Southern Comfort $$$	120 Main Street Waitsburg, WA 99361	509-337-9000 whoopemuphollowcafe.com info@whoopemuphollowcafe.com	Wed - Sun 3pm - 9pm

$ - less than $10 $$ - $10 to $20 $$$ - $20+

Pepper
Bridge

Winery Amenities

WineTrail	Winery	Gift Shop	Lodging	Picnic	Receptions	Restaurant	Tasting Room	Tours	Weddings	Wine Club	Pg #
	428			●			●				146
	Abeja		●			●	●	●			222
	Adamant Cellars			●			●			●	152
	àMaurice Cellars			●			●				168
	Amavi Cellars			●			●	●		●	184
	Ash Hollow Winery	●					●	●		●	156
	Balboa Winery			●			●			●	188
	Basel Cellars Estate Winery	●	●	●		●	●	●	●	●	178
	Beresan Winery			●			●	●		●	186
	Bergevin Lane Vineyards	●					●	●		●	110
	Bunchgrass Winery			●			●	●			60
	Buty Winery						●			●	144
	Cadaretta										222
	Canoe Ridge Vineyard	●					●	●		●	116
	Castillo de Feliciana			●			●	●	●	●	200
	CAVU Cellars			●			●			●	154
	Cayuse Vineyards						●				229
	Chateau Rollat Winery						●				88
	College Cellars of Walla Walla						●	●	●		164
	Cougar Crest Estate Winery	●		●			●	●		●	54
	Couvillion Winery						●				223
	DaMa Wines						●			●	90
	Doubleback										229
	Dowsett Family Winery										229
	Dumas Station Wines										223
	Dunham Cellars	●		●			●	●		●	130
	Dusted Valley Vintners			●			●	●		●	202
	El Corazon Winery						●			●	98
	Eleganté Cellars						●			●	134
	Ensemble Cellars										224
	Five Star Cellars	●					●	●		●	136
	Forgeron Cellars	●					●	●		●	104
	Fort Walla Walla Cellars	●		●			●	●		●	92
	Foundry Vineyards			●			●			●	112
	Gardena Creek Winery										229
	Garrison Creek Cellars			●			●				224
	Gifford Hirlinger Winery			●			●			●	212

Winery Amenities

Winery	Gift Shop	Lodging	Picnic	Receptions	Restaurant	Tasting Room	Tours	Weddings	Wine Club	P	Wine Trail
Glencorrie						●			●	52	
Gramercy Cellars			●			●				225	
Isenhower Cellars	●					●	●		●	204	
JLC Winery/Spofford Station						●			●	214	
K Vintners			●			●	●			166	
Kontos Cellars			●			●			●	148	
L'Ecole Nº 41	●		●			●	●		●	48	
Le Chateau Winery	●					●			●	126	
Leonetti Cellar						●				229	
Locati Cellars	●					●			●	70	
Lodmell Cellars			●			●			●	150	
Long Shadows Vintners			●			●	●		●	225	
Lowden Hills Winery	●		●			●	●		●	118	
Mannina Cellars						●			●	138	
Morrison Lane Winery						●	●			108	
Nicholas Cole Cellars						●	●		●	94	
Northstar Winery	●		●	●	●	●	●		●	196	
Otis Kenyon Wine						●			●	82	
Patit Creek Cellars	●		●	●		●	●	●	●	132	
Patrick M. Paul Vineyards						●	●		●	226	
Pepper Bridge Winery			●			●	●		●	198	
Rasa Vineyards										229	
Reininger Winery	●		●			●	●		●	56	
Revelry Vintners						●				226	
Reynvaan Family Cellars										229	
Robison Ranch Cellars						●			●	227	
Rotie Cellars						●				86	
Rulo Winery						●	●			206	
Russell Creek Winery						●	●		●	128	
Sapolil Cellars						●			●	80	
Sapphire Mountain Cellars										229	
Saviah Cellars			●			●	●		●	190	
Seven Hills Winery						●	●		●	72	
Skylite Cellars				●		●			●	62	
Sleight of Hand Cellars						●			●	76	
Spring Valley Vineyard						●	●			74	
Stephenson Cellars						●	●		●	100	

Winery Amenities

WineTrail	Winery	Gift Shop	Lodging	Picnic	Receptions	Restaurant	Tasting Room	Tours	Weddings	Wine Club	Pg #
	Sweet Valley Wines						●			●	78
	SYZYGY			●			●	●		●	142
	Tamarack Cellars						●	●		●	140
	Tertulia Cellars			●			●			●	208
	Thirsty Pagans										229
	Three Rivers Winery	●		●	●		●	●	●	●	58
	Tranche Cellars										228
	Trio Vintners	●		●			●			●	102
	Tru Cellars	●					●			●	227
	Trust Cellars			●			●			●	210
	Va Piano Vineyards	●		●			●			●	194
	Walla Faces Wines		●				●			●	96
	Walla Walla Village Winery	●		●			●	●		●	106
	Walla Walla Vintners			●			●	●			170
	Walla Walla Wine Works	●		●			●				84
	Waterbrook Winery	●		●	●		●	●	●	●	50
	Watermill & Blue Mountain			●			●			●	182
	Waters Winery			●			●				192
	Whitman Cellars	●					●	●		●	114
	Woodward Canyon Winery	●		●	●		●	●			46
	Zerba Cellars			●			●			●	180

Artist Series #16
Irene Yesley
WOODWARD CANYON
2007
Washington State Cabernet Sauvignon
ALC. 14.6% BY VOL.

DUSTED
VALLEY
MALBEC
Columbia Valley 2007

BeResAn
WINERY
2005 Semillon
WALLA WALLA VALLEY
ALC. 13.7% BY VOL.

SAPOLIL CELLARS
2006 SYRAH
Patina Vineyard, Walla Walla Valley

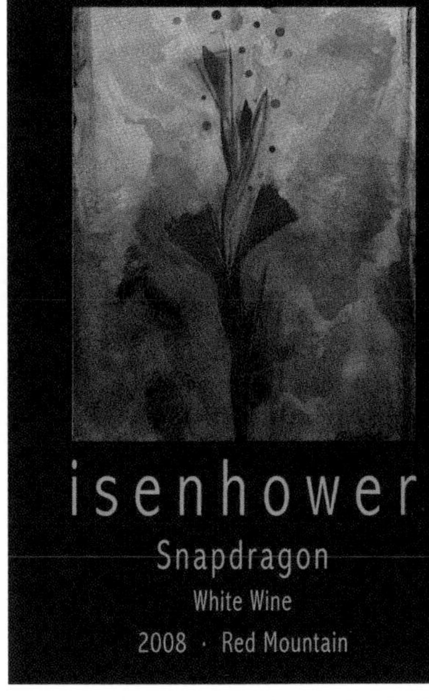
isenhower
Snapdragon
White Wine
2008 · Red Mountain

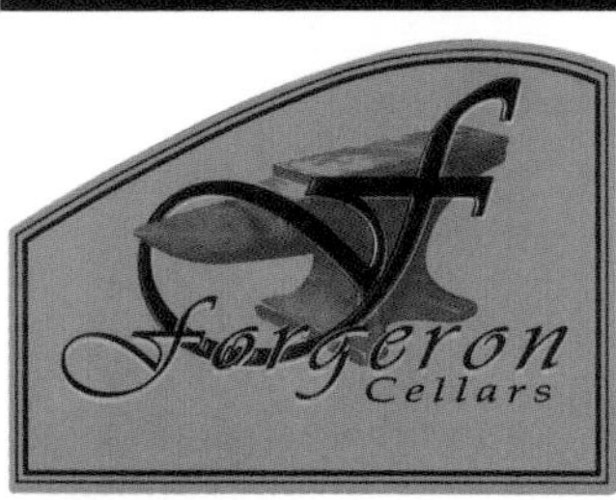
Forgeron
Cellars
2006 Roussane
Columbia Valley
Alc. 13.8% by vol.

WHITMAN
Cellars
2005 Narcissa Red
Walla Walla Valley
13.8% Alcohol by Volume

ROSÉ
cabernet franc
columbia valley
2008
TRUST

Dunham
Cellars
THREE
LEGGED
RED
2004
Alc 13.8% by Vol.
COLUMBIA VALLEY

SLEIGHT OF HAND
CELLARS
THE SPELLBINDER
2008
Columbia Valley Red Wine

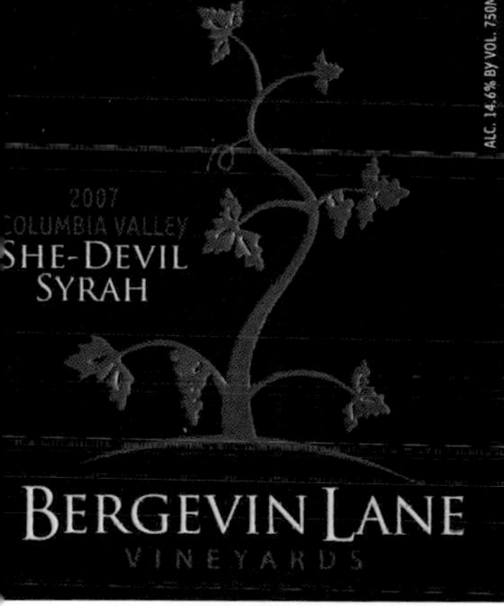
ALC. 14.6% BY VOL. 750ML
2007
COLUMBIA VALLEY
SHE-DEVIL
SYRAH
BERGEVIN LANE
VINEYARDS

WALLA WALLA
SPRING VALLEY VINEYARD
WASHINGTON
ESTATE
GROWN
2006
Uriah
WALLA WALLA VALLEY RED WINE
ALC. 14.9% BY VOL.

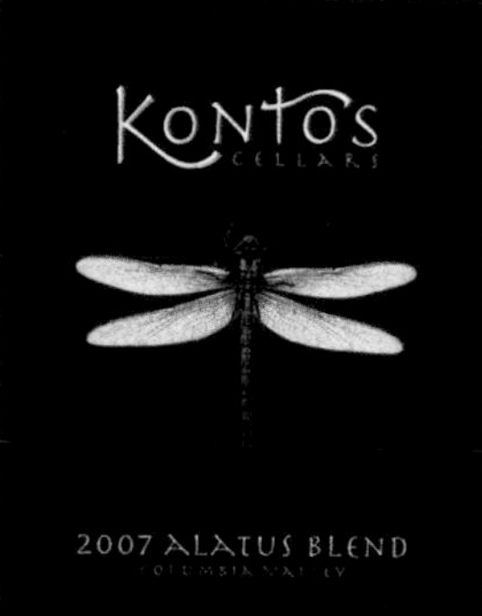
KONTOS
CELLARS
2007 ALATUS BLEND

NORTHSTAR
CABERNET
SAUVIGNON
COLUMBIA VALLEY
2006
ALC. 14.9% BY VOL.

SEVEN HILLS
Merlot
SEVEN HILLS VINEYARD
WALLA WALLA VALLEY
2006
ALCOHOL 13.7% BY VOLUME

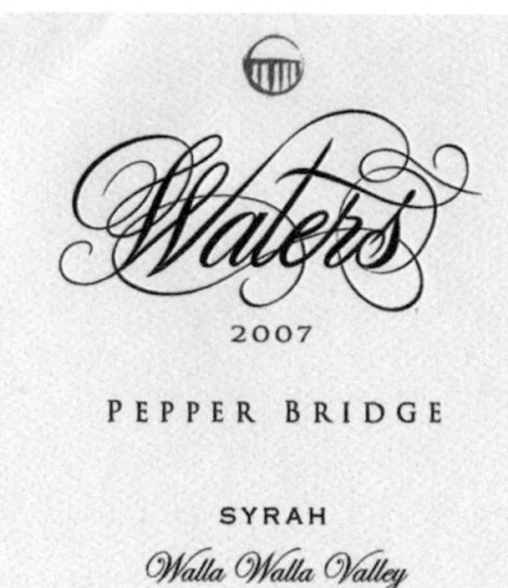
Waters
2007
PEPPER BRIDGE
SYRAH
Walla Walla Valley
ALCOHOL 14.1% BY VOLUME

tertulia cellars

2003
Columbia Valley
SYRAH

LEGENDS
Four Horsemen

WineTrail West

Walla Walla West WineTrail

Be sure to slow down going through the postage-stamp-size town of Lowden, and not just because of the speed limit. Lowden is the home of L'Ecole Nº 41 and Woodward Canyon wineries, and because they are located next door to one another, they are a convenient stop traveling to and from Walla Walla. However, realize that these are but two among a many splendid wineries on this WineTrail that offer a diversity of wines and tasting-room experiences. Many are well established, many are brand-new, but all possess a passionate desire to make great wine. At the end of the day, your biggest challenge could be identifying your favorite. All of these wineries are good and each offers some "Kodak moments".

WineTrail Tip: Plan to pack a picnic and visit the Whitman Mission National Historic Site, located just off Highway 12.

Walla Walla WineTrail West

1 Woodward Canyon Winery
2 L'Ecole Nº 41
3 Waterbrook Winery
4 Glencorrie
5 Cougar Crest Estate Winery
6 Reininger Winery
7 Three Rivers Winery
8 Bunchgrass Winery
9 Skylite Cellars

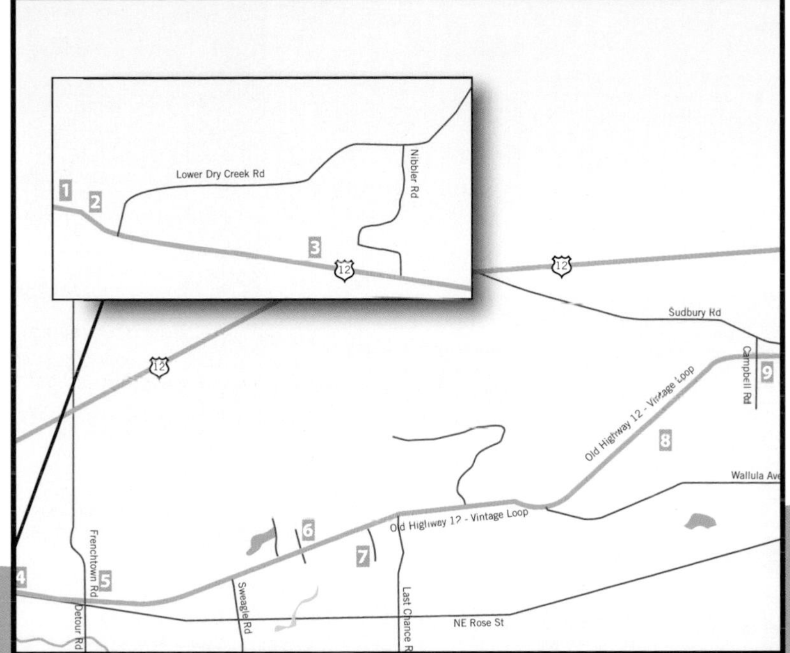

Region: **Walla Walla Wine Country**

# of tasting rooms on tour: **9**

Estimate # of days for tour: **2**

Getting around: **Car**

Key Events:

- **Events sponsored by Walla Walla Valley Wine Alliance: Spring Release Weekend (first full weekend of May); Balloon Stampede Weekend (second full weekend of May); Vintage Walla Walla (first full weekend of June); Entwine: An auction to support Walla Walla Arts, Wine, and Education (mid-October); and Holiday Barrel Tasting (first full weekend of December). See winetrailsnw.com for details.**

Tips:

- **Three Rivers Winery offers a mini 3-hole golf course (free).**
- **Be sure and view the artwork at Woodward Canyon.**
- **Consider using a limousine service (e.g., Black Tie Limo 509-525-8585, Blue Stocking Tours 509-522-4717, Sunset Coach Tours 509-303-0355, or Four Star Limousine Service 509-521-7849 are some of the many services to contact).**

Best:

- **Gift shop: L'Ecole Nº 41, Three Rivers Winery**
- **Picnicking: Cougar Crest Estate Winery, Reininger Winery, Three Rivers Winery**

Saffron Mediterranean Kitchen

Photo by Alan Ayers

The first thing you will notice when you walk into Saffron Mediterranean Kitchen is the tantalizing aromas wafting from the open kitchen. Next, you will sense the creative energy that fills the air. The source of this creative energy is Saffron's owners, Island and Chris Ainsworth, who were inspired to open Saffron Mediterranean Kitchen in 2007. What continues to inspire Chris and Island is the dedicated following of both locals and tourists, who love the adventurous and spirited dishes that Chris creates.

Photo by Alan Ayers

As chef, Chris uses the freshest local ingredients he can find and combines them in innovative ways, building a menu that conjures up visions of leisurely dinners along the Mediterranean coast. Island's charm shines as she helps diners navigate the menu, which at first might appear unfamiliar. A recent menu included three flatbreads with the exotic names of pastirma and onion pide pie, gozleme, and lahmacun.

Photo by Alan Ayers

The enticing flavors of the bold dishes at Saffron Mediterranean Kitchen call for wines that are equally enticing. Chris and Island are excited that more wines of Spanish origin, such as tempranillo, are being produced locally. These wines, says Chris, are perfect complements to Saffron's Mediterranean-inspired dishes.

What is the secret to making Saffron Mediterranean Kitchen such a fun restaurant? According to the Ainsworths, it is the family atmosphere they have created with their staff, their purveyors, and their customers. As Island so succinctly puts it: "Diners start their meals as strangers and end up sharing dessert."

Photo by Alan Ayers

125 West Alder Street
Walla Walla, WA 99362
509-525-2112
saffronmediterraneankitchen.com

Pho Sho

Need a break from wine tasting? Then head to Chris and Island Ainsworth's second restaurant, Pho Sho, for a glass of beer or a cup of sake and a delicious selection of Vietnamese small plates. The Ainsworths opened Pho Sho to cook up the foods that they missed eating. Judging from Pho Sho's local following, it appears that the Ainsworths aren't the only Walla Wallans who enjoy Vietnamese food.

Photo by Alan Ayers

The carefully selected beers that appear on the menu pair nicely with the spicy Vietnamese dishes. For a little variety, the Ainsworths occasionally hold sake tastings to demonstrate to diners how well this underappreciated drink complements Vietnamese food.

123 West Alder Street
Walla Walla, WA 99362
509-525-9794
phoshowallawalla.com

Woodward Canyon Winery 1

Located off Highway 12 in Lowden is the 1870s farmhouse that serves as Woodward Canyon's primary tasting room. Next to this charming room is the new Reserve House, built for private tastings and special events. If you get a chance to experience the Reserve House, do so. It's lovely, especially when owner Rick Small is pouring and sharing his zeal. In fact, the Reserve House definitely makes my top 10 list of winemaker-dinner venues.

Started in 1981 by Rick and his wife, Darcey Fugman-Small, Woodward Canyon is among the group of original wineries that served as the "starter dough" for the whole Walla Walla Valley wine industry. Rick honed his self-taught winemaking skills in the mid-'70s by collaborating with Gary Figgins, who would go on to create famed Leonetti Cellar. Rick believes that "intensity is key," and he is passionate about Woodward Canyon's vineyard, spending a great deal of time there as well as working with select vineyards in Columbia Valley, Horse Heaven Hills and, of course, Walla Walla Valley. His philosophy remains the same: quality over quantity, and the numerous awards throughout the years speak volumes about Woodward Canyon's success.

Woodward Canyon's winemaker, Kevin Mott, produces about 15,000 cases annually. Its premium wines include cabernet sauvignon, merlot, Bordeaux blends, chardonnay, sauvignon blanc, and riesling. In addition, Woodward Canyon diverges from Bordeaux-only wines, to make dolcetto and barbera wines as well. You don't need to store these wines in the cellar; enjoy them today with Italian food or red meat dishes, including your everyday backyard-grilled burger. Woodward Canyon also makes a second "declassified" label wine called Nelms Road, known for its excellent value.

Each year since 1992, Woodward Canyon has selected an original artwork to adorn the label of its top-quality cabernet sauvignon. That year's original vintage painting hangs in the tasting room through the year. Also found in the tasting room is the full line-up of the artist series of vintage wine bottles, with their distinctive labels. As noted on the winery website, the great French painter Paul Cézanne, in a letter written later in his life, asked, "Is art a kind of priesthood where only the most pure of heart are allowed to enter?" At Woodward Canyon, art is for everyone. For WineTrail enthusiasts visiting this winery, art can be seen on a canvas and tasted from a bottle.

WOODWARD CANYON WINERY
opened: 1981
winemaker(s): Kevin Mott
location: 11920 West Highway 12, Lowden, WA 99360
phone: 509-525-4129
web: www.woodwardcanyon.com
e-mail: getthedirt@woodwardcanyon.com
picnic area: Yes
wheelchair access: Yes
gift shop: Yes
tours: Yes
fee: Tasting fee refundable with purchase
hours: Daily 10–5
lat: 46.056098 **long:** -118.58174

DIRECTIONS: **From Walla Walla** take Hwy 12 west about 17 miles to Lowden. Look for Woodward Canyon Winery on the right next to L'Ecole Nº 41. in a restored farmhouse.

From Tri-Cities take Hwy 12 for about 34 miles, through the town of Touchet. Continuing east on Hwy 12 will take you through the small town of Lowden. Look for Woodward Canyon Winery on your left after you enter Lowden.

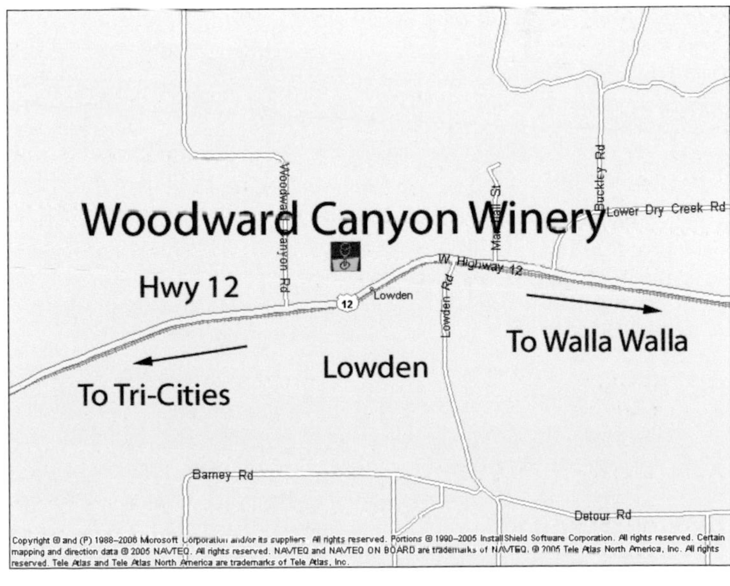

L'Ecole N° 41 2

Whatever you do, don't skip school whenever you pass through Lowden on old Highway 12. Specifically, be in attendance at the Walla Walla Valley's iconic L'Ecole N° 41 winery, housed in a former "Frenchtown" schoolhouse. A rendering of this 1915 building adorns L'Ecole N° 41's distinctive labels, drawn in 1983 by then-8-year-old Ryan Campbell when the winery was established. Ryan just happened to enter an art contest conducted by L'Ecole N° 41. They liked his drawing so much that they decided to use it for the label. Appropriately enough, Ryan now lives and works in Boston as a successful architect.

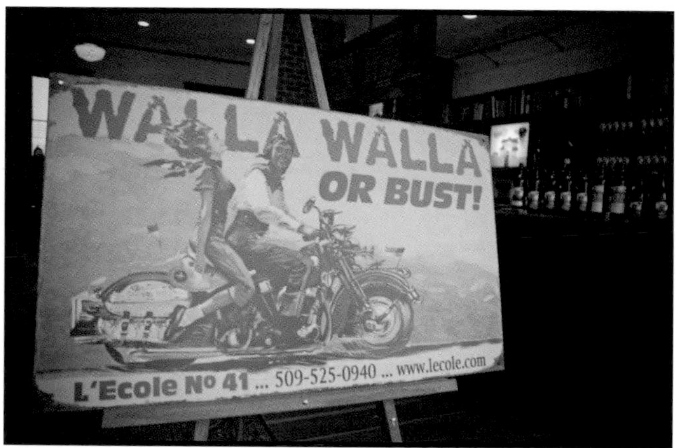

Established in 1983, L'Ecole N° 41 is the Walla Walla Valley's third-oldest winery, with only Woodward Canyon and Leonetti Cellar being a little older. Today, L'Ecole N° 41 produces about 35,000 cases annually, guided by a philosophy of traditional hands-on winemaking. Its owners, Megan and Martin Clubb, are clear about their goal: "To achieve clean, ripe, stylistically expressive and aromatic wines that let the individual site characteristics of our vineyards shine through." While Martin spends most of his time these days managing the vineyards, winemaker Mike Sharon is usually at the winery overseeing the punching, bottling, labeling, tasting, racking, de-stemming, and the rest of the ever-growing mountain of other chores that go into creating wine from grapes.

This schoolhouse of bygone days will take you back in time; the sounds, the smells, and even the fine craftsmanship of the building itself will have you imagining the sounds of laughing children playing at recess. As you walk inside, check out the cast-iron school bell at the entrance. In the upstairs tasting room, you will notice an old chalkboard now used to list L'Ecole N° 41's wines and prices. A stained-glass replica of L'Ecole N° 41 gracefully sits center stage behind the wine bar. The gift shop offers a variety of wine-related items and L'Ecole N° 41 logo–bedecked clothing and gear.

L'Ecole N° 41 produces a variety of red and white wines from estate grapes and fruit acquired from Columbia Valley and local vineyards. Given the vines established maturity, expect to see more estate- and single-vineyard wines forwarding the future. You will want to budget a good half-hour to sample these wines and visit with the friendly and well-trained tasting room staff. Fielding questions about L'Ecole N° 41 and the winemaking process with patience and engaging smiles, they are, by all appearances, very well schooled.

L'ECOLE Nº 41
opened: 1983
winemaker(s): Mike Sharon
location: 41 Lowden School Road, Lowden, WA 99360
phone: 509-525-0940
web: www.lecole.com
e-mail: info@lecole.com
picnic area: Yes
gift shop: Yes
tours: Yes
fee: Tasting fee refundable with purchase
hours: Daily 10–5; closed New Year's Day, Easter, 4th of July, Thanksgiving and Christmas; closed 1 p.m. December 24 and 31
lat: 46.048784 **long:** -118.591215

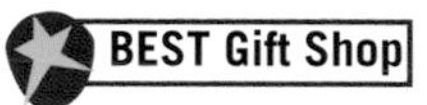

BEST Gift Shop

DIRECTIONS: **From Walla Walla**, head west on Hwy 12 for about 17 miles. L'Ecole Nº 41 is just off the highway at 41 Lowden School Rd on the right in Lowden.

From the Tri-Cities take Hwy 12 east for approximately 30 miles to the winery. You'll pass through the town of Touchet before coming to Lowden. L'Ecole Nº 41 is just off the highway at 41 Lowden School Rd on the left in Lowden.

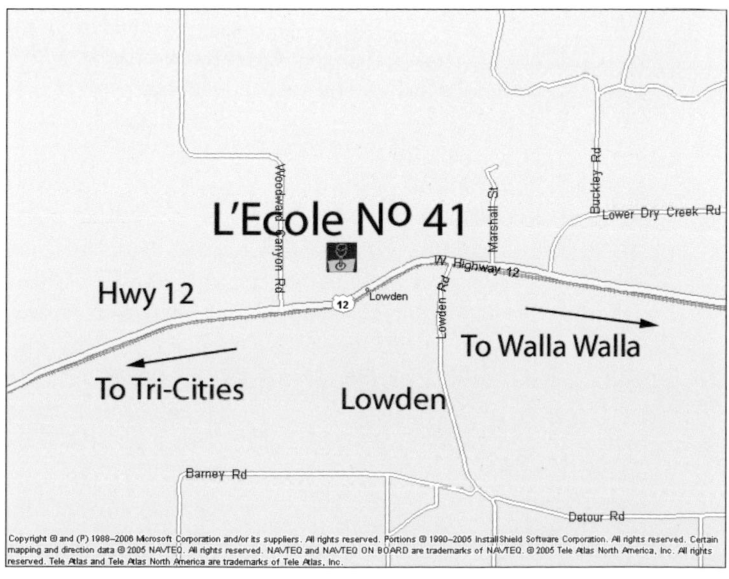

Waterbrook Winery 3

The new Waterbrook Winery tasting room might be 11 miles west of downtown Walla Walla, but it is a million miles away from its former digs. Its previous tasting room in downtown Walla Walla is now the site of Walla Walla Wine Works, where parent company Precept Wine Brands offers a variety of labels for visitors to sample, including Waterbrook's wines. But if you have an ounce of free time, hop in your car and head west, young wine traveler, and check out the results of a love affair with Washington wine and great business acumen.

Opened in 2009 (coincidently on its 25th anniversary), Waterbrook Winery's new tasting pavilion is much more than a simple tasting room. It's a statement — a statement about Waterbrook Winery's amazing success story as well as a commentary about the Washington wine industry as a whole. You can't help but be impressed by the contemporary Northwest-style, 5,000-square-foot facility and more than a little curious about experiencing the award-winning wines that brought you here.

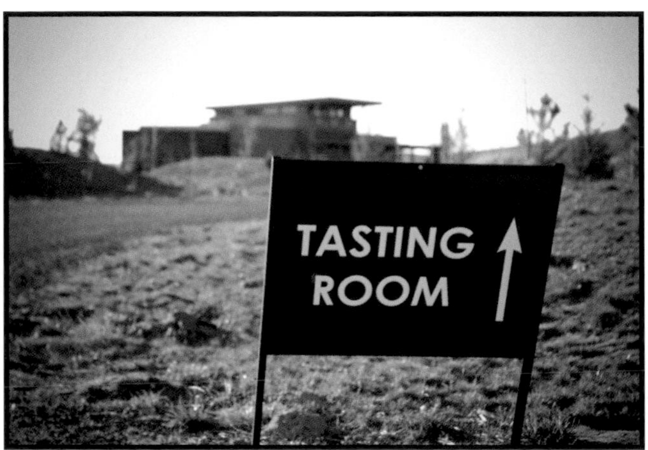

Situated on 75 acres, Waterbrook Winery's tasting center is where most visitors will come and linger. Expansive floor-to-ceiling windows provide a view of the 53,000-square-foot production facility beyond the pond. As you swirl and sip, try to imagine the 10,000 wine barrels resting in the production facility as they age wine for Waterbrook and other Precept Wine Brand labels. This is production on an advanced scale.

The friendly tasting room staff will guide visitors through a robust line-up of winemaker John Freeman's creations, which include dry whites, crisp rosés, and smooth but complex reds. My personal favorites are Waterbrook's varietally true chardonnay and its signature "Mélange Noir," which answers the age-old question "What do you get when you blend merlot, cabernet franc, cabernet sauvignon, and sangiovese?" Answer: liquid joy.

Inside the tasting room, there's plenty to marvel at, including the high ceiling with its huge beams, the natural earth tones, and the pleasing textures. The space mirrors the beauty of the surrounding Walla Walla Valley's rolling wheatfields and the Blue Mountains beyond. Lucky visitors on weekend nights can spring for a cheese plate and a glass (or two) of Waterbrook wines, and retreat to the outside patio and contemplate the meaning of life. Or, you can do what I do and relish the moment.

WATERBROOK WINERY
opened: 1984
winemaker(s): John Freeman
location: 10518 West Highway 12, Walla Walla, WA 99362
phone: 509-522-1262
web: www.waterbrook.com
e-mail: info@waterbrook.com
picnic area: Yes
wheelchair access: Yes
weddings: Yes
gift shop: Yes
tours: Yes
fee: Tasting fee applies
hours: Monday through Friday 10–6, Saturday 10–8, and Sunday 10–4
lat: 46.055239 **long:** -118.559073

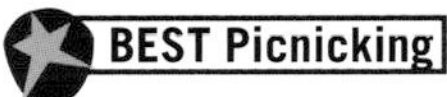

DIRECTIONS: **From Walla Walla**, head west on Hwy 12 for about 14 miles. Waterbrook Winery is on the right at 10518 West Highway 12.

From the Tri-Cities take Hwy 12 east for approximately 30 miles to the winery. You'll pass through the towns of Touchet and Lowden before reaching the winery. Waterbrook Winery is on the left at 10518 West Highway 12.

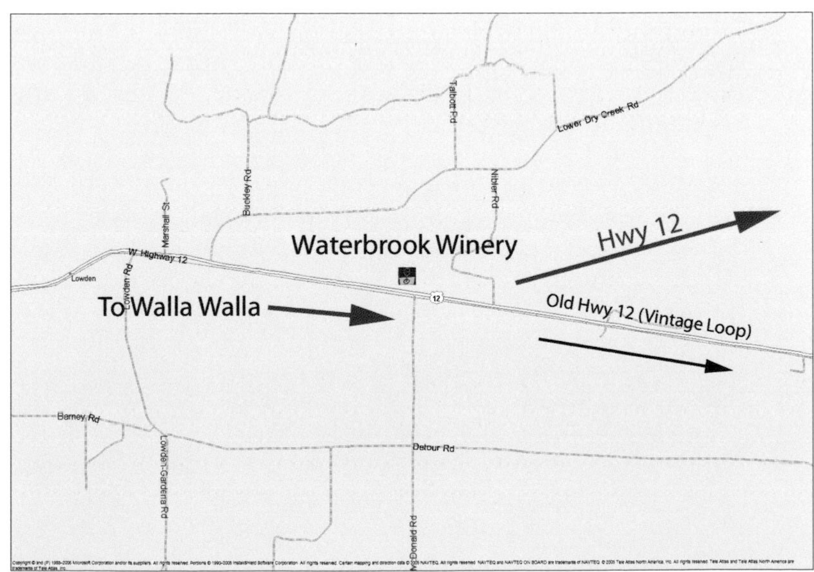

Glencorrie 4

As in life, finding the right balance in wine is the goal of all great winemakers; moderation is a good thing. Exceptional wines embody qualities of moderation: not too flabby, but not too sour either; just the right amount of oak; a fruit-forward taste on the front end and a long-lasting finish, perhaps with a lingering spice note (love that). All of these characteristics and more define a good, balanced wine. Such a wine can be rather elusive, but when found, it strikes a harmonious chord.

One evening in 2004, before they started Glencorrie winery, brothers Ronn and Dean Coldiron were having dinner in Spokane, and the Walla Walla merlot they ordered just so happened to perfectly complement their meat dish. The flawless pairing and their subsequent "aha" moment gave definition to the wine style they were seeking: food-friendly wine to match a beef dish or a meal with rich sauces. We're talking opulent reds with layered flavors, tannins for structure, and strong acidity. At the time, the brothers, who were living in the Bay Area, knew they wanted to act on their love of wine and open a winery, but deciding upon a wine style provided them with the compass they needed, and it directed them to Walla Walla to establish their vineyard and winery.

It was a stroke of luck when 13 acres of prime real estate became available west of Walla Walla along old Highway 12. The choice acreage is south-facing, with excellent air drainage and the ideal soil for planting food-friendly Bordeaux varieties. The brothers contracted with family-owned, well-established vineyards in the Columbia Valley for their fruit (and continue to do so while waiting for their own vineyard to mature). Armed with the best fruit, they then secured the services of Charlie Hoppes, the owner and winemaker of renowned Fidelitas Wines. Intentionally keeping production small — at only 650 cases — the brothers succeeded in hitting a home run with their initial release. In December 2009, *Wine Press Northwest* awarded the 2006 Glencorrie Cabernet Sauvignon a Double Platinum award, stating, "It's a beautifully *balanced* wine that should age gracefully for a decade or more." That's an auspicious beginning, and it doesn't hurt that Ronn has a Ph.D. in geology and brother Dean's background is in finance. Like peas and carrots, peanut butter and jelly, the two complement one another.

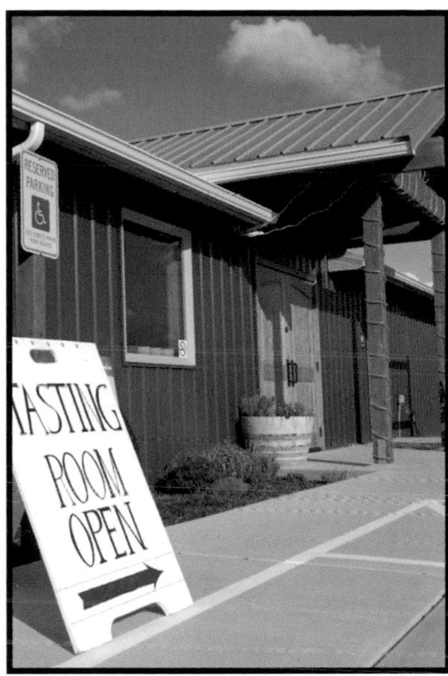

GLENCORRIE
opened: 2009
winemaker(s): Charlie Hoppes
location: 8052 West Highway 12, Walla Walla, WA 99362
phone: 509-525-2585
web: www.glencorrie.com
e-mail: via website
wheelchair access: Yes
fee: Tasting fee refundable with purchase
hours: Daily 10–5
lat: 46.049875 **long:** -118.502796

DIRECTIONS: **From Walla Walla**, head west on Hwy 12 for about 9 miles. Turn left on Frenchtown Rd. At the stop sign. turn right on Vintage Loop (Old Hwy 12) and Glencorrie is on the right.

From the Tri-Cities take Hwy 12 east for approximately 35 miles. Pass through the towns of Touchet and Lowden. Glencorrie is about 5 miles east of Touchet and a few miles east of Lowden. Past Waterbrook winery turn left onto Vintage Loop (Old Hwy 12) and continue for about a mile. Look for Glencorrie on the left.

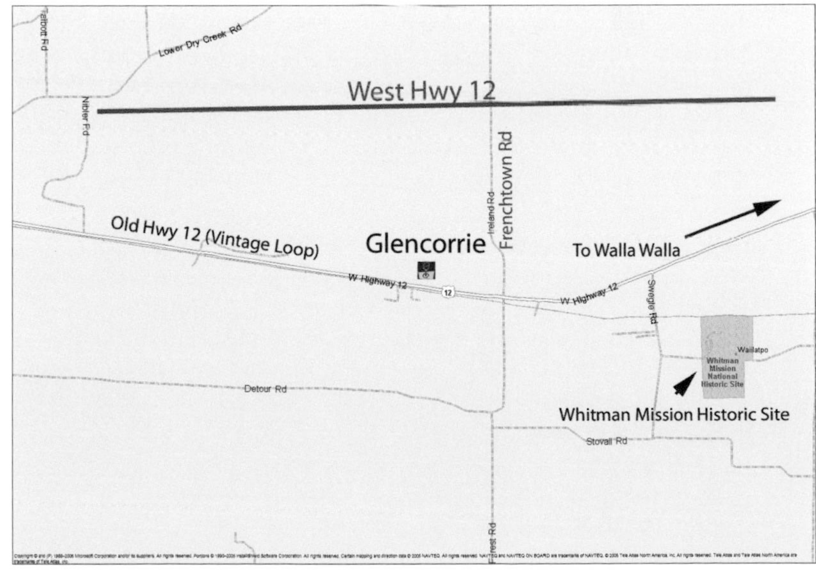

Cougar Crest Estate Winery 5

In the spring of 2008, Cougar Crest Estate Winery moved to its new 13,000-square-foot home on Frenchtown Road, right off the old Highway 12. To say that its new digs are an improvement over its original airport location in a Quonset hut is a major understatement.

This new, environmentally friendly $3.2 million facility is downright sumptuous. There's plenty of space to sit and relax, marvel at fine art, which includes selected works by Jeffrey Hill and Karen Ehart, and, of course, taste award-winning wine. Inside the Prairie-style facility, visitors bask in natural light from windows positioned in the dramatic cupola above. Here, you can purchase a glass of wine, camp out in front of the stone fireplace, and take in peek-a-boo views of the production area. You lose your sense of time here and before you know it, lunch plans give way to dinner plans.

Dave and Deborah Hansen, the owners of Cougar Crest Estate Winery, take pride in the fact that their labels bear the word "estate." Relying on earth-friendly, sustainable practices, Dave manages their vineyards, which are located just south of Walla Walla on the Oregon side of the state line. While most mortals would be sleeping, he might be turning on the wind machines to prevent a frosty cold snap from harming the vines. With fall's crush, it's time for winemaker Deborah to take over. In this role, her scientific training as a pharmacist comes in very handy. Deborah's minimalist winemaking style calls for careful extraction of the tannins and judicious use of oak to preserve the varietal character of the fruit. It's in the blending of the wine that science is set aside in favor of an experienced palate to derive the best blends.

For me, Cougar Crest Estate Winery's Dedication red table wines reflect this art of blending. The Hansens chose the wines' name to honor the sacrifice and professionalism shown by Portland-based Doernbecher Children's Hospital staff when saving their daughter's life following a life-threatening injury. With their layered complexity and wonderful mouthfeel, Cougar Crest's Dedication wines never disappoint.

To taste Cougar Crest Estate Wines, you need to make a beeline to its new place on Frenchtown Road. The name "Cougar Crest" is a natural extension of the Hansens' academic background. Both Dave and Deborah are Washington State University graduates. However, even if you are a diehard rival purple-and-gold Husky, you will want to brake for this Cougar.

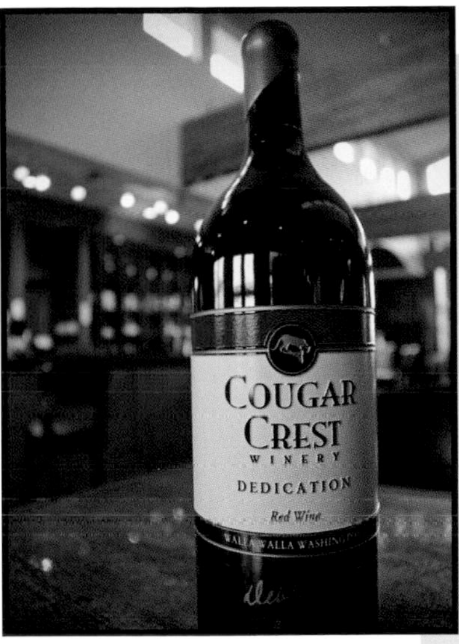

BEST Picnicking

COUGAR CREST ESTATE WINERY
opened: 2001
winemaker(s): Deborah Hansen
location: 50 Frenchtown Road, Walla Walla, WA 99362
phone: 509-529-5980
web: www.cougarcrestwinery.com
e-mail: info@cougarcrestwinery.com
picnic area: Yes
wheelchair access: Yes
gift shop: Yes
tours: Yes
fee: Tasting fee refundable with purchase
hours: Daily 10–5
lat: 46.064581 **long:** -118.343021
satellite location: 202 A Street, Walla Walla, WA 99362-8497
satellite hours: Friday and Saturday 11–4

DIRECTIONS: **From Walla Walla** go west on Hwy 12 for about 8 miles. Turn left on Frenchtown Rd exit and continue to Vintage Loop (Old Hwy 12). Cougar Crest winery is on your left at the corner of Frenchtown Rd and Vintage Loop (Old Hwy 12).

From the Tri-Cities take Hwy 12 east for approximately 35 miles to the winery. You'll pass through the towns of Touchet and Lowden. Take a right to get to Vintage Loop (Old Hwy 12) and continue about 5 miles. Cougar Crest winery is on the left at the Frenchtown Rd exit.

Another Cougar Crest Estate Winery tasting room is located at the Walla Walla Regional Airport Complex. **From Walla Walla**, take Hwy 12 going east for 3 miles. Take the Walla Walla Airport exit and go left (north) onto Airport Rd, which becomes A St. Arrive at 202 A St. on the right.

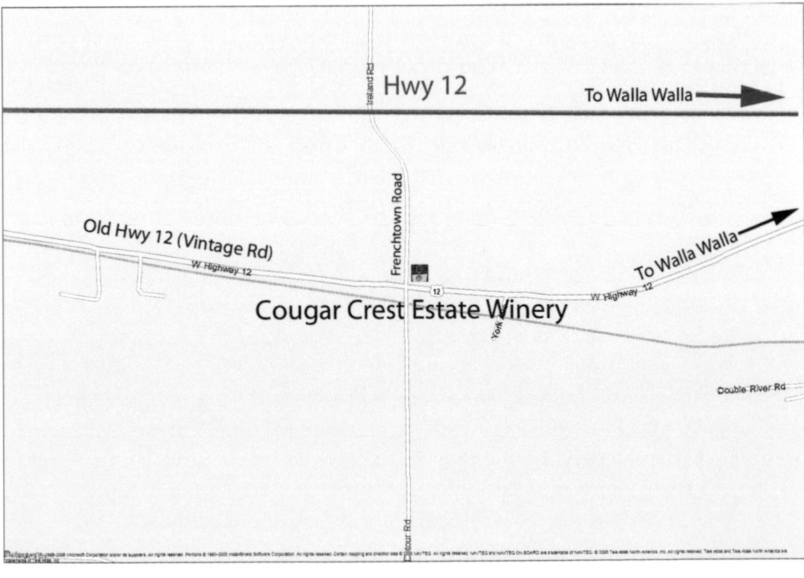

Reininger Winery 6

Winemaking has a way of attracting people from different career fields. Washington's wine scene includes many lawyers, doctors, engineers, and accountants who pick up winemaking as a second career. But how about adventuresome souls whose résumés include mountaineer and climbing guide? Such is the case with Charles Reininger of Reininger Winery.

After working as a mountain guide for many years, Charles hung up his ice axe, moved to the Walla Walla Valley, and married Tracy Tucker, a Walla Walla native. That was back in the early '90s. It was around this time that Charles caught the wine bug and began assisting at Waterbrook Winery, dabbling in home winemaking on the side. For most mountain guides, their reward is in the journey itself. For winemakers, their reward is to create the ultimate expression of the grape, its true varietal character. As Charles notes on the winery's website, "Wine is the adventure of the soul." We submit, however, that the destination can be great, too, whether it is a mountain summit or recognition by *Wine & Spirits* as being one of America's top 40 wineries (2005).

Reininger Winery produces small lots of Walla Walla Valley merlot, cabernet sauvignon, and syrah, in addition to its Helix-labeled wines, which are made with fruit from the Columbia Valley. Much of the fruit for the Reininger label comes from nearby Ash Hollow Vineyard, owned in part by the Reiningers. By the way, the name "Helix" honors the family's hardworking grandparents, Marvin and Erva Tucker. The proceeds from the sale of the Tuckers' farmland, near Helix, Oregon, provided the needed capital to launch the Helix wine label.

Located six miles west of Walla Walla right off the new Highway 12, the 15,000-square-foot Reininger Winery is actually a converted potato shed. However, there are no spuds in sight here. The Reiningers' newly designed tasting room is more of a tasting pavilion, featuring a fusion of basalt harvested from the Snake River in northern Walla Walla County; reclaimed potato-shed wood; zinc-covered countertops, and finely crafted cabinetry. One particularly aesthetic touch are the vines intertwined around the perimeter of the tasting bar. This is a grand tasting room that invites all who trek here to linger longer and enjoy the stellar line-up of wines. Just remember to remove your backpack and stow your climbing poles before imbibing at this wine summit.

REININGER WINERY
opened: 1997
winemaker(s): Chuck Reininger
location: 5858 West Highway 12, Walla Walla, WA 99362
phone: 509-522-1994
web: www.reingingerwinery.com
e-mail: info@reiningerwinery.com
picnic area: Yes
gift shop: Yes
tours: Yes
fee: Tasting fee refundable with purchase
hours: May through December, daily 10–6; January through April, daily 10–5
lat: 46.054556 **long:** -118.445825

DIRECTIONS: From Walla Walla, head west on Hwy 12 for 6 miles. Turn left on Spalding Rd (at the Whitman Mission exit). At the stop sign turn right onto Vintage Loop (Old Hwy 12) and Reininger Winery will be on the right.

From the Tri-Cities take Hwy 12 east for approximately 40 miles to the winery. Pass through the towns of Touchet and Lowden. Reininger Winery is about 9 miles east of Touchet and 4.5 miles east of Lowden. Turn right on Spalding Rd (at the Whitman Mission exit). Turn right at the stop sign onto Vintage Loop (Old Hwy 12) and Reininger Winery will be on the right.

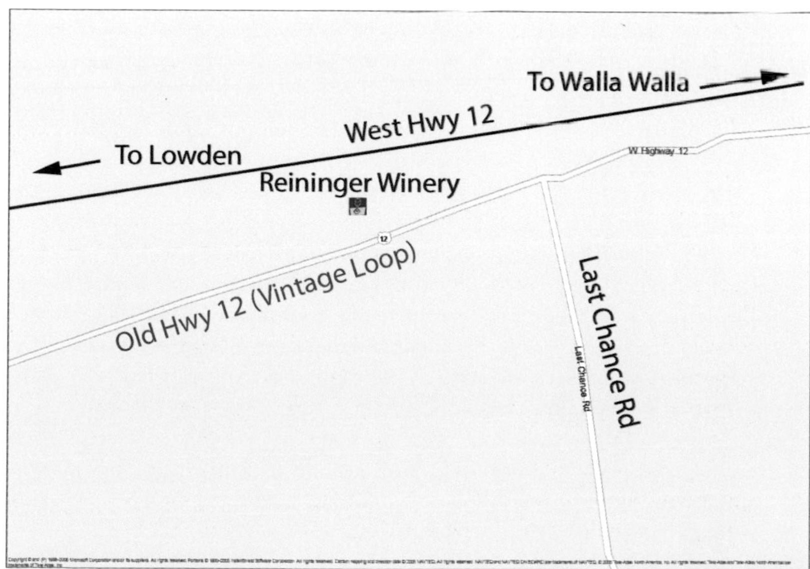

Three Rivers Winery 7

Midway between Lowden and Walla Walla sits the 16-acre site of Three Rivers Winery — plenty of space to sample wine, shop for merchandise, and play golf. Golf? Yes, Three Rivers is unique among Washington wineries; it comes equipped with a short, three-hole golf course. What's more, the golfing is free.

This is a destination winery for a variety of reasons. Foremost is the sheer size of the complex, which is composed of a winery, tasting room, gift shop, conference room, and outdoor deck. At 18,000 square feet, there's plenty of room to host your next corporate event or join a swarm of other wine tasters at the generous tasting room bar. The gift shop is one of the largest in the state, with enough stock to cross everything off next year's Christmas list. The buyer for Three Rivers Winery must have a discerning eye for great quality merchandise — schlocky trinkets are off-limits here.

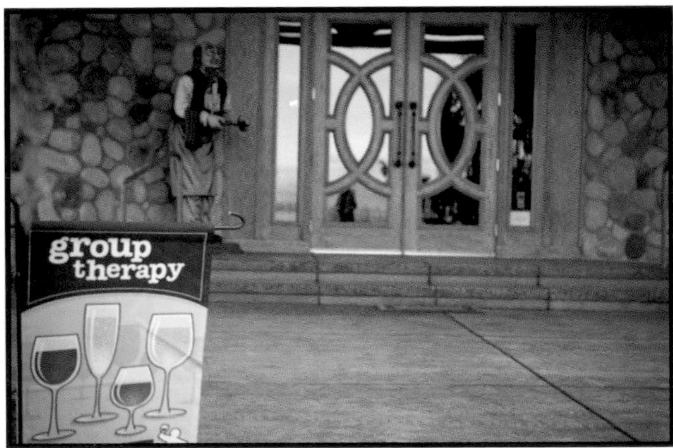

The structure itself is an inviting contemporary-style building with massive entrance doors, an interior with high-trussed ceilings, a huge stone-hearth fireplace, and an ample deck featuring one of the top views in Washington, courtesy of the Blue Mountains in the distance. In the past, Three Rivers Winery shunned weddings, trying to avoid the "bridezilla" syndrome. However, all that has changed under the ownership of William Foley, a California businessman who includes a number of other wineries in his portfolio, including Firestone.

The tasting fee varies depending upon what wines you sample, with a higher fee charged for reserve wines. We recommend that you indulge in the reserves and experience why winemaker Holly Turner has garnered so many awards and high praise. Since joining Three Rivers Winery in 2000, Holly has drawn upon her bachelor's degree in biology from Western Oregon State College and extended coursework in winemaking and wine grape production done at University of California–Davis. In addition, her résumé includes considerable hands-on working experience at Chateau Ste. Michelle and the Bodega la Rural winery in Mendoza, Argentina. All that experience goes into creating a style of wine that achieves balance — not too much wood or alcohol. Easy to drink, yet layered, food friendly, wonderfully quaffable.

Your visit will reveal why local readers of the Walla Walla *Union Bulletin Newspaper* voted Three Rivers Winery "Best Local Winery" five years in a row. Just remember to pack your 9-iron. Fore!

THREE RIVERS WINERY
opened: 1999
winemaker(s): Holly Turner
location: 5641 West Highway 12,
Walla Walla, WA 99362
phone: 509-526-9463
web: www.threeriverswinery.com
e-mail: info@threeriverswinery.com
picnic area: Yes
weddings: Yes
gift shop: Yes
tours: Yes
fee: Tasting fee applies; more for reserve wines
hours: Daily 10–5
lat: 46.054905 **long:** -118.437721

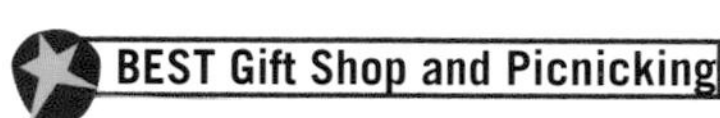

DIRECTIONS: **From Walla Walla** go west on Hwy 12 for 6 miles. Turn left on Spalding Rd (at the Whitman Mission exit.) At the stop sign, continue straight across Vintage Loop (Old Hwy 12) and into the Three Rivers Winery driveway.

From the Tri-Cities take Hwy 12 east for approximately 41 miles. Pass through Touchet and Lowden. Three Rivers Winery is 10 miles east of Touchet and 5.5 miles east of Lowden. Turn right on Spalding Rd (at the Whitman Mission exit). At the stop sign, continue straight across Vintage Loop and into the Three Rivers Winery driveway.

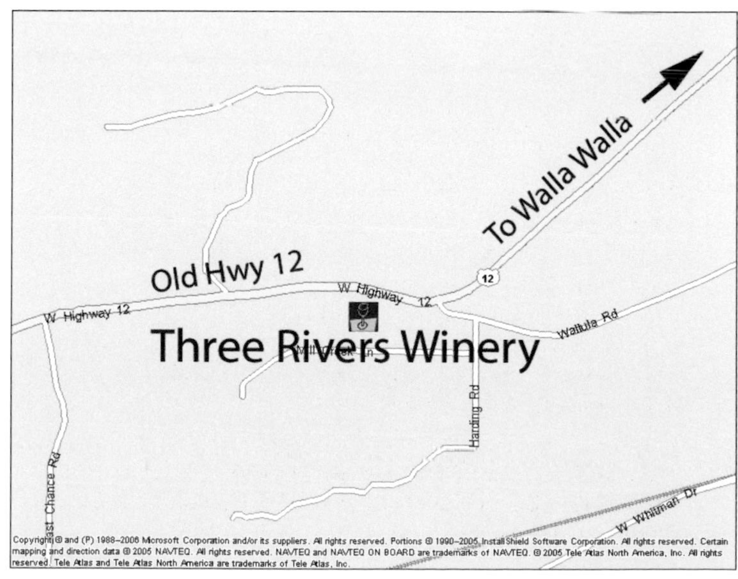

Bunchgrass Winery 8

Tom Olander, sales and marketing director for Bunchgrass Winery, uncorked a bottle of its Bordeaux blend with the intriguing name of "Triolet." Naturally, I had to ask my host from where the name Triolet derived. It would seem all five owners of Bunchgrass Winery are well-read individuals equipped with college degrees, teaching credentials and a shelf full of books in the tasting room as tribute to their love affair with the English language.

Pouring a deep purple sample of their red blend, Tom noted that a triolet is a one-stanza French poem of eight lines; the first, fourth and seventh lines are identical, as are the second and final lines. In a triolet, all the lines are in iambic tetrameter. Of course, I couldn't let this alone. So with apologies for the out-of-sync iambic meter, here's a triolet I penned for my new friends at Bunchgrass. I call it "Harvest Near":

Throughout the valley, the vines grow faster,
The warmth of summer sends tendrils twining
Among green grapes — each sun-lit cluster
Throughout the valley, the vines grow faster,
Swelling sugars turn pulp alabaster
Growers keep watch for weather's warning
Throughout the valley, the vines grow faster,
The warmth of summer sends tendrils twining.

Among Walla Walla Wineries, Bunchgrass Winery is a Lazarus of sorts. In 1997, Roger Cockerline began crafting small batches of premium wine with grapes from his now-dormant family vineyard. His plan was to eventually shut the winery down and enjoy his retirement. However, an unforeseen partnership came to pass to revitalize Bunchgrass Winery. The partners included the aforementioned Tom Olander, a certified sommelier and former restaurant manager at Whitehouse Crawford and more recently Inn manager at Abeja; Barb Commare, a business manager focusing on compliance paperwork; William vonMetzger, a Colorado transplant and winemaker at Walla Walla Vintners, and graduate of the Institute for Enology and Viticulture at Walla Walla Community College; Gordy Venneri, a longtime friend of Roger and cofounder of Walla Walla Vintners; and Roger himself.

Situated in a 1943 restored dairy barn Bunchgrass Winery is a tad small for moving barrels around, but just perfect for those visitors who are into quaintness. Quality over quantity is the mantra here. Long in barrel, long in bottle, Bunchgrass wines aren't rushed to market. Let's just say the owners are exercising their own take on poetic license.

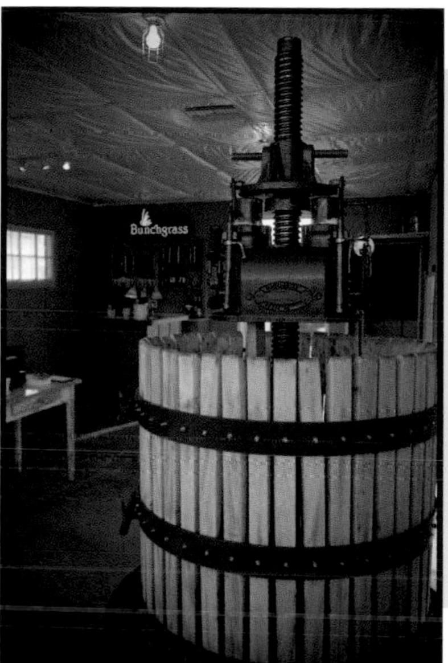

BUNCHGRASS WINERY
opened: 1997
winemaker(s): William vonMetzger
location: 151 Bunchgrass Lane,
Walla Walla, WA 99362-9588
phone: 509-540-8963
web: www.bunchgrasswinery.com
e-mail: info@BunchgrassWinery.com
picnic area: Yes
tours: Yes
fee: Tasting fee may apply
hours: From the first weekend in April to Holiday Barrel Tasting in December, Saturdays 1–4, or by appointment
lat: 46.063304 **long:** -118.335067

DIRECTIONS: Bunchgrass Winery is located 3.5 miles west of Walla Walla on the left side when traveling on Old Hwy 12 (Vintage Loop). Look for small sign on the left and follow the road a 1/4 mile to the winery.

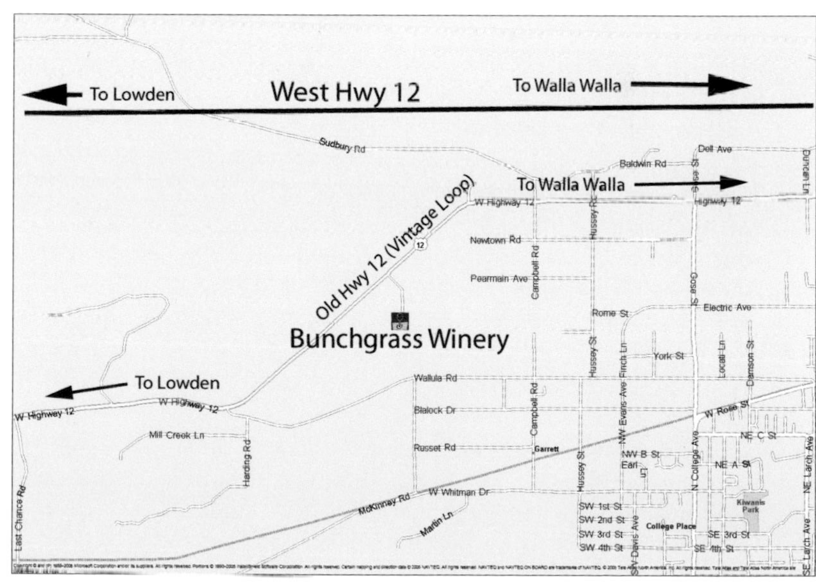

Skylite Cellars 9

With Skylite Cellars, you can double your pleasure. Visit Skylite Cellars at The Winery (main location off Old Highway 12 on Campbell Road) and then head to Skylite Cellars at The Gallery in downtown Walla Walla. The winery also produces wine under two different labels: the Skylite Cellars brand and the Hiney Wine label. Two tasting rooms, two labels — but one unifying theme: passion. A love story is behind the creation of Skylite Cellars, that of Tom Hodgins and his focus on growing a radio empire in Eastern Washington and his wife, Cheryl, whose farming background included driving tractors and planting gardens. As divergent as their backgrounds may have been, the couple has one vital interest in common, and that is wine.

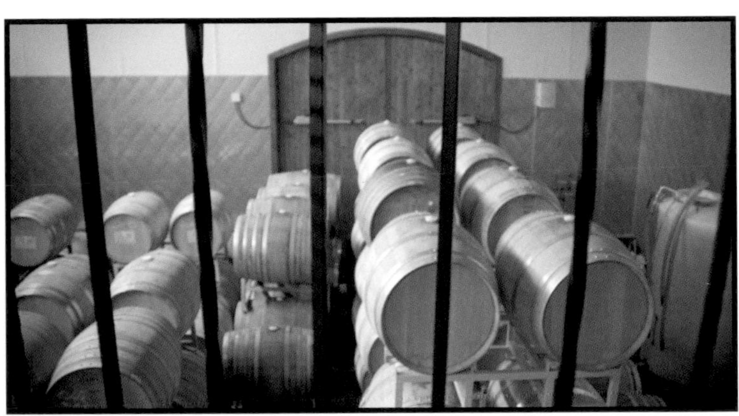

Skylite Cellars' main tasting room, just west of town on Campbell Road, is a high-ceilinged space with a spiral staircase taking center stage. Upon walking into this tasting room, your first reaction will likely be "Wow!" It is readily apparent that a lot of creative energy went into this space. There's ample parking, a peek-a-boo view of the barrel room from an upstairs window, and a terrific mural on an interior wall of the tasting room.

The downtown tasting-room location is on Second Street, down the street from the Marcus Whitman Hotel. Cheryl's parents — collectors of art and antiques gathered during their extensive globetrotting — started the eclectic antiques/art shop which shares the space with the downtown tasting room. While there, check out the distinctive wine-barrel bar and the surrounding art (particularly the painting of a tasting room scene). Upstairs, you'll discover a skylight that bathes the upstairs gallery with warm light, the source of the winery's name.

Winemaker Robert Smasne produces small quantities of "distinctive tasting wines for the discerning wine lover." The 5-acre Skylite Vineyard supplies the fruit for cabernet sauvignon and merlot, and other varieties are sourced from select vineyards in the Walla Walla and Columbia valleys. But Hiney Wine, Skylite's second label, is the real attention getter. With its "world famous" red wine and slogans such as "You only go around once in life, so grab all the Hiney Wine you can get!" "Feel my Hiney," and "Uncork the Hiney," it's obvious that Tom and his cohorts don't take themselves too seriously. They're all about having a great time while making great wine. Bottoms up!

SKYLITE CELLARS
opened: 2005
winemaker(s): Robert Smasne
location: 25 Campbell Road, Walla Walla, WA 99362
phone: 509-529-8000
web: www.skylitecellars.com
e-mail: info@skylitecellars.com
wheelchair access: Yes
fee: Tasting fee
hours: Monday through Saturday 12–5; Sunday 12–4
lat: 46.06777 **long:** -118.403309
satellite location: 7 North 2nd Street, Walla Walla, WA 99362
satellite hours: Weekends April through October 12–5

DIRECTIONS: **From Walla Walla** head west on Old Hwy 12 (Vintage Loop) for about 3 miles, then turn left onto Campbell Rd. The Skylite tasting room is on the left.

From the Tri-Cities take Hwy 12 east for approximately 43 mile. Pass by the towns of Touchet and Lowden. As you near Walla Walla turn right onto Sudbury Rd. Continue to Old Hwy 12 (Vintage Loop) and turn right. Drive a short distance and turn right onto Campbell Rd. The Skylite tasting room is on the left.

Skylite Cellars also has a tasting room in downtown Walla Walla on 7 North 2nd Ave.

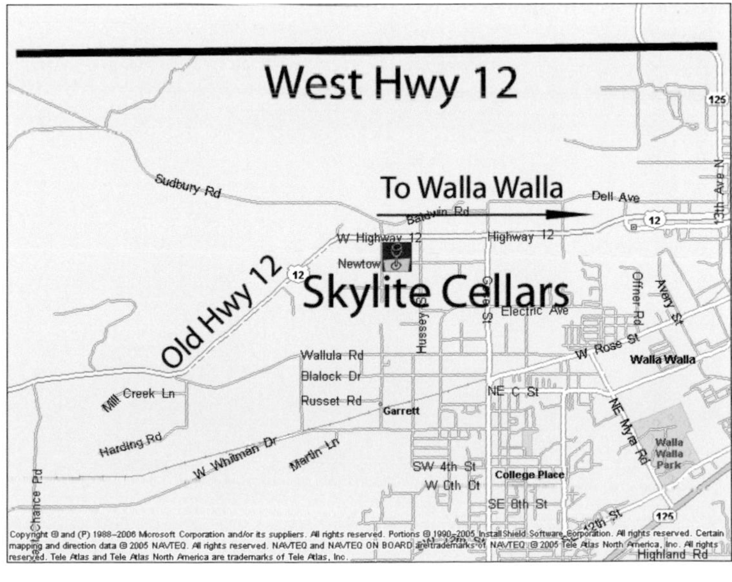

Downtown WineTrail

Walla Walla Downtown WineTrail

Amazingly, you can drive to downtown Walla Walla, park your car, and visit more than 20 wineries. With most hotels located downtown, it's the ultimate in wine-touring convenience. Don't forget to pack a good pair of walking shoes. And speaking of forgetting — after a day of wine tasting, good luck trying to remember where you parked your car!

Although devoid of vineyards, the Downtown WineTrail isn't missing any of the creature comforts. It has great restaurants, amazing shops, and coffee bars offering a double-tall afternoon pick-me-up. Along the way, you will discover historic architecture and real estate offices featuring wine-country homes for sale. You may find yourself daydreaming of what it would be like to live in Walla Walla — and making a life-changing decision!

Walla Walla Downtown WineTrail

1 Locati Cellars
2 Seven Hills Winery
3 Spring Valley Vineyard
4 Sleight of Hand Cellars
5 Sweet Valley Wines
6 Sapolil Cellars
7 Otis Kenyon Wine
8 Walla Walla Wine Works
9 Rôtie Cellars
10 Chateau Rollat Winery
11 DaMa Wines
12 Fort Walla Walla Cellars
13 Nicholas Cole Cellars
14 Walla Faces Wines
15 El Corazon Winery
16 Stephenson Cellars
17 Trio Vintners
18 Forgeron Cellars
19 Walla Walla Village Winery
20 Morrison Lane Winery
21 Bergevin Lane Vineyards
22 Foundry Vineyards
23 Whitman Cellars
24 Canoe Ridge Vineyard
25 Lowden Hills Winery

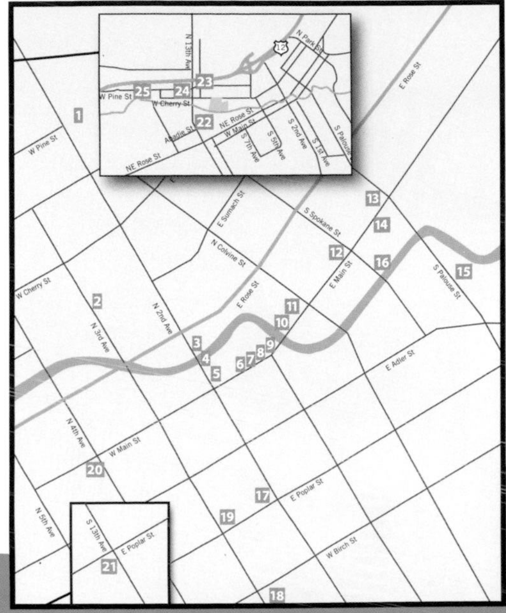

Region: **Walla Walla Wine Country**

# of tasting rooms on tour: **25**

# of satellite tasting rooms: **1**

Estimate # of days for tour: **4**

Getting around: **Car and foot**

Key Events:
- ❑ **Events sponsored by Walla Walla Valley Wine Alliance: Spring Release Weekend (first full weekend of May); Balloon Stampede Weekend (second full weekend of May); Vintage Walla Walla (first full weekend of June); Entwine: An auction to support Walla Walla Arts, Wine, and Education (mid-October); and Holiday Barrel Tasting (first full weekend of December). See winetrailsnw.com for details.**

Tips:
- ❑ **Saturdays are the best times to experience tasting rooms — most are open.**
- ❑ **Great restaurants to choose from — including Saffron Mediterranean, Brasserie Four, The Marc, Backstage Bistro, Vineyard Wine Bar, T. Maccarone's, Olive, Sweet Basil Pizzeria and Whtehouse-Crawford to name a few.**
- ❑ **Consider using a limousine service (Black Tie Limo 509-525-8585, Blue Stocking Tours 509-522-4717, Sunset Coach Tours 509-303-0355, or Four Star Limousine Service 509-521-7849 are some of the many services to contact).**

 **Best**
- ❑ **Eats: Sapolil Cellars**
- ❑ **Music venue: Walla Walla Wine Works, Stephenson Cellars, Walla Walla Village Winery, Sapolil Cellars**
- ❑ **Place to Stay: Walla Faces Wines**
- ❑ **Gift Shop: Forgeron Cellars**

T. Maccarone's

The warm tones of the dining room, soft lighting, and contemporary artwork blend beautifully to create the perfect backdrop for a memorable meal at T. Maccarone's. Owner Tom Maccarone is usually on hand to talk with diners and to welcome them back with each return visit. His outgoing personality also has allowed him to work closely with a number of local winemakers. Consequently, T. Maccarone's wine list includes several special local wines.

Photo by Alan Ayers

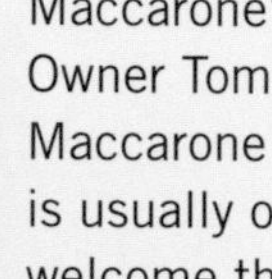

Photo by Alan Ayers

The menu at T. Maccarone's is an innovative seasonal menu. The dishes are based on the freshest locally grown ingredients available. During the winter months, the menu highlights comfort-food favorites, such as pasta with Grandma Maccarone's original meatballs and a hearty minestrone soup. By contrast, during the summer months, the menu highlights the fresh produce available at the local farmers' market. Whatever the season, however, diners can be assured that the pasta in the pasta dishes and the bread that accompanies the dinner are all freshly made in-house.

Photo by Alan Ayers

On Sundays, T. Maccarone's offers a brunch. The menu is filled with delicious traditional brunch selections along with a few twists. For example, not only can diners order the usual eggs

Benedict, but they also have the option of selecting a vegetarian Benedict or a prawn Benedict. This Sunday brunch provides a most satisfying way to ease into a day of wine tasting or maybe just a little nap.

4 North Colville Street
Walla Walla, WA 99362
509-522-4776
tmaccarones.com

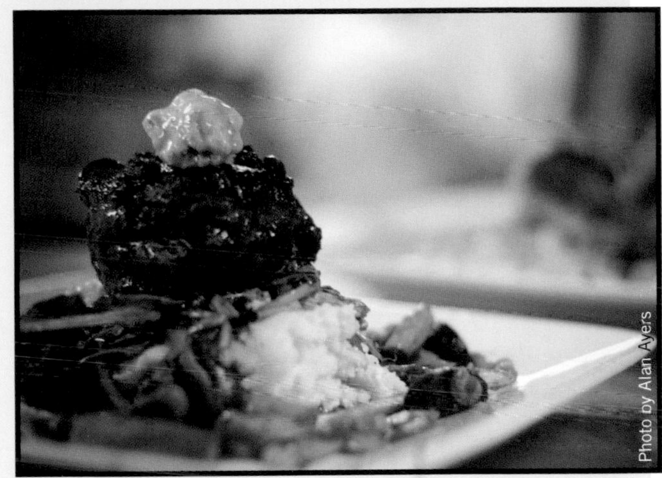
Photo by Alan Ayers

Olive Market Place & Café

The opportunities have expanded exponentially for Tom Maccarone, owner of T. Maccarone's restaurant, with his recent opening of Olive, which combines a Mediterranean-style marketplace and a café.

Olive is located on Main Street in downtown Walla Walla. With its awning-covered sidewalk seating, interior exposed-brick walls, and numerous seating areas, Olive is incredibly inviting. The restaurant sits in close proximity to several wine-tasting rooms and therefore is a perfect place for breakfast before wine tasting, a sandwich or snack between tasting, or a light dinner at the end of a day of wine tasting.

21 Main Street
Walla Walla, WA 99362
509-526-0200

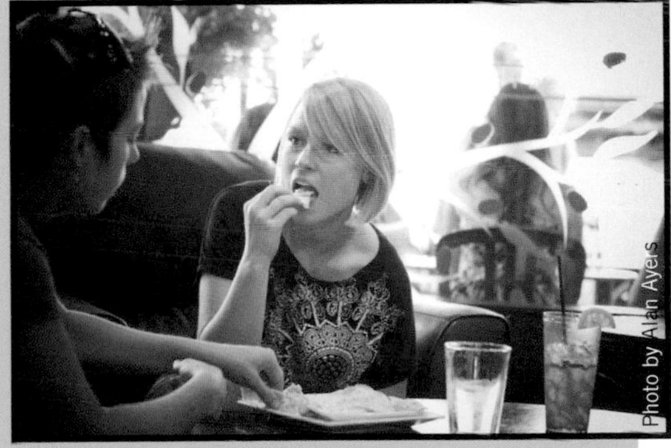
Photo by Alan Ayers

Locati Cellars 1

To those who have grown up in the valley, the name "Locati" is synonymous with Walla Walla sweet onions. The Locati family's roots (no pun intended) go back many generations to the pioneer settlers from Italy who made the Walla Walla Valley renowned for row crops — most famous of all, the illustrious Walla Walla sweet onion, which is harvested mid-June through September. The story goes that a French soldier stationed on the island of Corsica (which is part of France, but geographically closer to Italy) pocketed a sweet onion seed and brought it to Walla Walla.

However, like many farming families in the valley, the Locatis have gone beyond row crops to grow premium wine grapes, and not just any ol' wine grapes, but varieties that come from their native land, such as sangiovese and barbera. Relying on the winemaking expertise of Matt Steiner (owner and winemaker for Stella Fino Winery), Michael and Penne Locati produce pasta-friendly wines, including pinot grigio, orange muscat, barbera, and sangiovese. Maybe it was because of the warm spring day, but my sample of their crisp, oh-so-refreshing pinot grigio had me tipping the glass to get the last drop. As I savored the wine's citrus notes and nice acidity, Penne explained that she manages the tasting room and performs "other duties as assigned," in addition to her full-time job at a local bank.

Located in The Depot on Second Avenue, the Locati Cellars' tasting room features its distinguished logo on the entrance door, conveying the sense that visitors will be welcomed like family. The exposed brick walls provide a handsome backdrop to the wine bar and the display of wine-related merchandise (which reflects Penne's exceptionally good eye for such things).

Penne mentioned that her favorite sweet onion recipe calls for slicing the onion "bloomin' onion" style and adding butter, soy sauce, and Worcestershire sauce to the wedges; wrapping the onion in aluminum foil and then grilling it on the barbecue for about 20 minutes to let it cook down in its marinating juices. The final step is to layer the cooked onion on top of steak or hamburger and *voilà*, you're ready to eat. Of course, this meal isn't complete without a generous glass of Locati Cellars' sangiovese as the perfect complement. Salute!

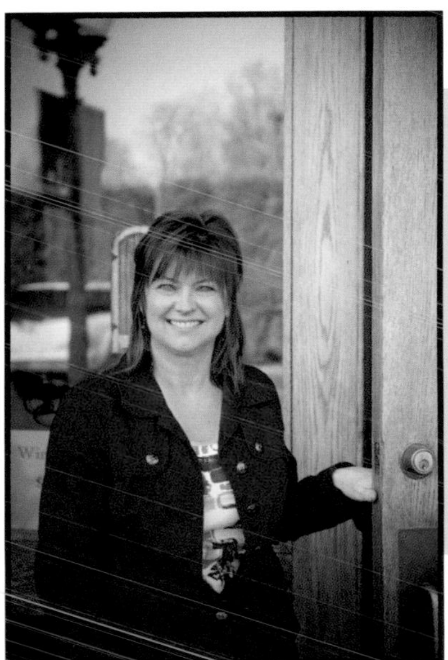

Penne Locati

LOCATI CELLARS
opened: 2009
winemaker(s): Michael and Penne Locati
location: 416 North 2nd Avenue, Suite O, Walla Walla, WA 99362
phone: 509-529-5871
web: www.locaticellars.com
e-mail: info@locaticellars.com
wheelchair access: Yes
gift shop: Yes
fee: Tasting fee refundable with purchase
hours: Tuesday through Saturday 10–6
lat: 46.070762 **long:** -118.342183

DIRECTIONS: Locati Cellars' tasting room is located in downtown Walla Walla in the historic Depot building. **From U.S. 12**, take the 2nd Ave./City Center exit and continue southeast on 2nd Ave. toward City Center for a tenth of a mile. Locati Cellars' tasting room is on the left.

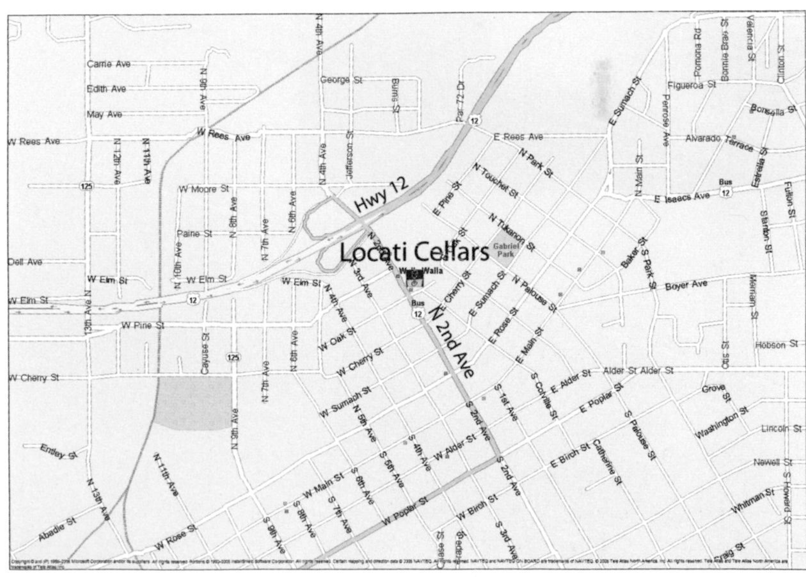

Seven Hills Winery 2

Perhaps you thought only Rome is known for its "Seven Hills." Not so fast, Eternal City. Walla Walla also has its Seven Hills, in the form of a winery.

The Seven Hills Winery is located in the superbly restored Whitehouse-Crawford building in downtown Walla Walla. The award-winning restoration of this former lumber mill preserved the 100-year-old brick building, including its posts, its beams, and most importantly, its charm. You can find it listed in the National Historic Register. It turns out that this historic building is an excellent venue for making fine wine and tasting the finished product. You can view the sky-lit temperature- and humidity-controlled barrel room from the tasting room itself, thanks to a strategically placed picture window. The barrels themselves are the traditional Bordeaux-style 225-liter oak barrels that are prevalent throughout the industry. The barrels are also the source of the Seven Hills wine club's name, the Barrique Society. Nice touch. **WineTrail Note:** Seven Hills Winery's Guild Society is a second-level wine club, giving members more wine per shipment than first-level wine clubs, more discounts and complimentary shipping.

Seven Hills Winery focuses on reds and enjoys a reputation for great balance, which it states is a "trinity of fruit, acidity, and tannin." This trinity of ingredients inspired the use of seven Irish trinity cross-knot symbols as part of the winery's logo — at least we at WineTrails Northwest choose to think so. Enjoy the wine right out of the bottle now or order it with your meal at the gourmet Whitehouse-Crawford Restaurant, also housed in the building. Alternatively, you can cellar this wine for years. Working closely with the grape growers of Red Mountain, Columbia Valley, and Walla Walla (especially the distinguished Seven Hills Vineyard), winemaker Casey McClellan makes single-vineyard wines and blends selectively to achieve, you guessed it, "harmony among fruit, acidity, and tannin." He also uses fruit from Oregon to make charmingly crisp riesling and pinot gris.

I was just pondering … it's a good thing the winery doesn't use the 300-liter barrels often used in Australia to age its wines. Otherwise, the name of the wine club would have to be the "Hogshead Society."

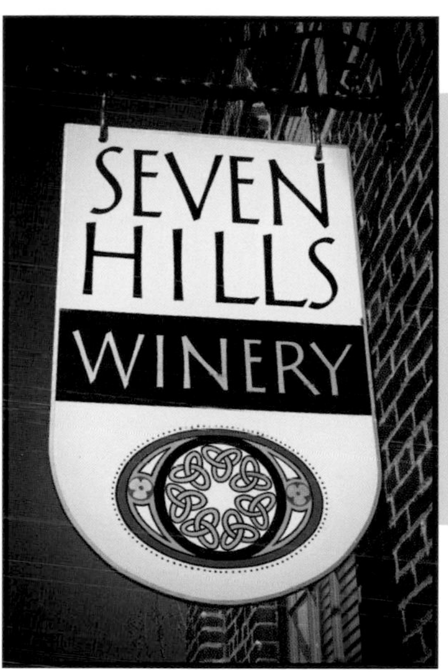

SEVEN HILLS WINERY
opened: 1988
winemaker(s): Casey McClellan
location: 212 North 3rd Avenue, Walla Walla, WA 99362
phone: 509-529-7198
web: www.sevenhillswinery.com
e-mail: info@sevenhillswinery.com
tours: Yes
fee: Tasting fee refundable with purchase
hours: Monday 11–4; Thursday through Saturday 11–4
lat: 46.068038 **long:** -118.341911

DIRECTIONS: Seven Hills Winery is located in downtown Walla Walla in the historic Whitehouse-Crawford Building. **From U.S. 12**, take the 2nd Ave./City Center exit and continue southeast on 2nd Ave. toward City Center for 0.3 miles. Turn right (west) onto W Sumach St. and arrive at 212 N 3rd Ave.

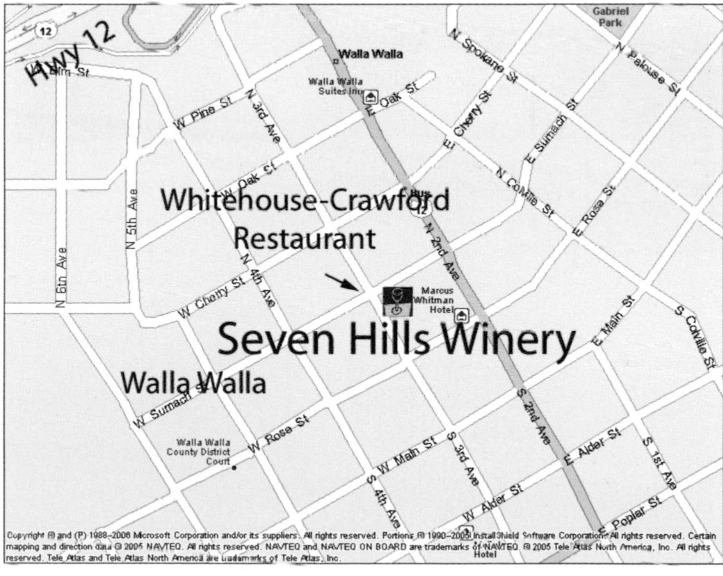

Spring Valley Vineyard 3

The tasting room of Spring Valley Vineyard is immersed in history. Spring Valley's story is one of a homesteading farm family, the Corkrums, who settled in Walla Walla Valley in 1865. Their offspring were later to marry and introduce the names of Derby and Elvin into the mix. On the tasting room walls, you see enlarged photos of the Spring Valley Vineyard, neatly kept rows of vineyards surrounded by golden wheatfields. Pictures of key family figures adorn the wine labels, as do their names, such as Uriah, Frederick, and Derby. Don't be surprised if one of the relatives is working the tasting room. My visit found a Derby granddaughter, Katherine Derby Raymond, in the tasting room, with her toddler son scampering about. **WineTrail Note:** Be sure to pick up a historical fact sheet that presents a chronology of the Spring Valley Vineyard story. It's chockfull of interesting factoids, including the wonderful tidbit about Dean Derby, who still holds the University of Washington record for the longest touchdown run from scrimmage (92 yards), set in 1956.

After the tragic death of winemaker/manager Devin Corkrum Derby in 2004, the Derbys turned to Ste. Michelle Wine Estates for assistance. In 2005, Ste. Michelle Wine Estates agreed to lease the vineyard and winery, and purchase the Spring Valley Vineyard wine brand. Ste. Michelle's decision to invest proved a smart business decision. Since that time, Spring Valley Vineyard has had four separate wines place on the prestigious *Wine Spectator* Top 100 list of the world's wines. Be sure to sample the "Uriah," a Bordeaux blend that *The Wine Advocate* described as "a complex fruitful mouth of blackberry, currant, and cherry with a hint of licorice and leather." Yum. And if you have the opportunity to sample them, the "Frederick," "Derby," "Katherine," "Nina Lee," and "Mule Skinner" vintages demonstrate the powerful and firm finish intensity of these 100 percent estate wines.

If time permits, take the short, 20-minute drive out of town and check out the 1,100-acre Spring Valley Vineyard and wheat farm. And take your camera. You may very well want to enlarge these pictures for one of your walls at home. Cheers to seven generations!

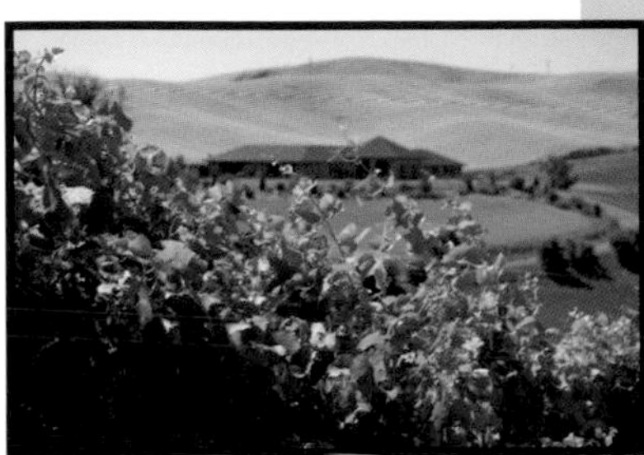

SPRING VALLEY VINEYARD
opened: 1999
winemaker(s): Serge LaVille
location: 18 North 2nd Avenue, Walla Walla, WA 99362
phone: 509-385-1495
web: www.springvalleyvineyard.com
e-mail: info@springvalleyvineyard.com
tours: Yes
fee: Tasting fee
hours: Friday and Saturday 11–4; Sunday 12–4; winery open by appointment only
lat: 46.066971 **long:** -118.339348

DIRECTIONS: Spring Valley Vineyard's tasting room is located in downtown Walla Walla on 2nd Ave. between E Rose and E Main St. across from the Marcus Whitman Hotel.

From Hwy 12, take the 2nd Ave./City Center exit and continue southeast on 2nd Ave. toward City Center for 0.3 miles. Arrive at 18 N 2nd Ave. Spring Valley Vineyard's tasting room is on the left.

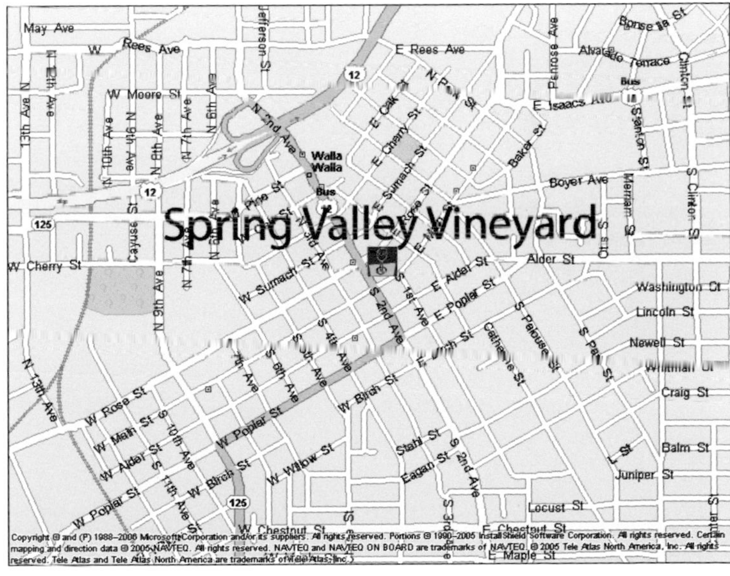

Sleight of Hand Cellars 4

Any new realizations would have to wait
'Til he had more time
More time
A time to dream
To himself
He waves goodbye
To himself
I'll see you on the other side
Another man moved by sleight of hand
— Pearl Jam, *Sleight of Hand*

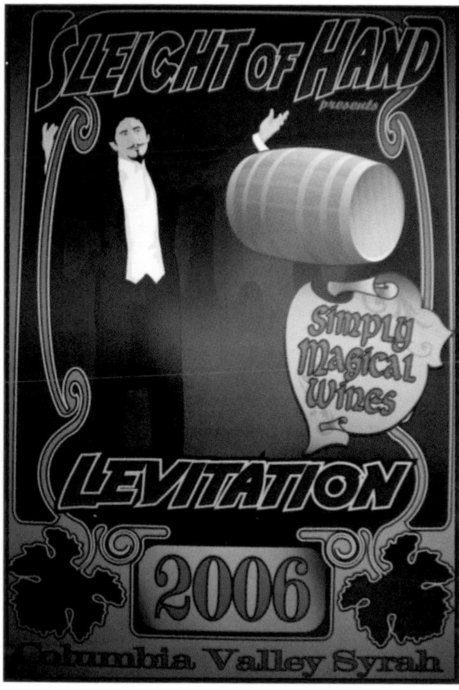

To say that co-owner and winemaker Trey Busch is a fan of Pearl Jam is an understatement. Pearl Jam holds cult status in Trey's mind and is the inspiration for Sleight of Hand's branding. With names and amazing label graphics for such wines as "The Magician" gewürztraminer, "Spellbinder" red blend, and "Levitation" syrah, you half expect the tasting room staff to pull a rabbit out of a hat. But there are no tricks up their sleeves. The real magic visitors experience are the premium small-lot wines.

It was Trey's chance encounter with Jerry and Sandy Solomon at a Sun Valley auction in 2002 that eventually led to the creation of Sleight of Hand Cellars. As the winemaker for Basel Cellars Estate Winery, Trey had established himself as one of Washington's up-and-coming young winemakers. Given his résumé, it was only natural for Trey to consider launching his own winery, with a focus on showcasing Washington *Vitis vinifera* fruit. He approached Jerry and Susan with the idea of a joint venture à la Walla Walla and the rest is Washington winemaking history.

Sleight of Hand's elongated, red brick tasting room on Second Avenue has only one problem. It's next door to gourmet food shop Salumiere Cesario, and during my visit someone must have ordered up a grilled panino; my nose caught the scents of salami and melted cheese as they wafted into the Sleight of Hand Cellar's tasting room, causing me to salivate like Pavlov's dog. Note to myself: Don't come hungry to Sleight of Hand Cellars in the future. Resisting a hot sandwich and reaching for a pretzel instead, I discovered that the "Spellbinder" pairs wonderfully with the aromas of meats, garlic, and herbs that I'm sure that even Eddie Vedder's great-grandmother Pearl would love.

Trey Busch

SLEIGHT OF HAND CELLARS
opened: 2007
winemaker(s): Trey Busch
location: 16 North 2nd Avenue, Walla Walla, WA 99362
phone: 509-525-3661
web: www.SofHCellars.com
e-mail: info@SofHCellars.com
fee: Tasting fee refundable with purchase
hours: April through November, Thursday through Saturday 11-5
lat: 46.066956 **long:** -118.339336

DIRECTIONS: Sleight of Hand Cellar's tasting room is located in downtown Walla Walla on N 2nd Ave. between E Rose and E Main St., across from the Marcus Whitman Hotel.

From Hwy 12, take the 2nd Ave./City Center exit and continue southeast on 2nd Ave. toward City Center for 0.3 miles. Arrive at 16 N 2nd Ave. The tasting room is on the left.

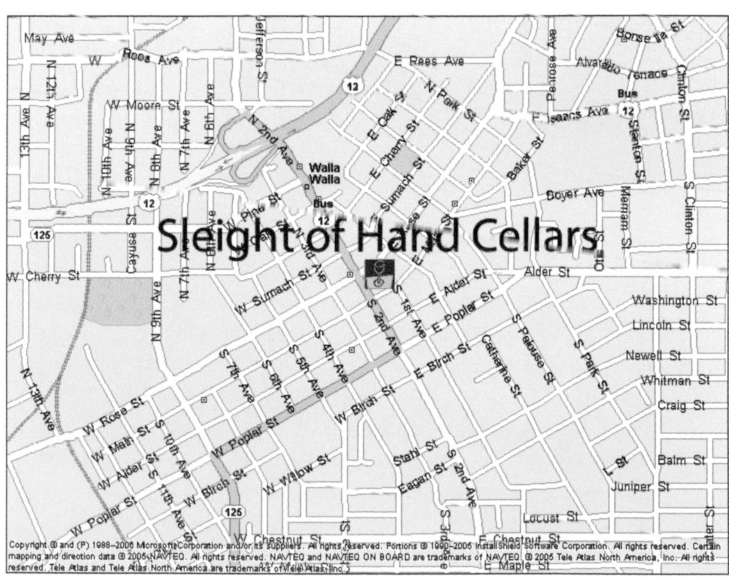

Sweet Valley Wines 5

Tall, lanky, with a great smile and barely legal: At 21 years of age, Josh McDaniels is just old enough to legally swirl and sip wine. Still, his youth belies his experience, which was gained growing up in Walla Walla, and working as a cellar rat for Don Redman at Mannina Cellars and then as an assistant winemaker at famed Leonetti Cellar. That working experience is in addition to the degree he earned from Walla Walla Community College's in-depth enology and viticulture program. Nevertheless, becoming a great winemaker is a lifelong endeavor, and to this end, at the time of my visit Josh was preparing to venture south to Argentina to work at Paul Hobbs' winery in Viña Cobos.

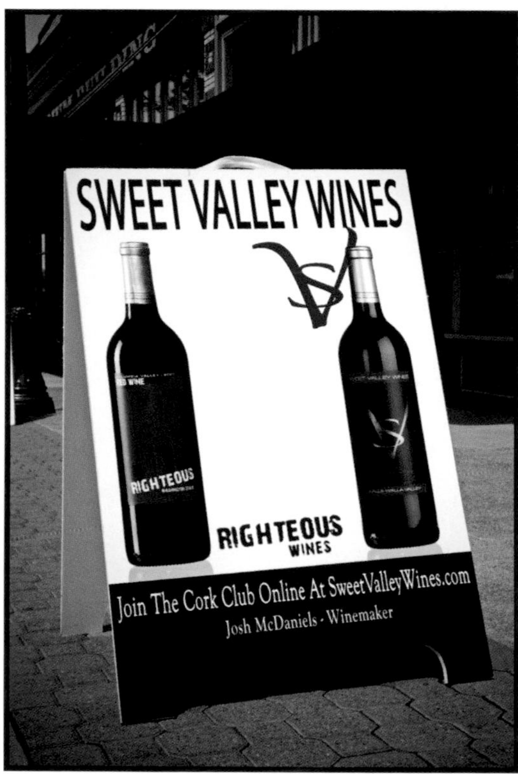

Josh isn't going solo in the Sweet Valley Wines venture. His parents and longtime family friends are partners in the business. They bring needed capital and complementary skills to the business of running a winery. What's more, Josh knows a host of key suppliers that provide essential ingredients for the winery, from the grape growers to the cork suppliers. Heck, he probably went to school with some of them.

As a seasoned taster, I appreciate it when there are only three or four wines to sample. I often feel overwhelmed when there's two dozen wines to choose from and you're already suffering from palate fatigue from the four previous wineries you visited that day. That's why it was such a delight to see a manageable number of wines to taste at the wine bar. With a Sweet Valley Wines' lineup of cabernet sauvignon, merlot, syrah and a red blend called "Double Barrel Red" (so named because Josh had only two barrels of wine to blend), I knew that I could take time to relish these beauties. Josh noted that this year's crop of wines included a viognier, which unfortunately wasn't available for tasting. It had sold out.

While I was eyeballing the deep red merlot, Josh's yellow Lab, Murphy, plunked down next to my feet. The dog's youthful appearance matched Josh's. These signs of young blood reflect Sweet Valley Wines' future; the many vintages to come with Josh at the winemaking helm. My curiosity compelled me to ask Josh how he intended to distinguish himself in such a competitive market as Walla Walla. To this question, he gave a one-word response. "Quality," he said. "Oh, the promise of youth!" I thought to myself.

Murphy

SWEET VALLEY WINES
opened: 2007
winemaker(s): Josh McDaniels
location: 12 North 2nd Street, Walla Walla, WA 99362
phone: 509-526-0002
web: www.sweetvalleywines.com
e-mail: info@sweetvalleywines.com
fee: Tasting fee may apply
hours: Fall and winter months, Thursday through Saturday 11–5; Spring and summer months, Tuesday through Saturday 11–5; also open on release and event weekends and by appointment
lat: 46.067323 **long:** -118.339551

DIRECTIONS: From U.S. Route 12, take the 2nd Ave./City Center exit and continue southeast on 2nd Ave. toward City Center for about half a mile. Turn left on Poplar St. and arrive at Sweet Valley Wines' tasting room.

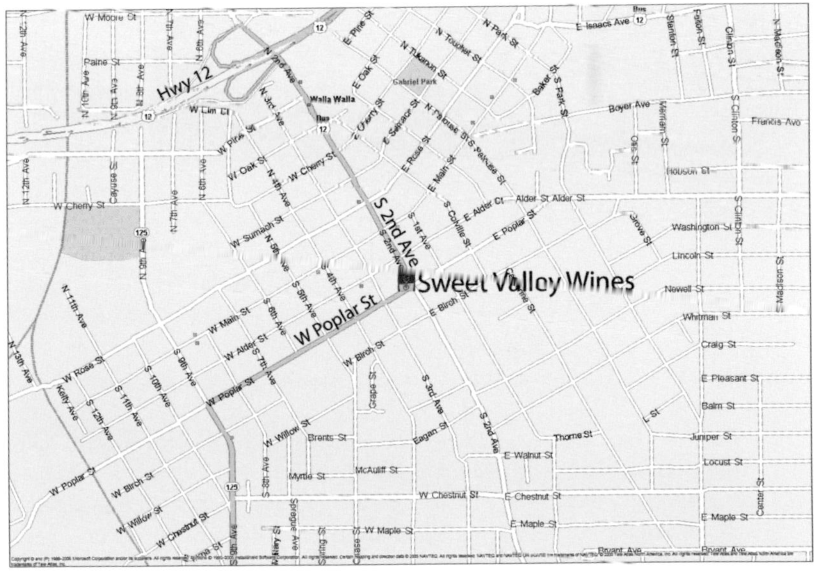

Sapolil Cellars 6

Blame it on Sapolil Cellars.

It used to be that downtown Walla Walla was deadsville: quiet, serene, little nightlife. Then in 2007, along came a little winery with a funny name that opened its tasting room doors on Main Street. Perhaps the first clue that things would never be the same was the winery's installation of a grand piano, along with plenty of tables and chairs at which patrons could sit and enjoy wine while listening to someone tickle the ivories. Since then, on most Friday and Saturday nights, many a visitor to downtown Walla Walla find themselves swaying to the music emanating from Sapolil Cellars.

Owner and winemaker Bill Scherwin, didn't have to venture far to come up with a name for his winery; the production winery is located on Sapolil Road about 10 miles east of Walla Walla. Sapolil was a Native American who served alongside Dr. Dorsey Syng Baker during the 1870s construction of the Walla Walla & Columbia River Railroad, from Wallula, on the Columbia River, to Walla Walla. One of its many railway stations, used for loading wheat and other merchandise, bore the name Sapolil Station to honor Sapolil.

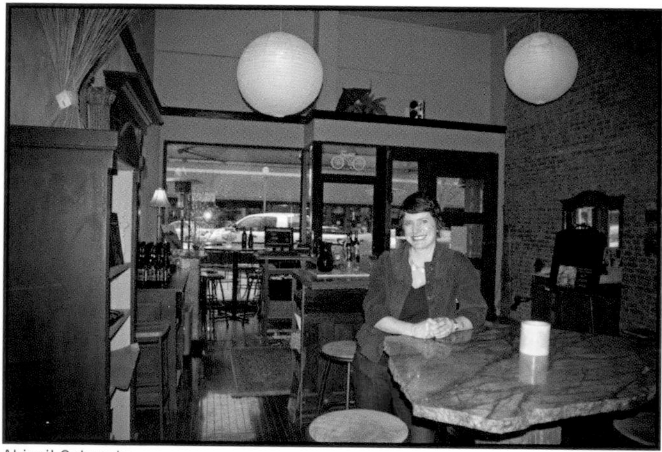

Abigail Scherwin

Sapolil Cellars is truly a family-run business. While Bill is instrumental in making the wine, his wife, Linda Scherwin, manages the tasting room/piano bar. Marketing and other duties fall on the experienced shoulders of their daughter Abigail Scherwin, and she's done a remarkable job. In a competitive wine market like Walla Walla, creating an identity that fuses full-bodied red wines with the sounds of Philly KingB & The Stingers, Dr. Mark Brown, Papa Loves Mambo, and the like was pure genius.

Sapolil Cellars' red blend "Gandy Dancer" features Jeffrey's artwork on the label. While I stuck my nose into a freshly poured glass of this New World blend, Abigail explained to me that "gandy dancer" is a slang term for a worker who maintained the railroad tracks, an expression that originated in the late 1800s. Moving together in a rhythmic dance, gandy dancers used a "gandy tool" to move displaced track back into place to prevent train derailment. It occurred to me that the gandy-dancer sounds of the past might jive nicely with the rhythmic blues and jazzy notes pulsating from Sapolil Cellars. Find out for yourself by sampling some great syrah and getting into the beat.

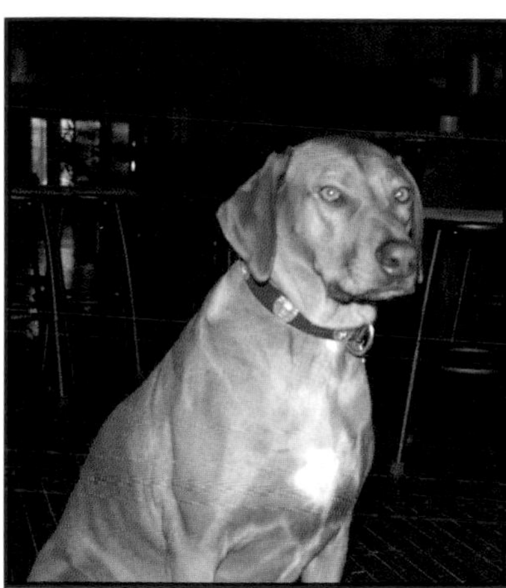

Queen Nefertiti

SAPOLIL CELLARS
opened: 2004
winemaker(s): Bill Schwerin
location: 15 East Main Street, Walla Walla, WA 99362
phone: 509-520-5258
web: www.sapolilcellars.com
e-mail: abigail@sapolilcellars.com
fee: Complimentary wine tasting
eats: yes
hours: Monday through Friday 11–4, Saturday 10–4, Sunday 1–4
lat: 46.066971 **long:** -118.339029

DIRECTIONS: From U.S. 12, take N 2nd Ave./City Center exit. Turn left onto E Main St. and travel half a block. Sapolil Cellars' tasting room is on the left.

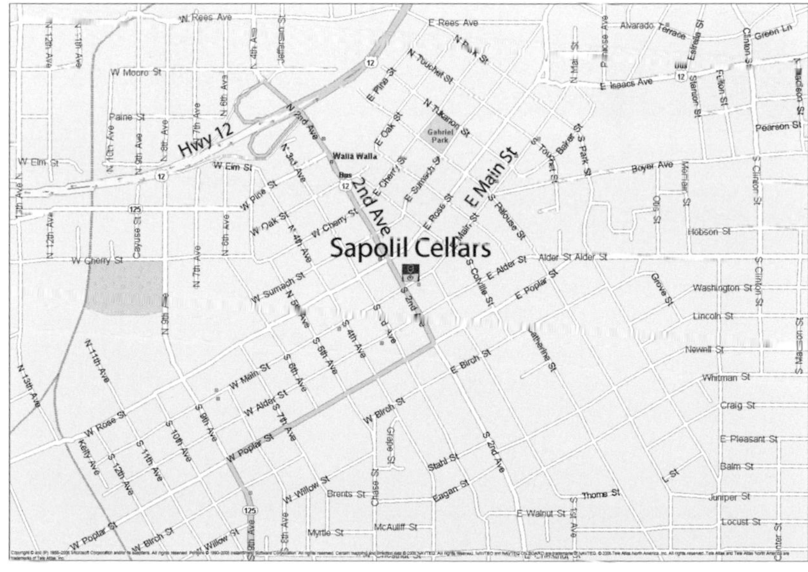

Otis Kenyon Wine 7

I was contemplating the silhouette of a man wearing a derby on a bottle of cabernet sauvignon when the tasting-room pourer asked, "Are you familiar with the Otis Kenyon story?" I mumbled something about a criminal past involving an ancestor in Milton-Freewater, but quickly came to the end of my recollection. As he poured me a sample of Otis Kenyon 2007 "Matchless Red," he wove a remarkable story — a story waiting to be told Hollywood style. Here's the 411.

In the early 1900s, James Otis Kenyon was a struggling dentist in nearby Milton-Freewater when a new dentist moved into town and became instant competition. Having a wife and two kids to fend for, James came up with the harebrained idea to burn down his competitor's dental office. As I was imagining James striking a match to flambé his nemesis's practice, the pourer noted that the derby-capped silhouette on the bottle is an image of old James Otis Kenyon himself.

The authorities arrested James, but rather than serving time in jail, he was "sentenced" to practice dentistry at a nearby hospital. During this time, his wife abandoned him and gave their two young sons the distinct impression that their father was dead. The wife and kids relocated to Walla Walla. As an adult, one of the sons, Robert, never spoke of his father, even to his own son, Stephen Otis Kenyon. However, as a young adult, Stephen discovered that, in fact, his grandfather was alive and living on the Oregon coast. Nearly 50 years to the day of the torching incident, James Otis Kenyon got a call from his grandson. Understandably, James was hesitant to meet him, but Stephen succeeded in reconnecting with his grandfather, and happily, James became a significant member of a family he had never known existed. James lived to age 101 — long enough to witness the birth of his first great-grandchild, Muriel, who now runs the winery's tasting room in downtown Walla Walla.

Today, owners Stephen Otis Kenyon and Deborah Dunbar produce small-lot premium wines, relying primarily on fruit from the Walla Walla area (including their own 10-acre Stellar Vineyard). Local winemaker Dave Stephenson handcrafts the wines for Otis Kenyon Wines with a clear focus on Bordeaux and Rhône varietal wines. Even crazy dentists with a penchant for torching things would love these wines.

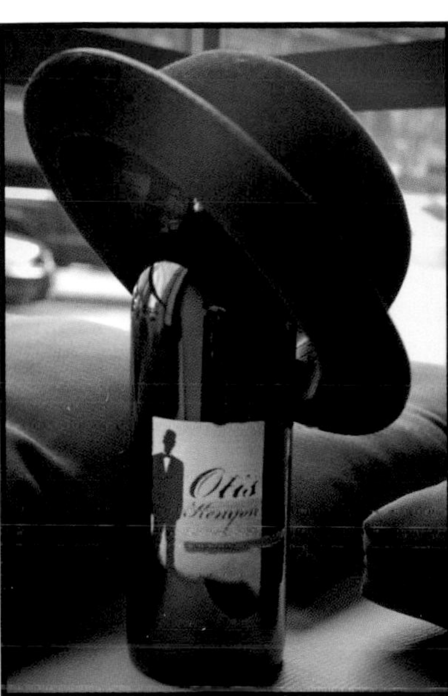

OTIS KENYON WINE
opened: 2004
winemaker(s): Dave Stephenson
location: 23 East Main Street,
Walla Walla, WA 99362
phone: 509-525-3505
web: www.otiskenyonwine.com
e-mail: info@otiskenyonwine.com
fee: Tasting fee may apply
hours: Thursday through Monday 11–5
lat: 46.067149 **long:** -118.338515
satellite location: 14525 148th Avenue Northeast #111, Woodinville, WA 98027
satellite hours: Friday through Sunday 12–5

DIRECTIONS: From U.S. 12 take N 2nd Ave./City Center exit. Turn left onto E Main St. and drive half a block more to arrive at Otis Kenyon Wine's tasting room on your left.

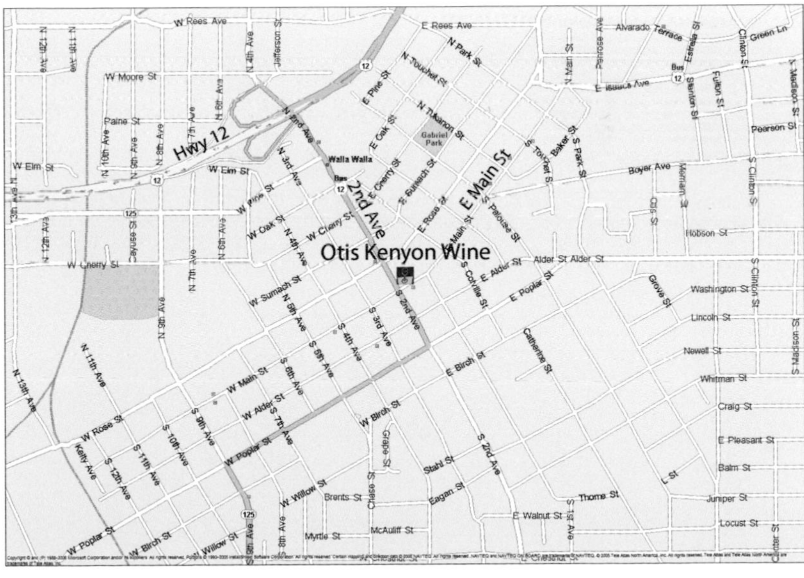

Walla Walla Wine Works 8

The sign outside reads, "7 wineries, 36 wines, 13 wines to taste." That got my attention, and I knew I was in for a unique tasting experience at the handsome red brick building at First and Main. Formerly the exclusive site of the Waterbrook Winery, the rebranded tasting room now offers a collection of wines made at the new Walla Walla Wine Works' 53,000-square-foot production facility just west of Walla Walla, off Highway 12.

If the purpose of your visit to the First and Main tasting room is to enjoy the luscious flavors of Waterbrook wines, fear not — you can sip those and a whole lot more. In addition to sampling winemaker John Freeman's Waterbrook creations, you also can sip your way through wines from Apex Cellars, The Magnificent Wine Company, Pendulum, Primarius, and SHIMMER. In so doing, you will be sampling from a who's who of noted Northwest winemakers, including the aforementioned John Freeman, as well as Peter Devison, Charles Smith, and Hal Landvoigt. There's a reason why, in 2008, *Wine & Spirits* gave The Magnificent Wine Company's The Original 2006 Syrah the "Year's Best Syrah" rating, and why *Seattle Metropolitan* magazine wrote that the Primarius 2006 Pinot Noir offered "Penny-wise Pinots — boasting intense flavors … worth every penny." These tributes are proof positive that fine wines can come from a high-production facility.

The truth is, Walla Walla Wine Works is more of a wine bar than a tasting room. Here you are encouraged to relax and spend quality time with a *New York Times* crossword puzzle or a good friend. But if you are one of the lucky ones to arrive on a Wednesday or a weekend evening, get ready for live (or DJ-mixed) music to accompany your glass of … whatever. For me, it's a glass of SHIMMER, a tasty blend of syrah and merlot.

Though you may come away thinking you have mastered the wines of Walla Walla Wine Works, be aware that it's just one component of Andrew Browne's Precept Wine Brands. Bursting on the winery scene in 2003, Seattle-based Precept Wine Brands is one of the nation's largest producers of wine, with such "value-driven" labels as Pavin & Riley, Washington Hills, Bloom, Avery Lane, Barrelstone, Big Sky, Grizz, Sweet Pea, Sol Duc, Sockeye, and Pine & Post. However, look for these labels in your local grocery store wine section, not at Walla Walla Wine Works. Only wines produced at the Highway 12 facility are uncorked here.

WALLA WALLA WINE WORKS
opened: 2009
winemaker(s): John Freeman, Charles Smith, Peter Devison and Hal Landvoigt
location: 31 East Main, 1st and Main, Walla Walla, WA 99362
phone: 509-522-5482
web: www.waterbrook.com/tasting/wallawallawineworks
e-mail: info@wallawallawineworks.com
picnic area: Yes
gift shop: Yes
fee: Tasting fee refundable with purchase
hours: Sunday through Thursday 11–6; Friday and Saturday 11–7
lat: 46.067092 **long:** -118.338724

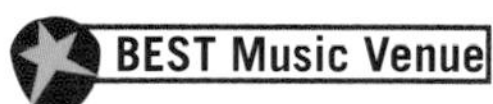

DIRECTIONS: Walla Walla Wine Works is located in downtown Walla Walla. **From Hwy 12** take the 2nd Ave. exit toward city center and go about half a mile. Turn left onto E Main St. Continue one more block to the tasting room, which is located in a red brick building on the left-hand side across from Starbucks at 1st and Main St.

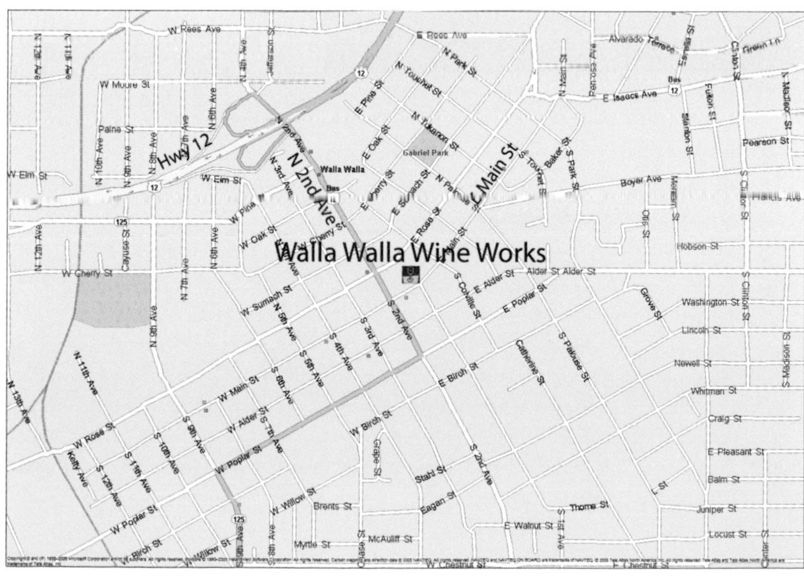

Rôtie Cellars 9

I'm a big fan of the Winepeeps wine blog, because it lends a critical palate to the Northwest wine scene. So I took notice when Winepeeps co-blogger Kori Vorhees made the following comment about a new Walla Walla wine, after she attended the packed 2009 Rhône Rangers soirée in Seattle: "Our most exciting discovery was the 2007 Rôtie Cellars 'Northern' Red Blend. It is a bold wine, yet exhibits remarkable finesse at the same time. I was blown away by its purity of fruit." Knowing Kori's discerning palate, I made a mental note to check out this new upstart when in Walla Walla.

Sean Boyd

However, I had one little obstacle. Rôtie Cellars lacked a tasting room. Thus, as I raced around visiting and drinking my way through all the wineries that appear in this book, I thought Rôtie Cellars would be destined for the book's appendix, at best. *Au contraire*! On my final visit to Walla Walla, I discovered Rôtie Cellars' new tasting room, located on the second floor of the red brick building across from Starbucks. The freshly painted tasting room had just opened, and lucky for me, owner/winemaker Sean Boyd was among the staff pouring for their "soft opening."

The affable, 6-foot-plus Sean poured a sample of his super-crisp southern Rhône white blend of roussanne and viognier. As I daydreamed of pairing this wine with pasta salad, Sean spoke of his days as a geologist, when he was deep into oil- and gas-exploration endeavors. The work was exciting, but the constant travel took him away from his wife, Annie, and their baby daughter, Bridget. Even as I savored the lingering notes of the white blend, it was clear to me that Sean is a family man to the core. But leaving a lucrative career and starting up a winery … now that takes guts.

Next up for the sampling were his two reds — a northern Rhône blend of syrah fermented together with viognier, which, by the way, has notes of floral and bacon (no kidding) reminiscent of the famed Côte-Rôtie in the northern Rhône; and a southern-Rhône-blend version featuring a backbone of grenache and smaller amounts of syrah and Mourvèdre. The southern blend, with its lighter, fruit-forward taste, provided an answer to that ever-troubling question: What to pair with chicken *à la Provençal?* I left that day with a fine case of Rhône rage, having chanced upon Walla Walla's most exciting new winery.

RÔTIE CELLARS
opened: 2010
winemaker(s): Sean Boyd
location: 31 East Main Street, Suite 216, Walla Walla, WA 99362
phone: 253-312-5991
web: www.rotiecellars.com
e-mail: via website
fee: Tasting fee refundable with purchase
hours: Typically Fridays and Saturdays; call ahead for hours
lat: 46.067159 **long:** -118.338326

DIRECTIONS: Rôtie Cellars is located in downtown Walla Walla. **From U.S. 12**, take 2nd Ave. exit toward city center and continue half a mile before turning left onto E Main St. Travel one more block to the tasting room located on the second floor of the red brick building on the left-hand side across from Starbucks at 1st and Main St. Rôtie Cellars is just above Walla Walla Wine Works.

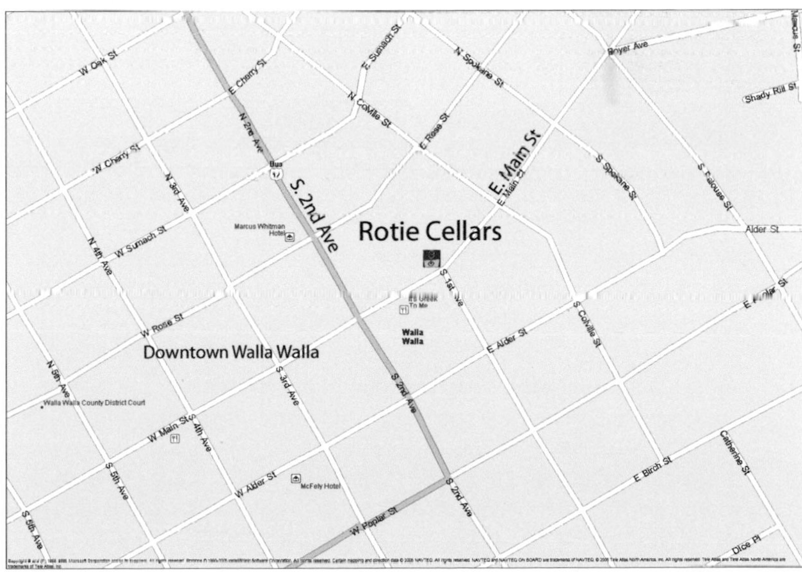

Chateau Rollat Winery 10

I came for the "Edouard de Rollat." Sometime ago, I read a review by noted *Seattle Times* wine columnist Paul Gregutt (October 17, 2007) in which he used the word "polished" to describe this Bordeaux blend; obviously relishing the wine, he noted that it was a *vin de garde* — a French term for wines that you can cellar for many years. Palate curiosity got the better of me and I decided to discover this wine for myself at the Chateau Rollat (pronounced ROLL-ah) tasting room in downtown Walla Walla.

Now, dear reader, it is not often that I splurge for a wine priced in the mid-$60s but maybe it was the intense fruitiness of the wine or the lasting finish that made me spring for a bottle of "Edouard de Rollat." Perhaps it was the friendliness of the pouring staff that encouraged my spendthriftiness as they wove a rich story about owner Bowin Lindgren and his great-grandfather Edouard.

If I could go back in time to early-1900s New York City, I would make a beeline for Café Martin, on 27th Street, and meet sommelier/wine steward Edouard Rollat in the flesh. Standing at more than 6 feet tall and sporting a neatly cropped mustache, the recent emigrant from France was an imposing figure of a man. It must have been disheartening to him when an amendment to the U.S. Constitution prohibited the manufacture and sale of wine during the 1920s. But he made the most of the dry spell and continued to teach and write about wine, and eventually the "Great Experiment" was repealed. Imagine the pride Rollat would have felt to learn that his great-grandson Bowin Lindgren would produce a highly acclaimed wine named after him.

There's another important character whom I heard about that day in the tasting room: one Christian LeSommer. Realizing he would need a consulting winemaker, Bowin succeeded in convincing Christian to come to Walla Walla and lend his winemaking expertise to create some great wines. Christian's résumé includes fulfilling the duties of general manager and wine master at Bordeaux's famed Chateau Latour. He is now the consulting manager for Domaines Barons de Rothschild's winemaking properties in such far-flung places as Italy, Argentina, and Chile. But Walla Walla, Washington? Clearly, Bowin is a great salesman, and I suspect he gets that from his great-grandfather Edouard. It's in his blood.

CHATEAU ROLLAT WINERY
opened: 2007
winemaker(s): Mike Golden and consulting winemaker Christian LeSommer
location: 43 East Main Street, Walla Walla, WA 99362
phone: 509-301-8596
web: www.chateaurollat.com
e-mail: sales@rollat.com
wheelchair access: Yes
fee: Tasting fee applies
hours: Thursday, Friday, Sunday 11–4, Saturday 11–5, or by appointment
lat: 46.067197 **long:** -118.338233

DIRECTIONS: **From U.S. 12** take N 2nd Ave./City Center exit. Turn left onto E Main St. and go one block. Arrive at 43 E Main St.,the tasting room is on the left.

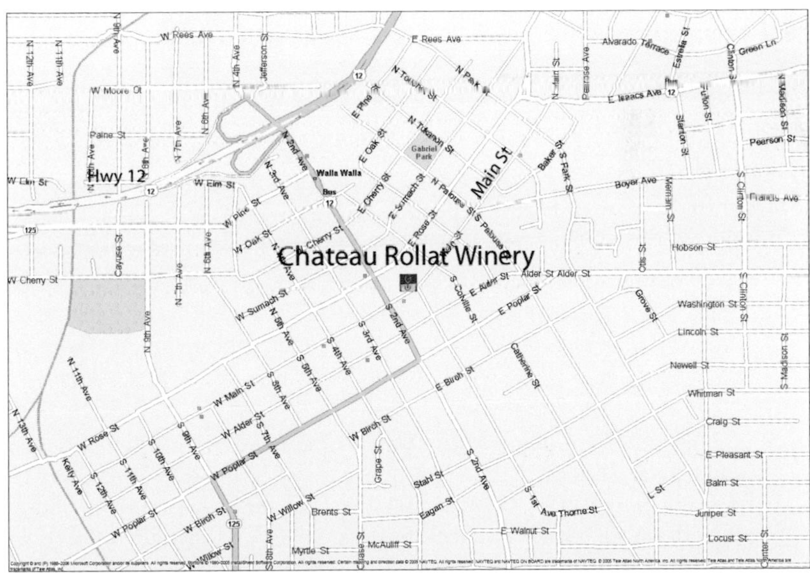

DaMa Wines 11

I always try to balance the light with the heavy — a few tears of human spirit in with the sequins and the fringes. Bette Midler

Perhaps the quotation above, one of several pithy sayings found on the DaMa Wines website, says it best about the winery's *raison d'être*. After all, co-owners and co-winemakers Dawn Kammer and Mary Tuuri Derby (the "Da" and "Ma" of DaMa) are always in the middle of a balancing act, with their shared goals of creating strong yet graceful wines; seeing to the financial needs of their winemaking operation while still giving back to the community; and meeting the challenges of being a female-owned business in a male-dominated industry. Despite these hurdles, DaMa Wines succeeds.

Dawn Kammer

Continuing the legacy of women winemakers in Washington, Dawn and Mary blend different backgrounds, training and ultimately different noses to create wines that are "full-bodied, true to the varietal taste with a smooth, rounded finish." Dawn grew up in Vacaville, California (near Napa Valley), and the "cowgirl" in her kept her out west, where she migrated from one prison town to another by random circumstance and eventually ended up in Walla Walla. She obtained a degree from the Institute of Enology and Viticulture at Walla Walla Community College before working at College Cellars and the iconic Marcus Whitman Hotel. Mary's route to DaMa included a long stint in the culinary arts working for renowned restaurants in San Francisco and Chicago. Eventually she, too, landed in Walla Walla, where she and her late husband, Devin Derby, launched Spring Valley Vineyard. Although their backgrounds and training are quite different, the two women possessed a common vision of the type of winery and wine style they sought to create.

Despite not having deep pockets Dawn and Mary make it a priority to give back to the community. Through their DaMa-Know Effect (a play on "domino effect") charity, they donate a portion of their sales to causes that support women, children and communities. Patrons of the DaMa Wines, including DaMa Nation wine club members, can take heart knowing that organizations such as Walla Walla's St. Mary's Cancer Care Center and the YMCA benefit when a bottle (or two) of Dawn and Mary's distinctively labeled wines are purchased. For me, the delightful "CowGirl Cab" ($21) had me reaching for my wallet, happy in the knowledge that someone's life would benefit.

DAMA WINES
opened: 2007
winemaker(s): Dawn Kammer and Mary Tuuri Derby
location: 45 East Main Street, Walla Walla, WA 98362
phone: 509-525-2299
web: www.damawines.com
e-mail: info@damawines.com
fee: Tasting fee applies
hours: Monday through Thursday 11–4; Friday through Saturday 11–6 and Sunday 11–2
lat: 46.067198 **long:** -118.338456

DIRECTIONS: **From Hwy 12** take N 2nd Ave./City Center exit. Turn left onto E Main St. and travel half a block. Arrive at 45 E Main St., home of DaMa Wines' tasting room.

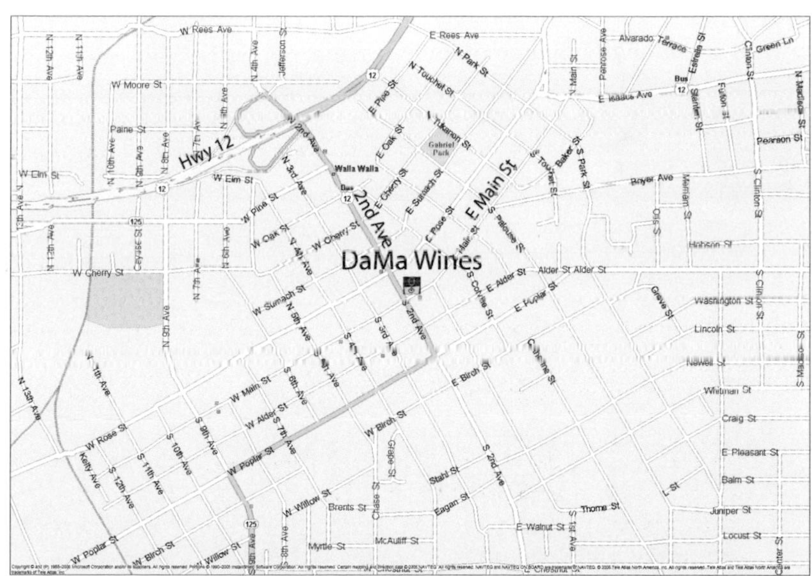

Fort Walla Walla Cellars 12

Owners Jim Moyer and Cliff Kontos appreciate tradition. As Walla Walla natives, they know a thing or two about the area's history and, in particular, it's grape-growing past, which goes as far back as the mid-1800s, when the early settlers in the area planted vines for wine production. Many of these pioneers emigrated from France and Italy, where winemaking is a centuries-old tradition handed down from one generation to the next. So in 1998, when Jim and Cliff began making wine together, they thought it would be fitting to name their winery to honor the past. They christened their new venture "Fort Walla Walla Cellars," paying homage to the landmark that helped establish Walla Walla.

According to the Fort Walla Walla Cellars website, a man by the name of Frank Orselli, who was stationed at the original Fort Walla Walla, opened what many historians agree was the area's first commercial winery. It produced approximately 1,000 cases of wine annually. Clearly, the Italian settlers needed some vino rosso to pair with vine-ripened tomatoes, onions and other delectables reminiscent of home!

Study Fort Walla Walla Cellars' wine labels and you'll see an illustration of Fort Walla Walla itself. The labels even have that "aged look," as if the bottles they adorn have been kept all this time in Orselli's own wine cellar. With Jim and Cliff's penchant for history, it's not surprising that they stick to a traditional winemaking style, using tried-and-true techniques passed down from generations of winemakers. Using these methods, they produce approximately 2,000 cases per year.

Located in the heart of downtown Walla Walla, the winery's fort-like red brick tasting room enjoys a steady stream of visitors. WineTrail enthusiasts will have an opportunity to swirl and taste premium cabernet sauvignon, merlot, syrah, and, my personal favorite, their award-winning Bordeaux blend "Treaty." Even with a dozen visitors milling about, the amiable tasting room manager, Terry Farley, finds time to pour, chat, and work the cash register with ease. Rarely do we see tasting room staff serving up second helpings, but at Fort Walla Walla Cellars, a second taste is commonly offered to guests. Yes, there is a spittoon on the wine bar, but Fort Walla Walla wines are too luscious to be wasted in a spittoon.

FORT WALLA WALLA CELLARS
opened: 1998
winemaker(s): Jim Moyer and Cliff Kontos
location: 127 East Main Street, Walla Walla, WA 99362
phone: 509-520-1095
web: www.fortwallawallacellars.com
e-mail: info@fortwallawallacellars.com
picnic area: Yes
gift shop: Yes
tours: Yes
fee: Tasting fee refundable with purchase
hours: 10–4:30 Thursday through Monday, or by appointment
lat: 46.068294 **long:** -118.337112

DIRECTIONS: From Hwy 12 take N 2nd Ave/City Center exit. Turn left onto E Main St. and go three blocks. Arrive at 127 E Main St. Fort Walla Walla's tasting room is on the left on the corner of Main St. and S Spokane St.

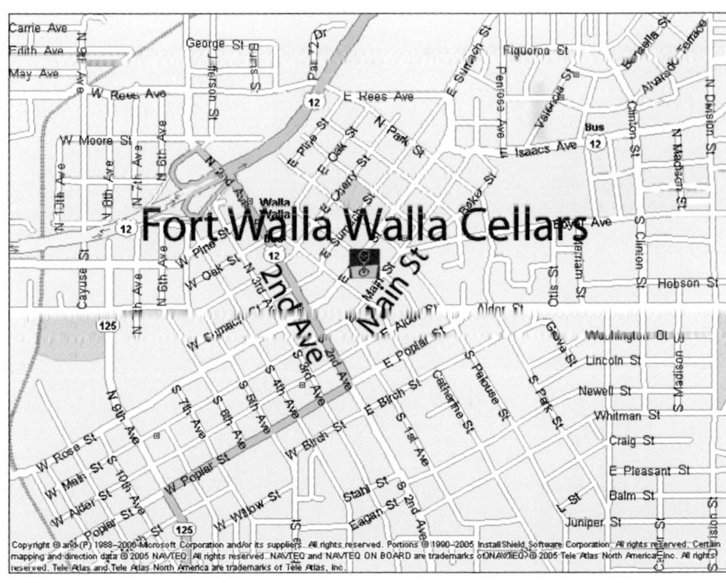

Nicholas Cole Cellars 13

"They're barrel staves," explained Mike Neuffer, owner and winemaker of Nicholas Cole Cellars. He was referring to the tasting room's interior wall, composed of spent barrel staves with handsome photos strategically placed here and there. With Nikon in hand, I was attempting to capture the sunlight's glow inside the contemporary-style tasting room when Mike's warm smile interrupted me. "Would you like to try some wine?" he offered. Uh, is merlot red?

Simple yet elegant, Nicholas Cole's Main Street tasting room mirrors Mike's wine style. Here, only red wines are offered for sampling — all of them unfiltered and unfined true to his minimalist approach to winemaking. He lets gravity remove the sediments in the barrel, preferring to rack his wines every three or four months to clarify and soften the finished product. He learned this style of winemaking from his mentor, Chris Camarda of famed Andrew Will Winery, as well as from a healthy dose of coursework at University of California–Davis. It's unquestionably a "less is more" approach to winemaking that reflects Mike's firm belief that it all starts in the vineyard. The challenge for the winemaker is to let the taste of the variety shine. In other words, don't mess with Mother Nature.

Speaking of vineyards, Mike planted his own 42-acre Neuffer Estate Vineyard in 2001. Situated at the eastern end of the Walla Walla Valley next to his well-known neighbor, Leonetti Cellar, Mike's vineyard is decidedly Bordeaux in its plantings, with cabernet sauvignon, cabernet franc, merlot, petit verdot and Malbec dominating the landscape. You will also find rows of sangiovese, which will eventually end up in his super-Tuscan blend, "Juliet," named after his sister. Of note is Mike's status as a founding member of Walla Walla–based Vinea, a group of winegrowers who have voluntarily embraced sustainable, earth-friendly practices.

Paying homage to his family, Mike named the winery for his two children, his son's first name "Nicholas" and his daughter's middle name "Cole". The names for his other wines also honor family members, including his Bordeaux blends "Michele" and "Camille," and his delectable "Dauphine," made from 100 percent syrah that even a Rhône Valley Hermitage loving fan would relish. His deliciously decadent right-bank Bordeaux blend (composed of primarily merlot and cabernet franc) is the oddball, bearing the name "Reserve." In my mind, however, I have rechristened this wine with a new name: Mike.

NICHOLAS COLE CELLARS
opened: 2001
winemaker(s): Mike Neuffer
location: 229 East Main Street, Walla Walla, WA 99362
phone: 509-525-0608
web: www.nicholascolecellars.com
e-mail: info@nicholascolecellars.com
tours: Yes
fee: Tasting fee applies
hours: Monday through Thursday 10–4; Friday and Saturday 10–5; closed Sunday
lat: 46.066874 **long:** -118.339453

DIRECTIONS: From Hwy 12 take N 2nd Ave. exit (city center). Turn left onto E Main St. and continue two more blocks. Nicholas Cole Cellar's tasting room is on the left.

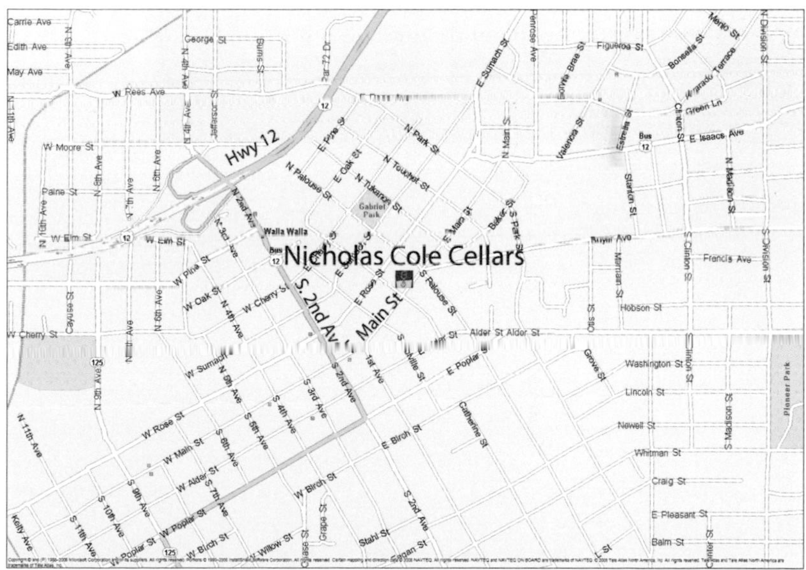

Walla Faces Wines 14

Sometimes dreams do come true.

Such is the case of Rick and Debbie Johnson, who got married on December 31, 1999 and a month later, honeymooned on the Oregon coast at Manzanita. While walking on the beach, the Johnsons had one of those "What shall we do next in life?" discussions, and the answer they arrived at was growing premium wine grapes. Not right away, mind you. Both of the Johnsons were invested in careers that demanded their full attention — he was in commercial real estate; she, in health care consulting.

It would take five more years before Rick and Debbie stumbled onto vineyard property in Walla Walla that suited their tastes as well as their life's goals. Once it was found, however, the Johnsons moved from Seattle to their new home — Walla Walla — and never looked back.

Walla Faces Vineyard Inn

Their "home" turns out to be a vineyard estate and luxurious inn east of town. It's the perfect place for realizing their dream — managing a 10-acre vineyard estate (8.5 acres of premium cabernet sauvignon and syrah under production) and running the elegant guesthouse, complete with outdoor pool. Here, Rick can apply his education and training in viticulture gained from Washington State University's viticulture program and his extensive coursework at the University of California–Davis. However, now that he's beyond the textbooks, Rick has real-world difficult decisions that come with the business of growing grapes.

For turning the grapes into fine wine, Rick and Debbie hired Matthew Loso, a legendary Washington winemaker. Walla Faces features a portfolio of delectable riesling, cabernet sauvignon, syrah, and a red blend called "Fusion Red," and visitors can sample these wines at its downtown Walla Walla tasting room, which includes yet another stunning second guest inn upstairs. Stylish and chic (thanks in large part to Rick's urban planning and commercial real estate background), the tasting room décor includes walls replete with the celebrated artwork of Rick's sister, Candice Johnson. Her "Faces" series is a visual representation of the winery's name and takes center stage on the labels of its wines. As I studied the label, Debbie mentioned that they recently had a clairvoyant in the tasting room giving readings for folks eager to get a sneak peak of their future. Although I am no soothsayer, I can easily see a bright future for the Johnsons in their adopted home.

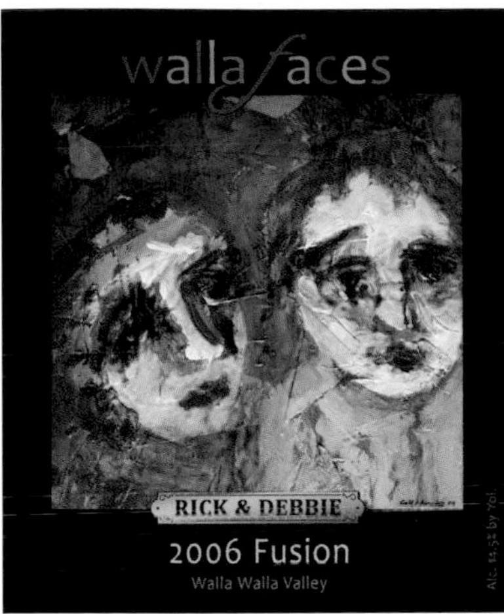

WALLA FACES WINES
opened: 2009
winemaker(s): Matthew Loso
location: 216 East Main Street, Walla Walla, WA 98362
phone: 509-301-1181
web: www.wallafaces.com
e-mail: info@wallafaces.com
wheelchair access: Yes
fee: Tasting fee may apply
hours: Monday through Saturday 12–8, Sunday 11–3 or by appointment. Winter hours (December through March) weekends only
lat: 46.068914 **long:** -118.336208

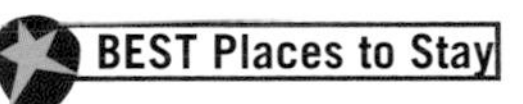

DIRECTIONS: From Hwy 12 take N 2nd Ave./City Center exit. Turn left onto E Main St. and go about two blocks to find Walla Faces Wines' tasting room on the right.

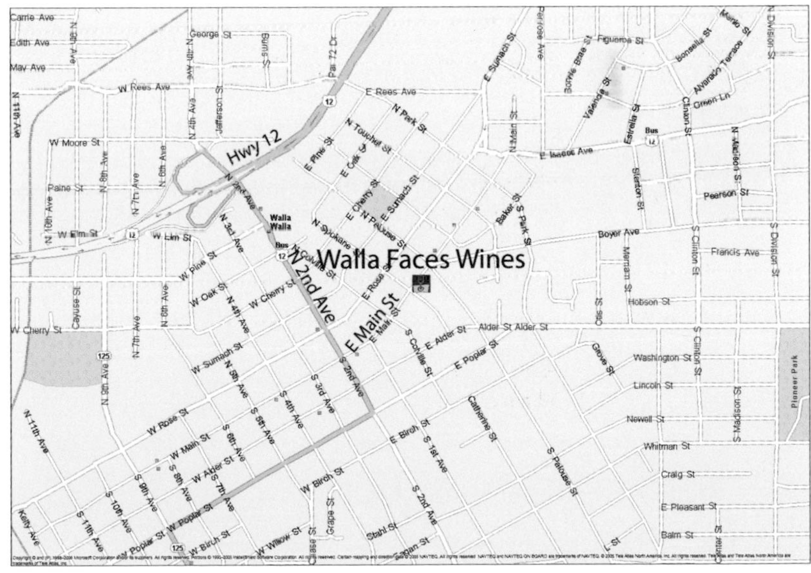

El Corazon Winery 15

"I want to be a volcanologist," said 6-year-old Tiger in answer to his mother's question about a future career. "How about being a winemaker?" his mom, Jennifer McKnight Sievers, asked. With a shrug of his shoulders, young Tiger gave a "Maybe, one day" response while eating a cup of yogurt and studying photos in a book he was perusing. Just like his mom and dad, Tiger has a can-do attitude.

Spencer Sievers

To say that Tiger's father, Spencer Sievers, has volcanic energy is the classic understatement. His fire instills a sense of *esprit de corps* in all those who are exposed to him. Tall and possessing a terrific smile, this lanky winemaker exudes great confidence, but not in a cocky way. Rather, it is a passion to try different things in life, such as moving to Kansas and opening a health food store in Lawrence (by the way, Jennifer owns Arizona Trading Co., a clothing reseller in Lawrence); living in Panama with Jennifer and toddler Tiger; and, in a leap of faith, relocating to Walla Walla to make wine. Winemaking wasn't altogether a new venture, however. While residing in Portland, Oregon, he and Jennifer would make occasional forays into the Willamette Valley and there, they fell in love with its vineyards. On one such tasting visit, he met a grape grower and purchased a half-ton of grapes two months before harvest. The fact that Spencer didn't know a lick about winemaking was incentive enough to devour winemaking how-to texts and talk the ears off winemakers. It was the classic Alfred E. Neuman "What, me worry?" approach.

At El Corazon (which means "the heart" in Spanish), handcrafted wine comes alive with small-lot productions of cabernet franc, syrah, Malbec, carmenere, and red blends. With his winemaking partner, Raul Morfin, Spencer works to keep El Corazon small (with production at 1,000 cases) but true to the fruit found in the Walla Walla Valley — varieties that grow wonderfully in this semi-arid location, which happens to share the same latitude as France's Bordeaux region and its Côte d'Or, in Burgundy.

With a tip of his wine glass toward his son, Spencer noted, "Tiger has a really good palate and picks up flavors that I don't." He was quick to add that Tiger tastes eyedropper-size samples. In this respect, it's only fitting that their 100 percent carménère wine bears the name "Tiger's Blood." At El Corazon Winery, the plan for succession is alive and well!

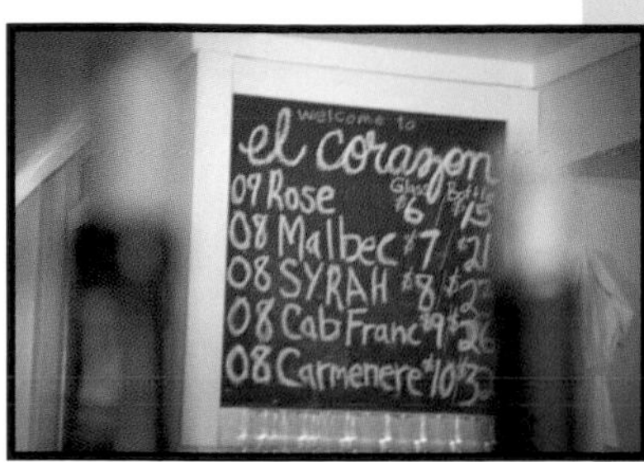

EL CORAZON WINERY
opened: 2008
winemaker(s): Spencer Sievers
location: 37 South Palouse Street, Walla Walla, WA 99362
phone: 509-240-5292
web: www.elcorazonwinery.com
e-mail: spencer@elcorazonwinery.com
fee: Complimentary wine tasting
hours: Friday and Saturday 12–7; Sunday 11–4, or by appointment
lat: 46.068834 **long:** -118.334205

DIRECTIONS: From U.S. 12 take N 2nd Ave./City Center exit. Turn left onto E Main St. and go four blocks. Turn right on S. Palouse St. and continue about a tenth of a mile. El Corazon Winery is on the left.

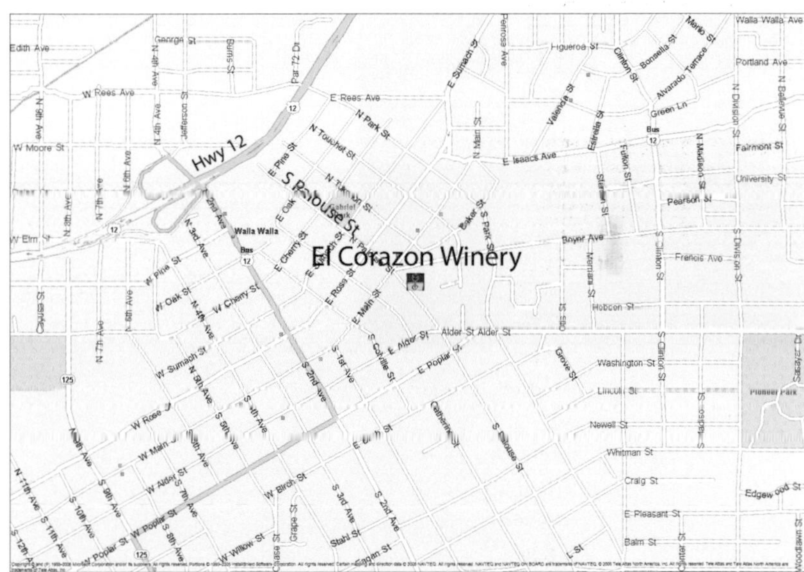

Stephenson Cellars 16

Stephenson Cellars' mission statement reads, "Pursuing the finest grapes, limited production, bottling poetry." Sounds simple enough, but the reality behind the statement is more blood, sweat and tears than romantic notions of owning a winery. To Dave Stephenson, it was cashing in everything, including his 401K, and selling his house, sailboat, and surfboard to start a winery east of town at the Walla Walla Regional Airport wine incubator complex.

Now, nearly 10 years later and producing just 1,200 cases annually, Dave can take pride in the numerous accolades he's won with plenty of 90+ scores from wine critics. To wit, Dan Radil, wine critic for *The Bellingham Herald*, nicknamed Dave "Mr. Syrah" and referred to his 2003 syrah as "mind-boggling, with an incredible nose of violets and smoky undertones and lush flavors of blackberry." Unfortunately for me, his reputation as one of Washington's finest syrah winemakers resulted in the two words that every WineTrail enthusiast hates to catch sight of: "sold out."

To realize his winery's vision of "limited production," Dave has a second career as a consulting winemaker, with Otis Kenyon Wine as a key customer. Given Otis Kenyon Wine's success, there's no doubt others will follow. As Dave notes on his website, "In two years, I can take anyone from zero to winery," and this includes not just pressing grapes but the business side of the winery as well. To be successful, you need to have the talent to vinify the juice, market your product, and manage a mountain of bureaucratic paperwork — one aspect I suspect the wine courses at University of California–Davis leave out. For starry-eyed people smitten by the wine bug, hiring Dave Stephenson may be the best investment you can make besides choosing the right grape growers to work with (Dave can help you with that, too).

Fortunately, if you're a Walla Walla wine tourist anxious to sample Dave's wares, you can enjoy a glass of wine at his airy, art-filled tasting room on Spokane Street. Not just a pour, mind you. There are plenty of tables where you can sit and uncork a bottle of Stephenson Cellars' finest. Even better, you can time your visit to coincide with live music performances, as my wife and I did on a Saturday night. As I sipped Dave's smooth cabernet and listened to the music and surrounding laughter, I found myself wondering if he misses that old surfboard at all.

STEPHENSON CELLARS
opened: 2004
winemaker(s): Dave Stephenson
location: 15 South Spokane Street, Walla Walla, WA 99362
phone: 509-529-8200
web: www.stephensoncellars.com
e-mail: stephenson@bmi.net
tours: Yes
fee: Tasting fee applies
hours: Tuesday through Sunday 11–5, Saturday evening reopens 7–10 for live music, or by appointment
lat: 46.068679 **long:** -118.335622

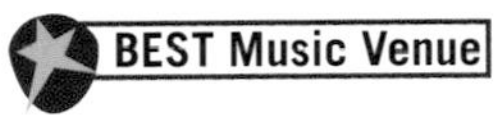

DIRECTIONS: From downtown Walla Walla (2nd and Main St.) go three blocks east on Main St. and turn right onto Spokane St. The tasting room is on the left a half block down.

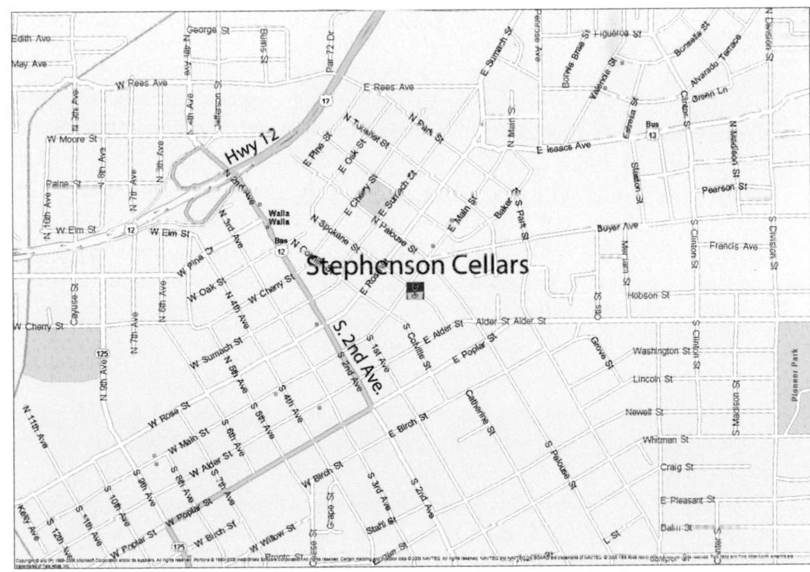

Trio Vintners 17

"We'll be moving to the 'financial district' of Walla Walla. At least that's what Denise [Slattery] calls it," quipped 6-foot-something Steve Michener, in reference to their new downtown location near the main offices of Walla Walla–based Baker Boyer Bank and Banner Bank. Moving from the "incubator" to the heart of the commercial district defines a success story of sorts for the husband-and-wife winemaking team of Trio Vintners.

The fact that Denise and Steve still have a couple of more years left on their non-renewing lease at the airport winery incubator location speaks volumes about their hard work and ingenuity. Sure, the rent is low (at least it was in the beginning years), but everything else — from the equipment and the grapes to the marketing prowess — is in the hands of the winemaker. And in the crowded field of top-notch winemakers who populate this valley, the bar is set even higher. But how this transplanted couple from the Bay Area came to Walla Walla in 2004 without a lick of winemaking training to achieve *Wine Business Monthly's* top 10 ranking for "Hot Small Brands of 2008" is a story that other fledging wineries can only hope to emulate.

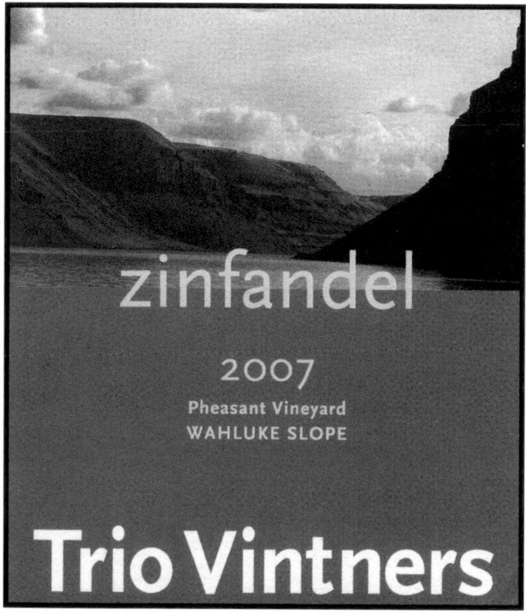

A sip of their dense but oh so delectable 2007 zinfandel tells it all. First, it reflects the fact that both Denise and Steve were very good students at Walla Walla Community College's Institute for Enology and Viticulture. The degrees earned demonstrate a command of the region's terroir in terms of its unique soil, perfect climate, and variety of grapes. The trio of earth, climate, and fruit is the source of the winery's name but more importantly, this triad guides their winemaking style. Because of the diversity of climate and soil, the couple is free to choose the grape varieties to use as well as the style of wine to make. With Trio Vintners wines, your taste buds experience the varieties of the hotter European zones, such as zinfandel, Mourvèdre, syrah, tempranillo, and sangiovese.

The Wallula Gap image on Trio's wine labels highlight this sense of place. The Micheners deeply appreciate the geological fact that the Wallula Gap, between present-day Oregon and Washington, corked the flooding headwaters of the Missoula Floods (occurring about 12,000 years ago), resulting in the alluvial soils of the Columbia Valley. Without the Wallula Gap, perhaps we'd all be drinking cabernet and chardonnay from California, and be left wondering what we were missing. In short, Trio Vintners offers the perfect cure for palate fatigue.

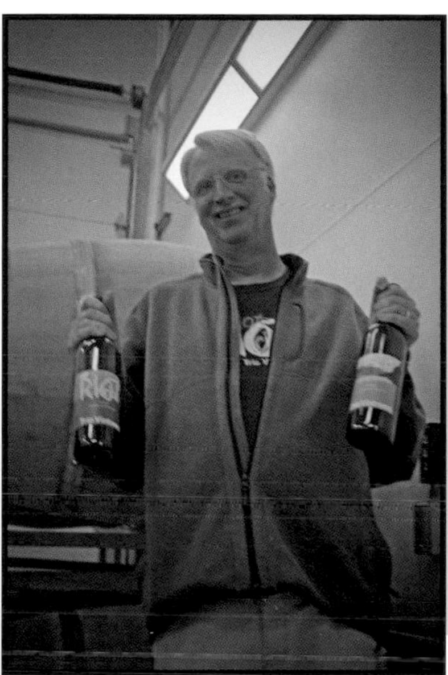
Steve Michener

TRIO VINTNERS
opened: 2007
winemaker(s): Denise Slattery and Steve Michener
location: 102 South 2nd Avenue, Walla Walla, WA 99362
phone: 509-529-8746
web: www.triovintners.com
e-mail: wine@triovintners.com
picnic area: Yes
wheelchair access: Yes
gift shop: Yes
fee: Complimentary wine tasting
hours: Saturday and Sunday 11–4:30, or by appointment
lat: 46.065754 **long:** -118.338609

DIRECTIONS: Trio Vintners' tasting room is located in downtown Walla Walla on S. 2nd Ave.

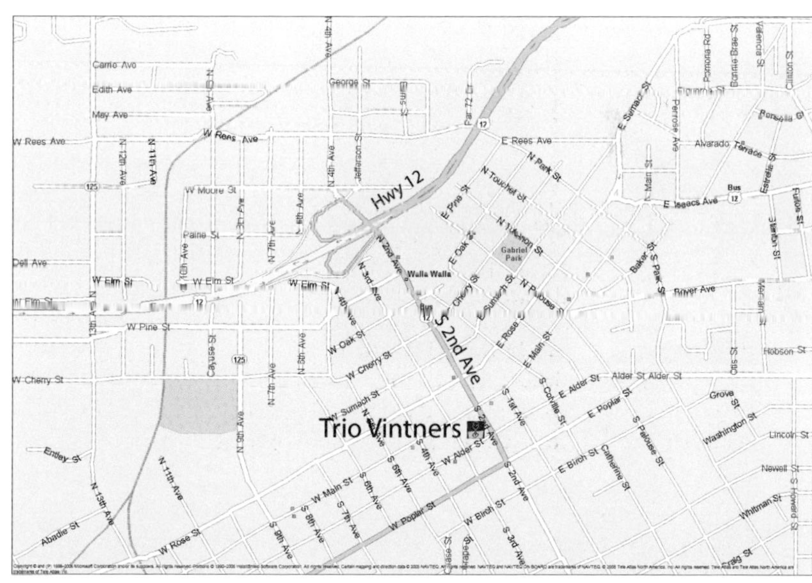

Forgeron Cellars 18

If you're a fan of chardonnay, your ship has come in — and docked at Forgeron Cellars. Early on, winemaker and co-owner Marie-Eve Gilla insisted that Forgeron Cellars make chardonnay. At the time, this decision was somewhat controversial; after all, Walla Walla is mecca for big, intense reds. Fortunately, for the other 50-plus investors in Forgeron, she got her way. Today, if you ask the locals where to find great chardonnay, they would steer you to Forgeron. With chardonnay production at 1,400 cases a year to meet demand, those same investors are celebrating Marie-Eve's success.

Forgeron's chardonnay is made from Columbia Valley grapes, using neutral French oak to create luscious "variety expressive" chardonnay. The fact is Marie-Eve happens to hail from the part of France that's famous for its chardonnay: Burgundy, where the white wines of Chablis and Côte de Beaune enjoy a bit of a reputation. When I taste her chardonnay, my mind immediately goes into "foodie" mode with thoughts of chicken, seafood and summer salads. Priced in the mid-$20 range, her exquisite chardonnay is an affordable luxury.

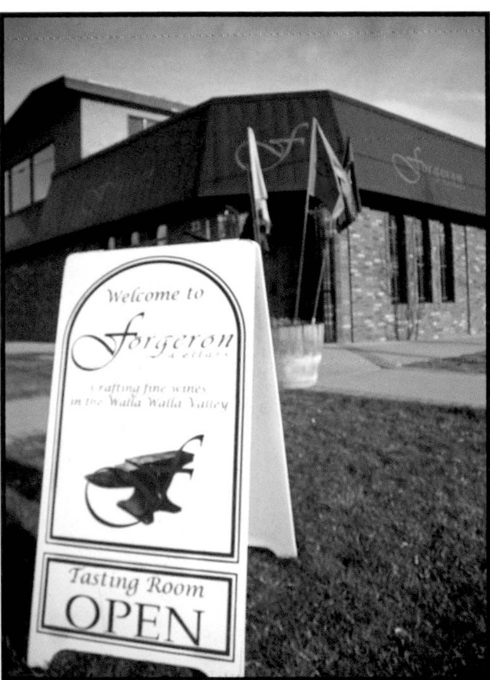

However, if you are a devotee of red wines, Forgeron Cellars will not disappoint. After all, three-quarters of the wines produced at Forgeron are red — bold, layered, fruit-forward explosions with lingering finishes. In fact, it's Marie-Eve's Bordeaux blends, her syrah and her barbera that get many a visitor to join the winery's Anvil Wine Club — that, and the fact that the wine club offers a number of primo benefits.

Colorful flags adorn the winery entrance and serve as a landmark for WineTrail seekers. As you step into Forgeron's tasting room, you will most likely find yourself in the presence of a dog; the Lab's name is Salsa. A Mexican crew working in one of the vineyards discovered the lost dog and fed her tortilla chips. When Marie-Eve came to the dog's rescue and offered her a home, she named her Salsa.

Forgeron's winery/tasting room was once the site of a blacksmith's workshop, hence its name, which is French for "blacksmith." Rumor has it that horseshoes were discovered during the renovation of the former blacksmithy. As you are swirling, sipping, and yakking with the friendly staff, you might just ask to see one of the horseshoes. Some of the good luck it has brought Forgeron is bound to rub off.

FORGERON CELLARS
opened: 2001
winemaker(s): Marie-Eve Gilla
location: 33 West Birch Street, Walla Walla, WA 99362-3004
phone: 509-522-9463
web: www.forgeroncellars.com
e-mail: info@forgeroncellars.com
gift shop: Yes
tours: Yes
fee: Complimentary wine tasting; tasting fee may apply to reserve wines
hours: Daily 11–4 excluding major holidays
lat: 46.063817 **long:** -118.337629

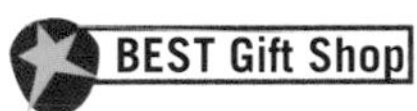

DIRECTIONS: **From U.S. 12** take S 2nd Ave. exit and continue about half a mile before turning right onto W Birch St. Look for Forgeron's red and black flags marking the entrance.

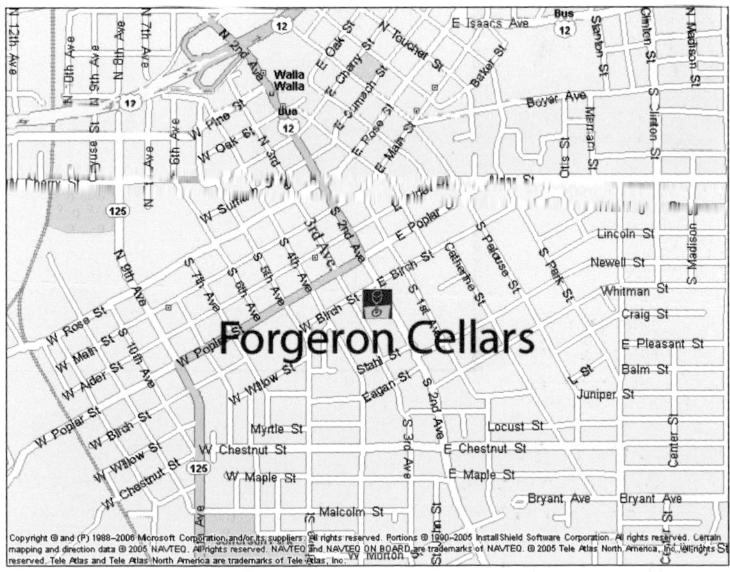

Walla Walla Village Winery 19

It was the summer of 1967. I was 15 at the time, and my dad and mom had thrown two of my three sisters and me into the two-tone blue Ford Fairlane 500 to drive from Spokane to the Bay Area. We were going to visit my older brother, who was stationed at Fort Ord. The nightly news was reporting the latest body counts in Vietnam. Eric Burdon and The Animals' "San Francisco Nights" was a huge hit on the radio, and my dad begrudgingly turned up the volume when the song played. We were heading to a music mecca, where The Fillmore was the venue for Jefferson Airplane, The Doors, Janis Joplin, The Grateful Dead, and other acid-rock icons. Our city tour included Haight-Ashbury, where I saw plenty of hippies and psychedelic posters announcing upcoming concerts. I was to learn later that Stanley Mouse was the artistic creator behind many of the posters. Today, serious collectors wage bidding battles on eBay for his work.

So imagine my delight nearly 40 years later when I walked into the Walla Walla Village Winery tasting room and saw that its labels were designed by none other than Stanley Mouse. The same guy whose art embodied quintessential '60s rock had loaned his talents to the creation of Walla Walla Village's wine labels. Just as a music poster can evoke memories of events, feelings, and ideas, a wine label can also define a moment in time.

Barb and Lynn Irish Clark, owners of Walla Walla Village Winery, had Mouse create the label for their first 2003 release of gewürztraminer. His label designs also capture the spirit of other wines they offer. I was to discover that the eye-popping sunburst label perfectly represented the spiciness of the gewürztraminer, as well as the luscious, rich flavor of their "Bordello Red." The Clarks' son, Joel, is their winemaker, and he has created a full sleight of wines using grapes from Washington's Columbia Valley.

Located in a renovated 1900 building, the Walla Walla Village Winery tasting room beautifully complements Walla Walla's downtown architecture. Inside, the high ceilings feature still-shiny copper tiles, and the refurbished tasting bar dates back to an era that honored artisanship. As you sample the delectable offerings and gaze through the arched windows, you can almost imagine a horse-drawn carriage passing by. It would be the perfect moment to hear "On a warm San Francisco night ... "

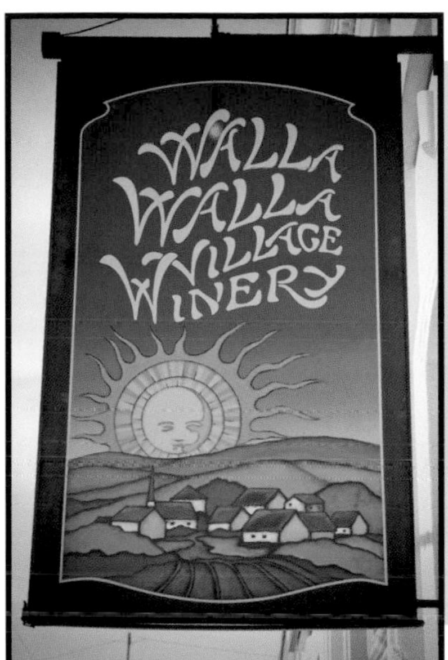

WALLA WALLA VILLAGE WINERY
opened: 2003
winemaker(s): Joel Clark
location: 107 South 3rd Avenue, Walla Walla, WA 99362
phone: 509-525-WINE (9463)
web: www.wallawallavillagewinery.com
e-mail: info@wallawallavillagewinery.com
picnic area: Yes
gift shop: Yes
tours: Yes
fee: Tasting fee refundable with purchase
hours: Tuesday through Saturday 12–6, extended hours on Thursday evening 7–11 for live music; hours subject to seasonal change so call ahead
lat: 46.065266 **long:** -118.339645

DIRECTIONS: **From U.S. 12** take 2nd Ave. exit toward city center and go half a mile. Turn right onto W Alder St. and continue to 3rd Ave. The tasting room is just around the corner on the right-hand side.

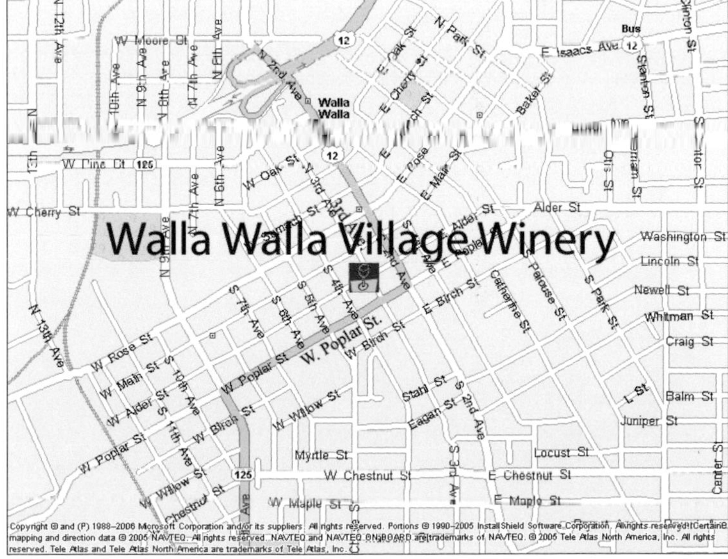

Morrison Lane Winery 20

Often, wineries are successful because owner and winemaker march together to the beat of a different drummer. When your lineup of wines includes such uncommon choices as cinsault, carménère, barbera, nebbiolo, and counoise, you distinguish yourself immediately. Such is the case with Morrison Lane.

Since 1997, Dean and Verdie Morrison have supplied a number of wineries with premium grapes of Rhône and Italian origins from their 23-acre vineyard, located just south of Walla Walla. In 2002, the couple took the plunge themselves, not only growing the fruit, but also turning it into fine wine. Today, Morrison Lane wines are produced from the "Morrison family committee." Dean and Verdie manage their vineyards and winery, and sons Sean and Dan manage the winemaking tasks. When not performing Morrison Lane Winery duties, Sean is the cellar master at Abeja Winery, working under John Abbot. Dan fulfills the role of cellar master at nearby Canoe Ridge Vineyard.

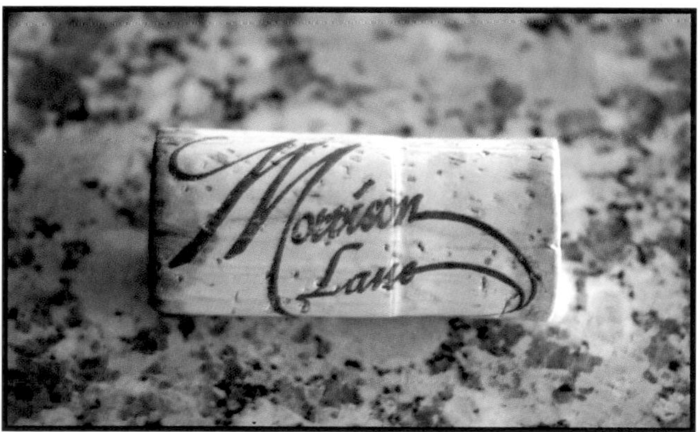

The Morrisons still use the winemaking facilities of other wineries and therefore technically can't label their wines as "estate." The fed's Alcohol and Tobacco Tax and Trade Bureau would slap their wrists. Nevertheless, by any other name, the Rhône varietal counoise (pronounced koon-WAHZ) would taste just as delicious. It actually tastes like the syrup from canned Bing cherries — very fruit forward, yet not sweet.

The Morrison Lane tasting room is situated downtown in the historic Dacres Building, on the corner of Main and Fourth streets. Wine pairs wonderfully with music, and it's no accident that a baby grand piano graces the tasting room. In the past, the Morrisons hosted live performances and open-mike evenings, but all that changed in 2009 when the American Society of Composers, Authors and Publishers (ASCAP) threatened legal action if the Morrisons didn't pay a licensing fee. ASCAP is the same organization that threatened to sue the Girl Scouts of America for singing copyrighted songs at camps without paying a licensing fee!

Because Morrison Lane is a small, family-owned and -operated winery, you will often find Verdie and Dean working the tasting room. When I asked Verdie if they had a wine club she noted, "We don't have a wine club per se, but we do have a baseball bat under the bar." We discovered that she wasn't kidding. Under the bar, there is a bat inscribed with the words "Wine Club" on its barrel.

MORRISON LANE WINERY
opened: 2002
winemaker(s): Dan Morrison
location: 201 West Main Street, Walla Walla, WA 99362
phone: 509-526-0229
web: www.morrisonlane.com
e-mail: verdie@morrisonlane.com
tours: Yes
fee: Complimentary wine tasting
hours: Friday through Sunday 12–5, or by appointment; Closed January and February
lat: 46.065535 **long:** -118.341986

DIRECTIONS: The Morrison Lane tasting room is located in the historic Dacres Building. **From N 2nd Ave. (U.S. 12 Business)** turn right onto W Main St. and go a tenth of a mile to find Morrison Lane tasting room on the corner.

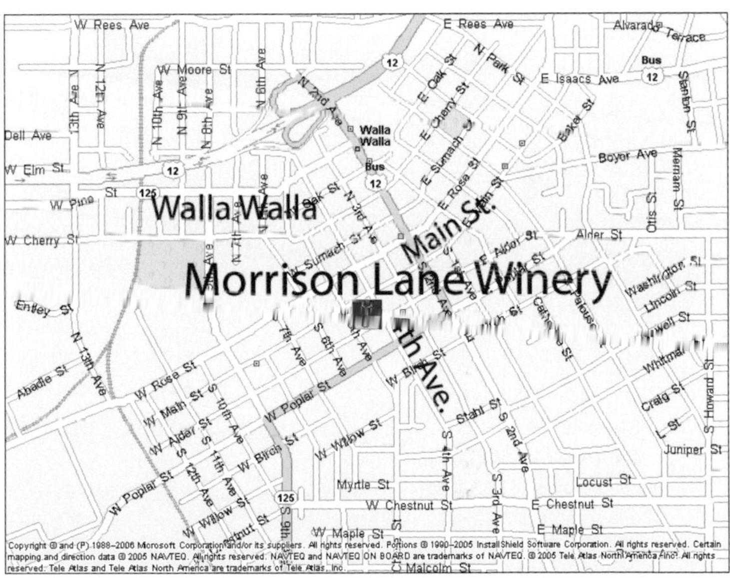

Bergevin Lane Vineyards 21

If you spend any time in Walla Walla and dine at some of the city's finer restaurants, you may notice that one establishment serves a Bergevin Lane viognier. Another offers a Bergevin "Calico" syrah. A trip to a nice bottle shop in town reveals a row of Bergevin wines, which includes the winery's top-selling "Calico" Red and its reserve blend "Intuition." You might find yourself in the downtown Starbucks and overhear someone mention that they had Bergevin Lane's "Calico" White last night with their fresh halibut. By day three, you begin to detect a pattern and you ask, "'Where the hell is this Bergevin Lane Vineyard?"

Bergevin Lane is a key stop on the downtown Walla Walla WineTrail, but you won't arrive by foot. To get to 1215 West Poplar, you will need to get into the car and drive. As you pull up, you'll see that, unlike the many other tasting rooms found in downtown Walla Walla, Bergevin Lane's tasting room shares a space with the winery's production facility. The facility comes fully equipped with a spacious winemaking/testing area and barrel storage area. Co-owner Gary Bergevin has learned from his experience with other wineries, including Canoe Ridge Vineyards, that size does matter. So there's no need to play real-world Tetris with the barrels here.

Danish-born and -bred Steffan Jorgensen oversees the winemaking duties for Bergevin Lane Vineyards. With ample space and advanced equipment, Steffan plies his extensive experience gained from winemaking stints in France, Chile, and Sonoma. A peek into the production area often finds Steffan, with his shaved head and energetic smile, working his magic — perhaps close to achieving a final blend, with nose stuck in a just-swirled glass of red.

Bergevin Lane's story is one of a collaborative effort between two women to produce premier wines. Gary's daughter, Annette Bergevin, and her partner, Amber Lane, have formed a hugely successful team to manage the sales and marketing, as well as the day-to-day operations, of Bergevin Lane. They must be doing something right. The emperor of wine himself, Robert M. Parker Jr., had this to say about Bergevin Lane's cabernet sauvignon, "Edge-free, fruit-driven decadence." Five simple words, but certainly just the right verbiage to convince WineTrail enthusiasts to stop in and take a swirl.

Amber Lane

BERGEVIN LANE VINEYARDS
opened: 2001
winemaker(s): Steffan Jorgensen
location: 1215 West Poplar Street, Walla Walla, WA 99362-2780
phone: 509-526-4300
web: www.bergevinlane.com
e-mail: info@bergevinlane.com
gift shop: Yes
tours: Yes
fee: Tasting fee refundable with purchase
hours: Monday through Saturday 11–4, or by appointment
lat: 46.058346 **long:** -118.354196

DIRECTIONS: **From downtown Walla Walla** head west on W Poplar St. and continue about a mile. Arrive at 1215 W Poplar St. where the winery and tasting room can be found on the left-hand side.

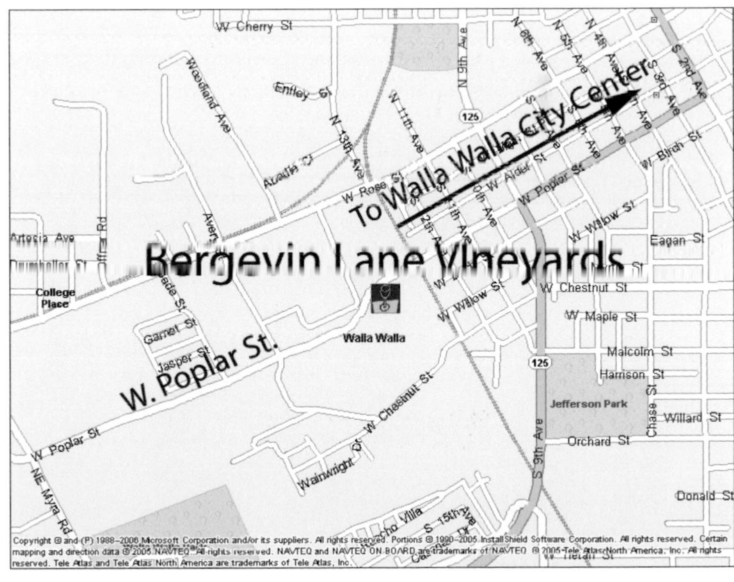

Foundry Vineyards 22

Imagine a "creative blending of fine wine and contemporary art" and you have Foundry Vineyards, or FV for short. It's true. At Foundry Vineyards, art takes many forms, from bronze sculpture and colorful glasswork to estate wines. Even the labels on the bottles reflect modern art, as exemplified on FV's 2006 Artisan Blend label, featuring Deborah Butterfield's horse-inspired sculpture (see **Appendix B — Decoding a Walla Walla Wine Label**).

Located a short drive west of downtown, FV's tasting room is Northwest contemporary in style, designed with lots of glass, steel, and concrete — a perfect space for showcasing the art within. The style also lends the room a sense of airiness and light. Here, visitors sampling Foundry Vineyard wines can't help but pause in their sipping and gawk. Works of art hang on the wall or rest handsomely on pedestals. Of particular note are FV co-owner Squire Broel's works, which include imaginative paintings and sculpture (also celebrated on the Artisan Blend label, for the 2007 vintage). As you taste and gaze, you are reminded that art takes many forms, be it in bronze, on a canvas — or from the fruit of the vine. As Robert Mondavi stated in *Harvest of Joy*, "Making good wine is a skill. Fine wine is an art."

The brainchild of Walla Walla native Mark Anderson, Foundry Vineyards relies on grapes from the valley, including the fruit of his own 3.5-acre estate Stonemarker Vineyard, to produce premium wine. Mark and Squire's goal is to produce small lots of wine using traditional means, and to focus on a few select wines. This isn't the Baskin-Robbins of wineries, with 31 flavors to sample. I discovered a manageable sampling of their many-layered cabernet sauvignon, a Bordeaux blend called "Fire Red" (was it the Malbec that gave it some spice notes?), and a white blend of chardonnay and viognier possessing just the right acidity. Mark makes fabulous wines, but then, it seems that all his projects turn into works of art.

If Mark or Squire happens to be at Foundry Vineyard, your visit just got a big upgrade. Both are exceptionally friendly as well as knowledgeable about art history and culture as it relates to the valley and beyond. As you'll discover, FV's partners are eclectic, creative, and always striving for artistic expression. Who needs the Guggenheim after a pour of FV's delectable art?

FOUNDRY VINEYARDS
opened: 2006
winemaker(s): Mark Anderson
location: 13th Avenue & Abadie Street, Walla Walla, WA 99362
phone: 509-529-0736
web: www.foundryvineyards.com
e-mail: info@foundryvineyards.com
picnic area: Yes
fee: Complimentary wine tasting
hours: Tuesday through Saturday 11–5
lat: 46.06353 **long:** -118.355889

DIRECTIONS: **From downtown Walla Walla** travel west on W Rose Ave. to 13th Ave. Turn right and drive approximately four blocks to 13th and Abadie St. where Foundry Vineyard's tasting room can be found.

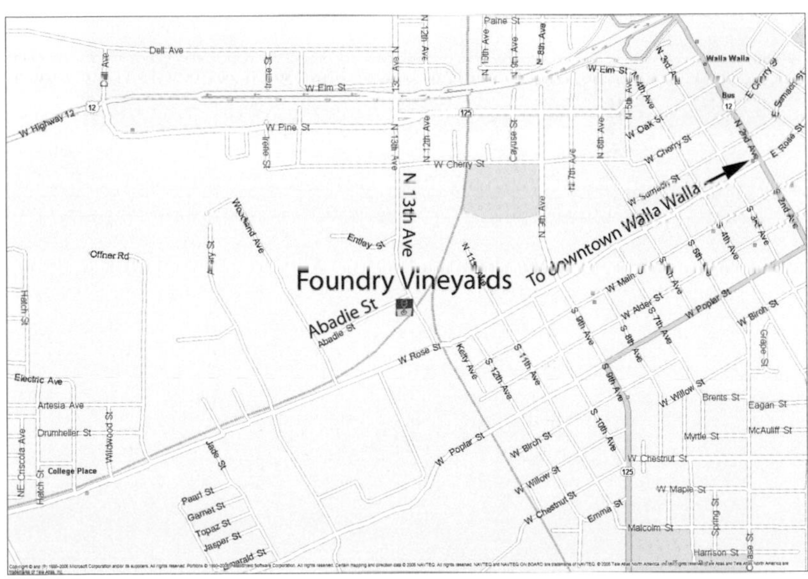

Whitman Cellars 23

In 1990, Sally and John Thomason delivered two trucks to Gary Figgins at Leonetti Cellar. That experience introduced them to the winemaking world and ignited their love affair with wine. The eventual result was the creation of Whitman Cellars with business partner John Edwards.

Located on the outskirts of town near Canoe Ridge Winery, Whitman Cellars is a boutique winery (producing about 5,000 cases annually) that has gained a loyal following and a long list of awards. As Sally Thomason explains it, "We're the Olympics of wineries — we 'medal' well." Whitman Cellars' long list of golds, silvers, and bronzes can be attributed to winemaker and partner Steve Lessard, who brings to the mix a rich background in food science and a résumé that includes a period at California's Stag's Leap Wine Cellars as an enologist (wine chemist).

It takes only a few minutes with Steve to realize how serious he is about winemaking and to discover that the real secret to making great wine is paying attention to the details. As he states on the Whitman Cellars website, "The most important word used in describing my wines is 'balance.' A wine reflects balance in a similar way to a vineyard, or I should say — its fruit reflects its *terroir*. It's an all-encompassing word in which the character of the varietal, the vineyard terroir, the structure of the wine, the chemistry of the wine, and the oak integration all harmonize together to produce a wine of seamless depth and interest."

In the tasting room, you will experience traditional Bordeaux- and Rhône-style wines. Be prepared to taste the "balance" of Whitman Cellars' viognier, syrah, cabernet sauvignon, merlot, Bordeaux blends (including my favorite, "Narcissa"), and a lip-smacking port-style wine. And you will likely discover that there is a balance struck in the tasting room itself. Yes, the Thomasons are serious about their wines, but they are equally concerned that your experience at Whitman Cellars is a truly enjoyable one. The tasting room finds that balance with a relaxed, friendly atmosphere suitable for even the neophyte wine drinker.

WHITMAN CELLARS
opened: 1998
winemaker(s): Steve Lessard
location: 1015 West Pine Street, Walla Walla, WA 99362
phone: 509-529-1142
web: www.whitmancellars.com
e-mail: info@whitmancellars.com
gift shop: Yes
tours: Yes
fee: Tasting fee refundable with purchase
hours: Daily 11–5
lat: 46.068881 **long:** -118.355309

DIRECTIONS: **Heading east on Hwy 12**, take the W. Pine St. exit. Continue to 13th Ave., the cellars is on the right-hand side.

Coming into Walla Walla from State Hwy 125, follow direction to 9th Ave., turn left on Rose St. Take a right on 13th Ave. and Whitman Cellars will appear a quarter mile down the road at the stop sign.

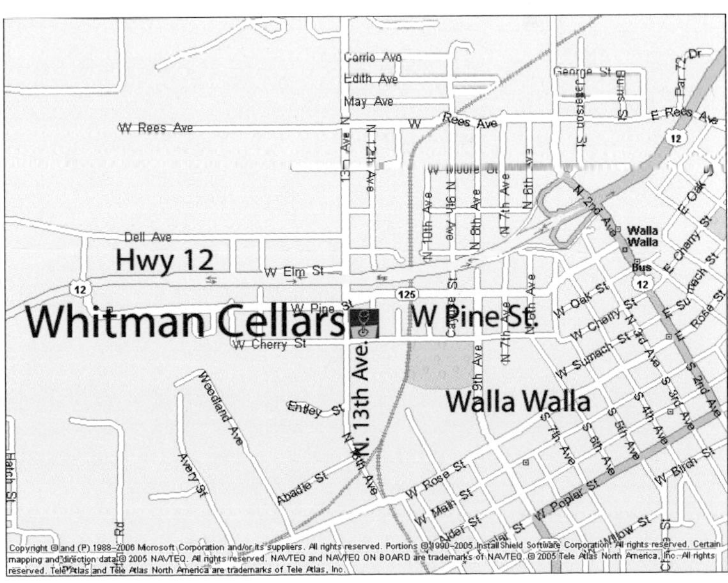

Canoe Ridge Vineyard 24

Merlot is such an elegant wine, great by itself or paired with food. Rich and velvety, with flavors of chocolate, cherry, and raspberry — what's not to like? Merlot loves to grow in eastern Washington, particularly in the Horse Heaven Hills American Viticultural Area (AVA), which also happens to be the home of Canoe Ridge Vineyard. (**WineTrail Note:** Canoe Ridge was named by explorers Lewis and Clark on their historic journey west. From the Columbia River, the massive ridge looks like an upside-down canoe.) Here, the proximity to the weather-moderating Columbia River, hot summers, cool nights and dry conditions all conspire to create the perfect growing conditions for merlot, cabernet sauvignon and other European varieties.

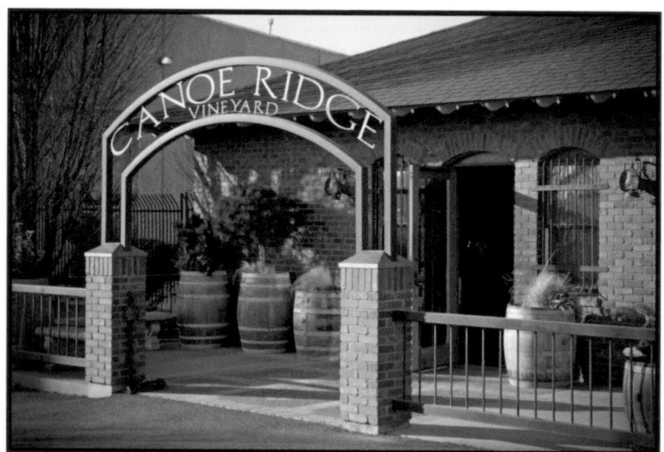

A visit to the Canoe Ridge winery, on the outskirts of downtown Walla Walla, offers a study in merlot. True, Canoe Ridge Vineyard does produce a full line-up of elegant, easy-to-quaff red wines, but at the winery, you have the opportunity to sample merlot of different vintages and qualities. And while the winery focuses on red wines, it does make a limited quantity of whites, including chardonnay, gewürztraminer and riesling.

Canoe Ridge is owned by the Diageo Corp. (perhaps you've heard of Tanqueray, Smirnoff, J&B, Guinness, and Sagelands, to name a few Diageo properties), but the corporate giant gives Canoe Ridge winemaker Ned Morris the independence he requires to craft premium wines. Incidentally, this winemaker happens to be one of the nicest individuals you'll find in the business. Not that you have to be a nice guy to make great wine; that's not a requirement for graduating from any enology program. But it's ironic that Ned was the assistant winemaker for another genuinely friendly winemaker, John Abbott of Abeja Winery. Both happen to have attended Oregon State University and, interestingly, John Abbott's résumé includes a stint at Canoe Ridge Vineyard as the chief winemaker. Coincidence? We think not.

Canoe Ridge's winemaking philosophy begins in the vineyard, where the level and quality of ripeness become the foundation of every new vintage. Each winemaking effort aims to honor the uniqueness of the Canoe Ridge vineyard site, reflecting its individuality through the depth, nuance, concentration, and balance of Canoe Ridge wines. It's a winning formula that brings together a big corporation, exceptional fruit and local talent to create wonderfully approachable wines.

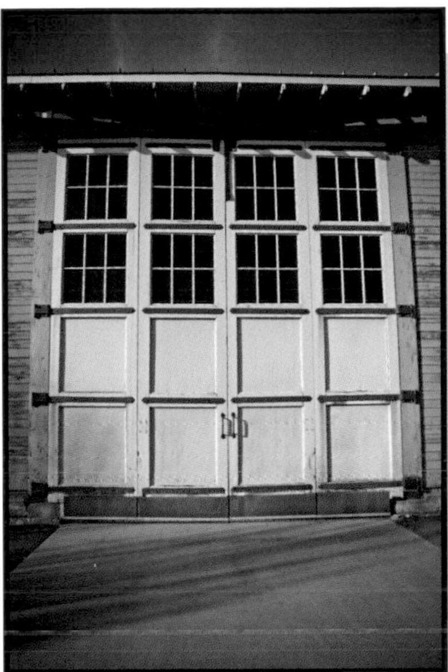

CANOE RIDGE VINEYARD
opened: 1989
winemaker(s): Ned Morris
location: 1102 West Cherry Street, Walla Walla, WA 99362
phone: 509-527-0885
web: www.canoeridgevineyard.com
e-mail: CRVinfo@canoeridgevineyard.com
wheelchair access: Yes
gift shop: Yes
tours: Yes
fee: Tasting fee refundable with purchase
hours: May through September, daily 11–5; October through April, daily 11–4; closed major holidays and December 24 through January 1
lat: 46.067656 **long:** -118.356929

DIRECTIONS: **Heading east U.S. 12**, take the W Pine St. exit. Follow to 13th Ave., take a right and you will find Canoe Ridge Winery one block down on the right-hand side.

From downtown Walla Walla, go west on W Pine St. for about half a mile. Turn left (south) onto SR-125 [N 9th Ave.] followed by a quick right (west) onto W Cherry St. Continue 0.3 mile to 1102 W Cherry St. and arrive at the winery.

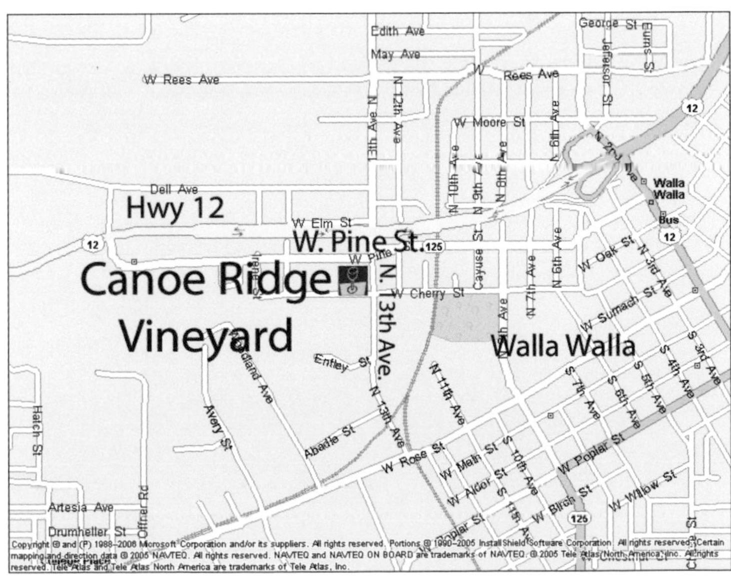

Lowden Hills Winery 25

Lowden Hills' 2006 "See You There" Syrah grabbed my attention with its label, which bears the photo of a smartly dressed, confident young woman waving from her perch on the front of a Model T. A quick perusal of the tasting notes revealed that this northern Rhône-style blend consists of 92 percent syrah co-fermented with 8 percent viognier. I had to try it. Perhaps it was my "puppy dog with an empty belly" approach to asking for a sample, but I lucked out with a generous pour of dark, inky blue wine. A rapid swirl and sniff gave way to dark fruit and spicy notes on the palate.

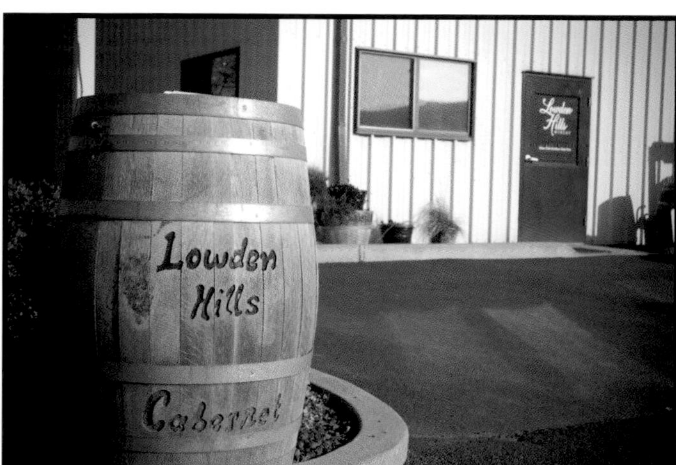

As I sampled this delicious treat, I could not help but reflect on my first visit to Lowden Hills Winery in 2007, when the winery and tasting room were shoehorned into an old barn on Spitzenburg Road in Walla Walla. As I noted in *WineTrails of Washington*, "The original barn, built in 1938 by Emilio Gugliemelli Sr., stored vegetables and other crops. As Jim [Henderson, Sonja's husband and winery co-owner] notes, 'What once housed workhorses and livestock is now the main-floor barrel room.' The foundation footprint is rather small, but a cellar door leads down a steep set of stairs to the barrel room below. It's in these tight quarters that Jim plays Tetris with the barrels, racking and topping off the barrels as needed." In relation to the old digs, the new space, west of downtown Walla Walla on Pine Street, is colossal in size.

To understand Lowden Hills Winery is to appreciate family history. The Hendersons' vineyard, Win Chester Vineyard, is located on Woodward Canyon Road just outside the small town of Lowden. On these 18 acres, they grow merlot, cabernet sauvignon, syrah, and viognier. The vineyard's name honors Sonja's mother, Susanne Estes, and her mother's late husband, Win Chester Estes. Win was a well-respected wheat farmer with a true pioneering spirit, and his family homesteaded in the Clyde area of Walla Walla County in the 1860s. A picture of Win Chester Estes is on the wall at the winery. It turns out that the aforementioned picture of the woman on the "See You There" Syrah is Sonja's mom, Susanne. A nice touch.

Honoring the past with the great wines of today is the driving force behind Jim and Sonja's labor of familial love.

LOWDEN HILLS WINERY
opened: 2002
winemaker(s): Jim Henderson
location: 1401 West Pine Street, Walla Walla, WA 99362
phone: 509-527-1040
web: www.lowdenhillswinery.com
e-mail: info@lowdenhillswinery.com
picnic area: Yes
gift shop: Yes
tours: Yes
fee: Refundable tasting fee may apply
hours: Thursday through Monday 11–5, or by appointment
lat: 46.068554 **long:** -118.366765

DIRECTIONS: **From downtown Walla Walla** take Hwy 12 west about 1.2 miles. Turn left onto SR-125 [W Pine St] and proceed about one tenth of a mile to the tasting room, located on your right.

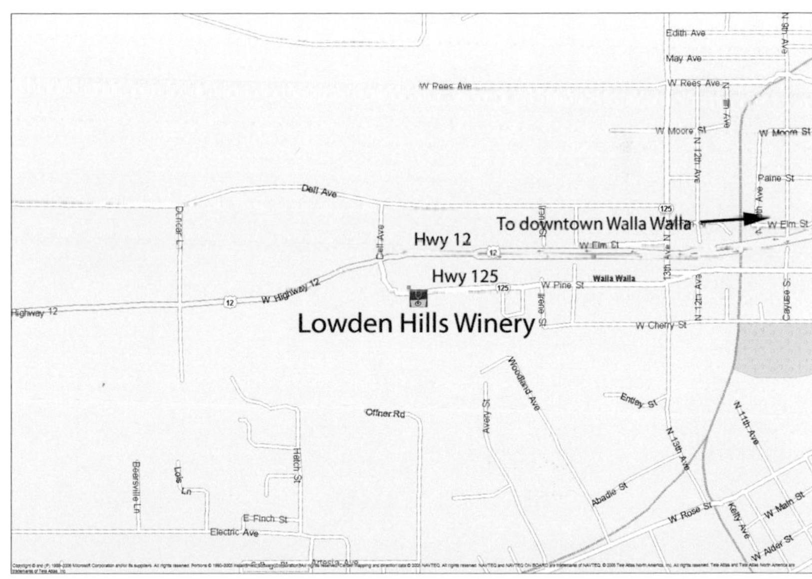

Airport WineTrail

Walla Walla Airport WineTrail

During World War II, the regional airport near Walla Walla housed more than 10,000 military personnel. After the war, most of these properties sat idle, and the Port of Walla Walla had a major problem deciding what to do with all the buildings left behind, including barracks, mess halls, and fire stations. The answer was a low-cost solution, allowing start-up businesses to rent space in the buildings. Today, more than a dozen wineries make and sell wine at the Walla Walla Regional Airport and Industrial Park, also referred to as the "wine incubator" complex, and more are on the way. You can easily spend a weekend trekking the Airport WineTrail, and unless you bring a bike or a good pair of hiking boots, plan to use your car to get from one tasting room to the next.

Walla Walla Airport WineTrail

1 Le Chateau Winery
2 Russell Creek Winery
3 Dunham Cellars
4 Patit Creek Cellars
5 Eleganté Cellars
6 Five Star Cellars
7 Mannina Cellars
8 Tamarack Cellars
9 SYZYGY
10 Buty Winery
11 428
12 Kontos Cellars
13 Lodmell Cellars
14 Adamant Cellars
15 CAVU Cellars
16 Ash Hollow Winery

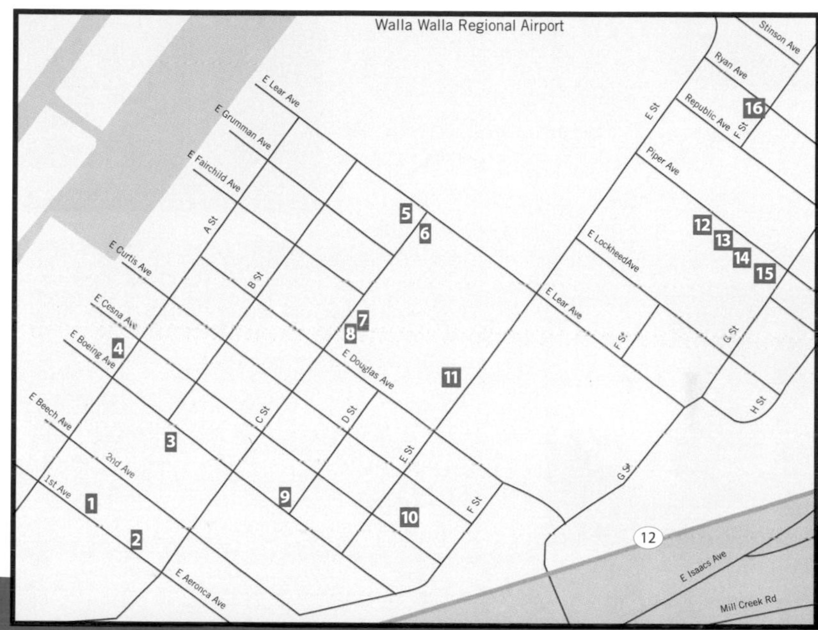

Region:	**Walla Walla Wine Country**
# of tasting rooms on tour:	**16**
# of satellite tasting rooms:	**1**
Estimate # of days for tour:	**2 or 3**
Getting around:	**Car and foot**
Key Events:	❑ **Events sponsored by Walla Walla Valley Wine Alliance: Spring Release Weekend (first full weekend of May); Balloon Stampede Weekend (second full weekend of May); Vintage Walla Walla (first full weekend of June); Entwine: An auction to support Walla Walla Arts, Wine, and Education (mid-October); and Holiday Barrel Tasting (first full weekend of December). See winetrailsnw.com for details.**
Tips:	❑ **Purchase one or two inexpensive Styrofoam chests to store your wine purchases. In the summer, interior car temperatures easily get over 100°F.**
	❑ **Consider using a limousine service (Black Tie Limo 509-525-8585, Blue Stocking Tours 509-522-4717, Sunset Coach Tours 509-303-0355, or Four Star Limousine Service 509-521-7849 are some of the many services to contact).**
 Best:	❑ **Gift shop and picnicking: Dunham Cellars**

Brasserie Four

Photo by Alan Ayers

By definition, a brasserie is an informal, typically French restaurant serving meals and as well as single dishes. Brasserie Four is all of that and more. From the wonderful menu filled with savory French favorites to the wine list replete with both Walla Walla and French wines, to the French music playing in the background, eating at Brasserie Four is like a brief escape to Paris.

Photo by Alan Ayers

Its chef, Hannah MacDonald, readily admits that she is a Francophile. The attention she pays to each of the menu items is evidence that not only does she like all things French, but she understands French culture.

According to Hannah, the most popular items are the steak *frites* and the *moules* (mussels) *frites*. Although the *moules* pairs wonderfully with several of the whites on Brasserie Four's wine list, for the steak, the wine of choice is the 2007 Domaine Catherine Le Goeuil "Cairanne." The *assiette de fromage* or "cheese plate" is another on of their specialties. Be sure to check the chalkboard behind the bar for the daily selections. Hannah is passionate about cheese, and it shows in the excellent and unique artisan varieties she had discovered and serves. The servers,

Photo by Alan Ayers

who are well versed in wine and cheese parings, can provide thoughtful suggestions to enhance your culinary experience.

Photo by Alan Ayers

In true French style, Brasserie Four does not forget the kids. Any item on the menu can be prepared in a child's portion for these very important young guests. Brasserie Four truly is a little slice of Paris and a perfect place to while away an evening.

4 East Main Street
Walla Walla, WA 99362
509-529-2011
brasseriefourrestaurant.com

Sweet Basil Pizzeria

If you are looking for a casual alternative for dinner or lunch, then follow the locals and line up at Sweet Basil Pizzeria for some of the best New York-style pizza in the Northwest. Whether you are salivating over the combo pizza, considering the vegetarian, or contemplating the calzone, you can't go wrong. The crust will be as light as a feather and topped with the freshest ingredients.

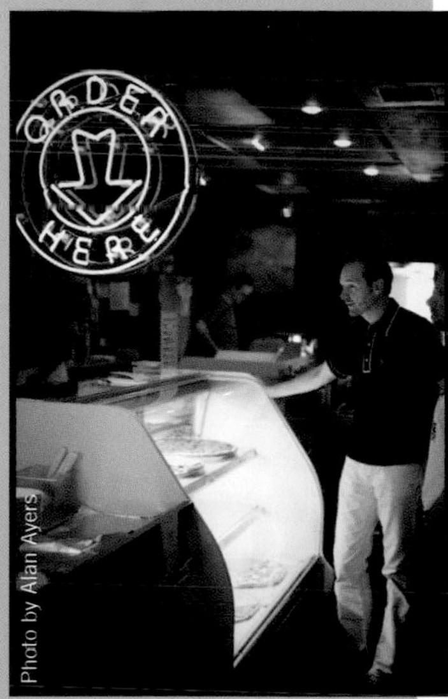

Photo by Alan Ayers

To complement your pizza, Sweet Basil Pizzeria offers a concise selection of wonderful local wines and beers on tap. Although you can order your pizza to go, the pizzeria, with its walls and ceiling painted the color of fresh sweet basil, is a fun and lively place to eat. Sweet Basil Pizzeria is clearly a local favorite.

5 South 1st Avenue
Walla Walla, WA 99362
509-529-1950
sweetbasilpizzeria.com

Le Chateau Winery 1

I'm always a little suspicious of wineries with the word "chateau" in their monikers. I like winery names that give a sense of place or family. Thus, when I drove to the Walla Walla Regional Airport's winery district to visit Le Chateau Winery, my expectations weren't high. However, life does throw us curveballs, and as I drove into the winery's parking lot, my eyes took in the whimsical faux chateau mural covering the façade of the 1940s barracks building. Any thoughts that I was visiting a pretentious winery quickly dissipated. Instead, the artist's wonderfully executed tongue-in-cheek rendering of a French castle had me immediately snapping pictures and grinning.

Once inside, a friendly tasting room employee greeted me. Her two miniature dogs, Lulu and Remi, were wrestling with each other, and it was hard to tell which dog had the upper paw. I placed camera and notebook down on what I surmise as Walla Walla's finest wine bar and responded affirmatively to her question "Would you like to do some wine tasting?" I proceeded to smell, taste and spit my way through a portfolio of white and red wines.

To maintain my rep as a cheap date, as well as to keep my wits, I generally spit rather than swallow. But whatever discipline I had melted away when I took in a mouthful of Le Chateau's Masterpiece Red, a blend of merlot and cabernet sauvignon made from grapes sourced in the Walla Walla Valley. This one I swallowed, relishing its full mouthfeel, huge black fruit notes and long finish.

Now more open to learning, I discovered that Kennewick's Dick and Diane Hoch own the winery. Under the banner "Wines from the Scablands," they created Le Chateau Winery to sell their wine, display original art, and provide a winery event room for private parties and winery-sponsored functions. However, the *pièce de résistance* of Le Chateau Winery is the Hochs' wine, made by French winemaker Bruno Corneaux. Although the winery is relatively new (opening in 2008), it's clear that Bruno has years of experience to create such delicious wines.

While saying my goodbyes, I recalled that other Northwest wineries include "chateau" in their titles, such as Chateau Lorane, Chateau Bianca Winery, Chateau Faire Le Pont Winery and a little Woodinville-based winery called Chateau Ste. Michelle. I realized then that by any other name, Le Chateau's wines would taste just as good.

LE CHATEAU WINERY
opened: 2008
winemaker(s): Bruno Corneaux
location: 175 East Aeronca, Walla Walla, WA 99362
phone: 509-956-9311
web: www.lechateauwinery.com
e-mail: info@lechateauwinery.com
gift shop: Yes
fee: Tasting fee refundable with purchase
hours: December through April, Thursday through Sunday 10–4; May through November 30, Thursday through Sunday 10–6
lat: 46.086345 **long:** -118.277925

DIRECTIONS: Le Chateau Winery is located at the Walla Walla Regional Airport Complex. **From Walla Walla**, take U.S. 12 east about three miles. Follow the Walla Walla Airport exit and turn left (north) onto Airport Rd., which becomes A St. Turn right onto Aeronca Ave. to find Le Chateau Winery on the left.

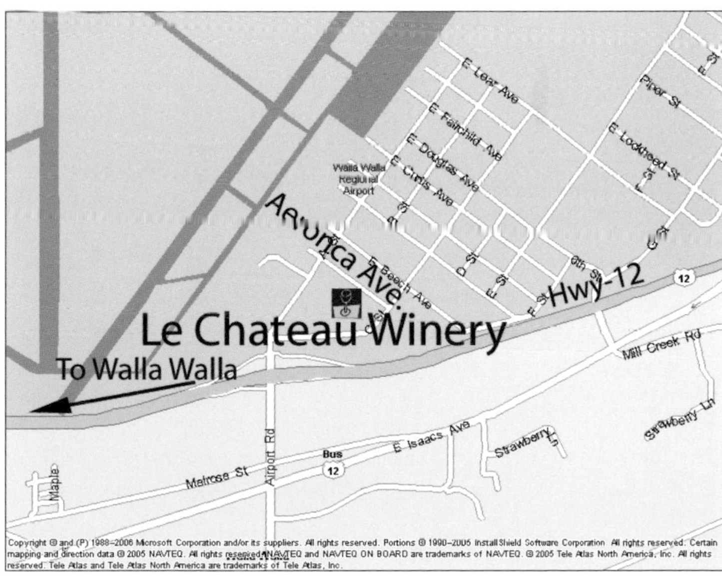

Russell Creek Winery 2

For wine-country travel writers like *moi*, one of the joys of reporting about the Northwest wine industry is that it is forever changing. However, that is also the problem with reporting about the Northwest wine industry. It's the classic double-edged sword. Take Russell Creek Winery as exhibit A. When I first met Larry Krivoshein in 2007, he was both owner and winemaker of Russell Creek, having launched the winery in the early days of the Walla Walla wine boom back in 1998. Fast-forward to 2010, and although Larry is still involved as the chief winemaker (while he trains the new winemaker, Carl Potter), the winery is under new ownership and has received a boost of new energy.

With majority owner Eileen Crosby at the helm, loyal fans of Russell Creek Winery will still find their remarkable sangiovese, as well as the winery's number-one seller, "Tributary," a blend of cabernet sauvignon, merlot, and syrah. That's reassuring. However, a closer inspection of the Russell Creek Winery wine label revealed a portrait of Bing Crosby with his iconic smoking pipe. That's new. Being slow on the uptake, I looked over at Eileen's brother, Samuel Crosby, and started to ask why the old crooner was on the label. Then it dawned on me that, duh, the two share the same last name, Crosby. It turns out that Bing was their dad's uncle. Bing's face adorns the labels for their Crosby series of wines, and this series is featured on the menu at California-based Bing Crosby Restaurants.

Visitors to Russell Creek Winery's Walla Walla Regional Airport location discover the continuing trend of blending the old with the new. For example, on display are wine bottles bearing the famous "Diggers" label, showing a shovel stuck in the ground near Walla Walla, a nod to Larry's former career as a funeral director. Even the hand-operated wine press that Larry first used sits on public display in the winery. But along with the familiar accoutrements, there clearly is a sense of new energy in the air. Under Eileen's direction, look for new marketing initiatives, regular wine events, and a wine club offering compelling reasons to join.

While working my way through Russell Creek's portfolio of wines (opting to swallow rather than spit), it occurred to me that all of these wines have a trademark charm not unlike their celebrity namesake. Russell Creek Winery's distinctive reds are imbued with the same effortless grace and versatility so reminiscent of Bing.

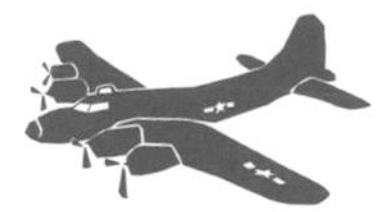

Samuel Crosby with Beau

RUSSELL CREEK WINERY
opened: 1998
winemaker(s): Larry Krivoshein and Carl Potter (assistant)
location: 301 Aeronca Avenue, Walla Walla, WA 99362
phone: 509-301-0061
web: www.russellcreek-winery.com
e-mail: russellcreekwinery@gmail.com
tours: Yes
fee: Tasting fee refundable with purchase
hours: Daily 11–4; special events 10–5
lat: 46.087012 **long:** -118.279037

DIRECTIONS: Russell Creek Winery is located at the Walla Walla Regional Airport Complex. **From Walla Walla**, take U.S. 12 east about three miles. Take the exit towards the Walla Walla Airport and turn left (north) onto Airport Rd., which becomes A St. Turn right onto Aeronca Ave. to find the winery on the left.

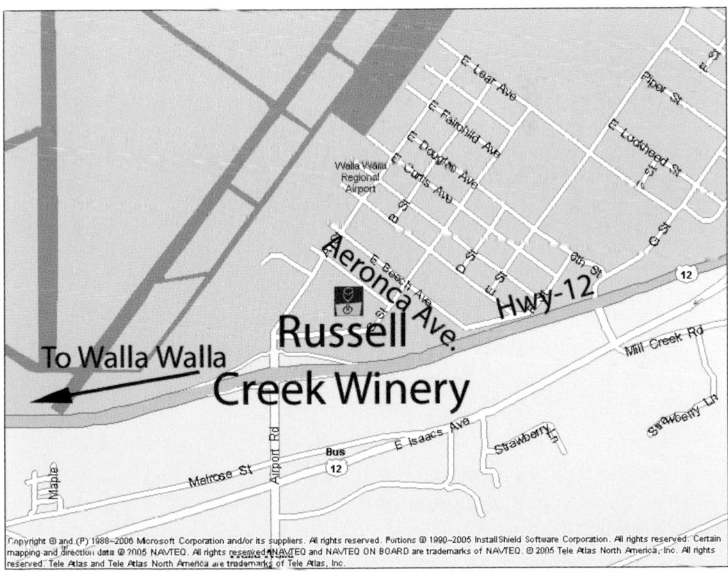

Dunham Cellars 3

Dunham Cellars is dog friendly — just as friendly as co-owner and winemaker extraordinaire Eric Dunham, but we'll get to him in a bit. This is border collie heaven, with angelic canines Konnie and Maysy circling underfoot. While Maysy is pictured on the "Four Legged White" label, Eric's dog Port, now deceased, still graces the label of his delectable "Three Legged Red." All these dogs share something special: They are rescue dogs and they won the lottery by being taken into this loving home.

Located at the Walla Walla Airport Complex, Dunham Cellars' tasting room is one of my favorite wine stops along the Walla Walla Airport WineTrail. Named by *Sunset* magazine in 2009 as one of the top tasting rooms in the West, Dunham Cellars' provides relaxed comfort inside its oh so nicely decorated Hangar Lounge or, weather permitting, outside at one of many picnic tables.

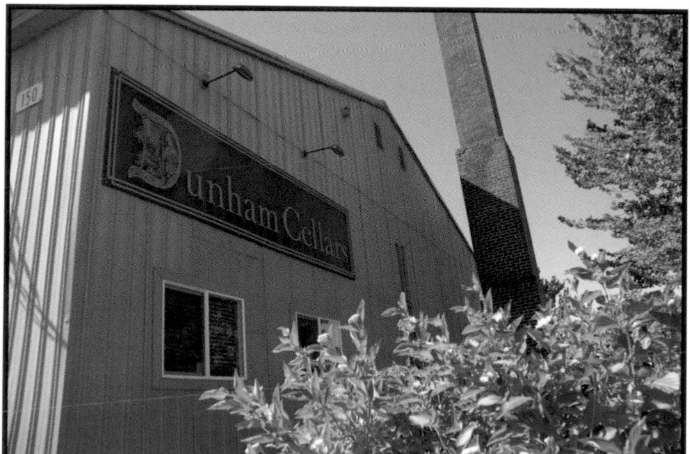

Eric is often at the winery, tending to the never-ending duties of winemaking, but he still manages to find time to visit with guests, whether they are novice wine drinkers or experienced connoisseurs. Eric is one of the friendliest winemakers in the valley. His roots are in Walla Walla, and in 1999, together with his parents, Mike and Joanne Dunham, he began the winery in this former World War II airplane hangar. His is an inclusive enterprise as well — dozens of folks in the valley involved in winemaking either volunteered as cellar rats or worked as assistant winemakers at Dunham Cellars.

The Dunhams are fortunate in that they need never go searching hither and yon for the best fruit; they own several vineyards that produce renowned grapes. Indeed, theirs must be excellent grapes, because they possess a laundry list of prestigious awards too numerous to list here. In addition to the "Three Legged Red," you have an opportunity to sample their renowned syrah, cabernet sauvignon, sémillon, "Shirley Mays" chardonnay, a crisp rosé, as well as a Bordeaux blend called "Trutina" (the Latin word for "balance"). By the way, the vivid artwork that graces the single-vineyard-designated wines is the work of Eric himself. In addition, the staff at Dunham Cellars vouch that Eric is also a fabulous cook. Culinary artist, fine-arts painter, celebrated winemaker — the guy is multitalented. Does he ever sleep? I'm dog-tired just thinking about it.

DUNHAM CELLARS
opened: 1999
winemaker(s): Eric Dunham
location: 150 East Boeing Avenue, Walla Walla, WA 99362-7400
phone: 509-529-4685
web: www.dunhamcellars.com
e-mail: wine@dunhamcellars.com
picnic area: Yes
gift shop: Yes
tours: Yes
fee: Tasting fee refundable with purchase
hours: Daily 11–4
lat: 46.086666 **long:** -118.273076

DIRECTIONS: Dunham Cellars is located at the Walla Walla Regional Airport Complex. **From Walla Walla**, take Hwy 12 east about three miles. Take the exit toward the Walla Walla Airport and go left (north) onto Airport Rd. Airport Rd becomes A St. Turn right onto E Boeing Ave. Dunham Cellars is on the right.

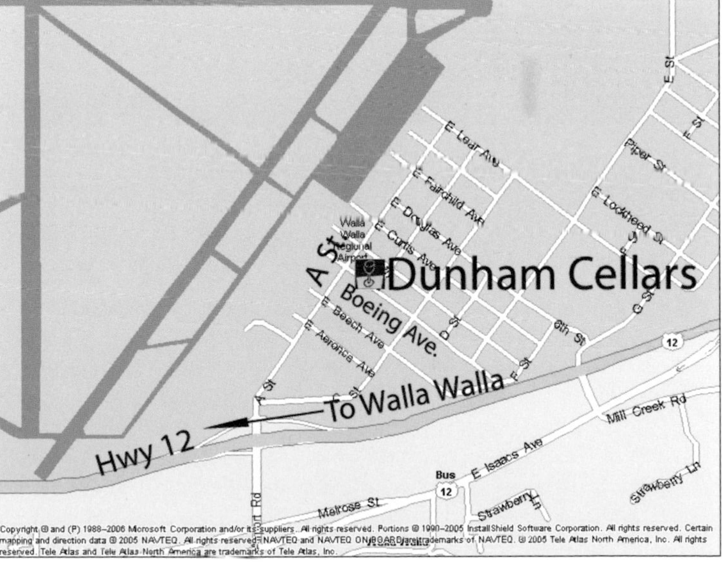

Patit Creek Cellars 4

"Sure!" I blurted to the question "Would you like to try our 2008 Semillon Ice Wine?" As I watched Ed Dudley pour a golden sample of Patit Creek Cellars' dessert wine, I reflected that until recently, Patit Creek Cellars had produced just two wines — cabernet sauvignon and merlot. But that was the focus of the former ownership group, before Ed and his business partner, Karen La Bonté, purchased the winery in 2007.

Prior to acquiring Patit Creek Cellars, Ed and Karen worked in the communications industry: he in Virginia, and she in California. Both had more than a mere interest in wine; they shared something closer to a fervor. They studied all aspects of the wine industry, read books, volunteered at crush, and bent the ears of winemakers from coast to coast. Their desire to purchase an existing winery eventually led to the purchase of Patit Creek Cellars. Papers were signed, dollars transferred, and Ed and Karen were the proud parents of a Walla Walla winery. As part of the team, Ed is the numbers guy handling the myriad paperwork duties, and Karen's natural people skills make her the winery's goodwill ambassador and tasting room manager.

Once the ink had dried on the sales contract, one of Ed and Karen's first moves was to relocate the downtown Walla Walla tasting room and the Dayton, Washington–based production facility into a common 6,000-square-foot facility at the Walla Walla Region Airport wine incubator complex. Visitors will ooh and ah at the Tuscan-style interior, with its warm colors and an inviting fireplace, where you can enjoy a glass of wine.

Visitors will also discover a variety of red and white wines to sample, the products of their up-and-coming winemaker, Joe Forest. Early on, the Patit Creek team added to its cabernet and merlot line-up by introducing a citrusy riesling and a barrel-fermented chardonnay, both of which pair very nicely with Northwest seafood, chicken and summer salads. Grapes were acquired from the prestigious Les Collines Vineyard to produce a wonderfully spicy dark-ruby zinfandel. Not to leave out Rhône-style wines, the team introduced a red blend of syrah, grenache, and Mourvèdre. All of them are luscious pleasures on the palate, but the semillon ice wine buckled my knees with its silky smooth finish and satisfying sweetness. With a final gulp, I felt a smile growing across my face, happy in the knowledge that Patit Creek Cellars is under good stewardship.

PATIT CREEK CELLARS
opened: 1999
winemaker(s): Joe Forest
location: 325 A Street, Walla Walla, WA 99362
phone: 509-522-4684
web: www.patitcreekcellars.com
e-mail: info@patitcreekcellars.com
picnic area: Yes
weddings: Yes
gift shop: Yes
tours: Yes
fee: Complimentary wine tasting
hours: Tuesday through Saturday 11–5; Sunday 11–4; Closed Monday
lat: 46.089878 **long:** -118.279318

DIRECTIONS: Patit Creek Cellars is located at the Walla Walla Regional Airport Complex. **From Walla Walla**, take Hwy 12 east about three miles. Take the Walla Walla Airport exit and turn left (north) onto Airport Rd, which becomes A St. Arrive at 325 A St.

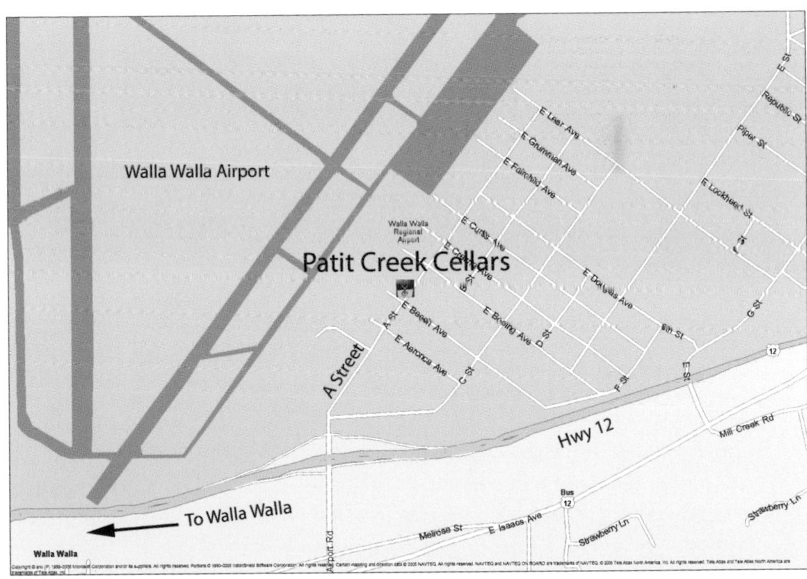

Eleganté Cellars 5

Doug Simmons, a native Walla Wallan, had a problem. In 2002 when he retired from teaching, Doug still had his health, an inquisitive mind, and a desire to start his own business. What's more, after 30 years of teaching chemistry in the Walla Walla School District, he was left with a sense of emptiness, and he realized he wasn't finished being a scientist. Doug had a serious case of "science deficit," something that most people don't experience. He clearly needed a lab in which to mix and match potions.

Doug's résumé also includes a long stint of farming. For 49 summers, Doug stained his fingers red while working at a local Walla Walla institution, Klicker's Strawberry Acres. He became intimate with the land and understood its climate. He appreciated that the ground is not simply dirt; it is soil. Moreover, he understood why farmers obsess over weather forecasts. Occasional frosts and dry summer days have a way of doing that.

Thus, when Doug retired from teaching high school, becoming a winemaker was a no-brainer solution to his life's dilemma. The fact that Walla Walla Community College just happens to offer a superb enology and viticulture program helped to cement his career decision. He graduated from Walla Walla Community College with an A.A. degree in enology and viticulture. Soon thereafter, in 2007, he created Eleganté Cellars, following a practicum at Five Star Cellars. Now he just needed a name for his winery. Recalling that a fellow teacher in Walla Walla always said "elegant" when asked how his day was going, Doug added the "é"on the end of that word to give it a Euro feel. Thus, Eleganté Cellars was christened.

I met Doug in late January 2010 at his winery, located in the Walla Walla Airport Complex. His faithful Boston terrier, Bing, was at his side (it's hard to find such loyal help these days!). Trim, with graying temples, Doug possesses a youthful look belying his 60-some years. Doug has the good fortune to know many nearby grape growers, whom he probably either went to school with or taught their kids. What got my attention were his sources: Seven Hills for his merlot and Les Collines for his cabernet sauvignon. It's clear that Doug specializes in these Bordeaux beauties. However, for a nice treat to cap your tasting experience at Eleganté, be sure and check out his slightly sweet but lovely strawberry wine. There's no doubt about the source of his strawberries — Klicker's, of course.

Doug Simmons

ELEGANTÉ CELLARS
opened: 2007
winemaker(s): Doug Simmons
location: 839 C Street, Walla Walla, WA 99362
phone: 509-525-9129
web: www.elegantecellars.com
e-mail: simmondl@yahoo.com
fee: Complimentary wine tasting
hours: Daily 11–4
lat: 46.052983 **long:** -118.376711

DIRECTIONS: Elegantè Cellars is located at the Walla Walla Regional Airport Complex. **From Walla Walla**, take U.S.12 east about three miles. Take the Walla Walla Airport exit and turn left (north) onto Airport Way. Continue about 1 mile before turning right onto Douglas Ave. Continue to C St. and turn left to arrive at 839 C St. The cellars is on the left.

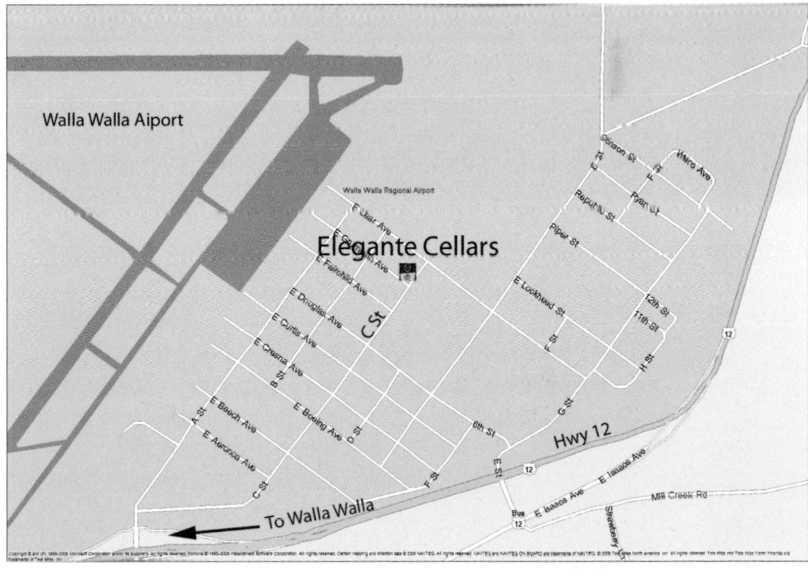

Five Star Cellars 6

"It is a wise father that knows his own child." — William Shakespeare, *The Merchant of Venice*

Along the WineTrails of Washington, you come across a number of retirees who traded in the tedium of retirement to create fine wines. Such is the story of David Huse. He didn't have to launch Five Star Cellars, but his passion won out. In 2000, following his career as a farm equipment provider and a few stints assisting at other wineries, David started Five Star Cellars. He hasn't looked back.

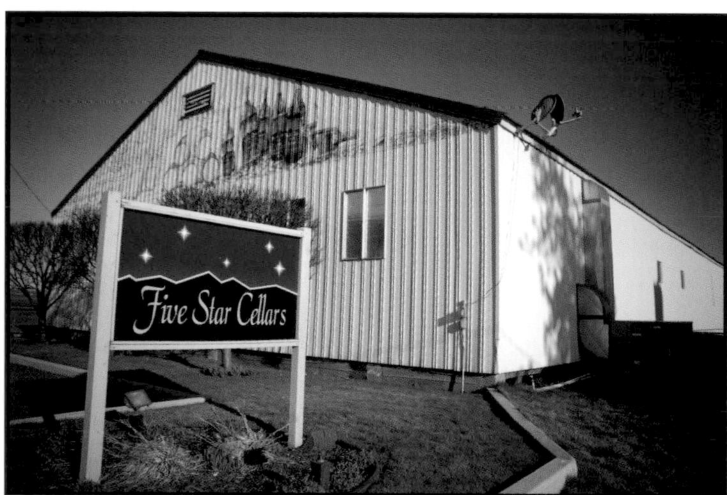

Of course, when you name a winery "Five Star," you'd better deliver wines worthy of that premier rating. To achieve this level of quality, David needed a helping hand. He didn't have far to look. In 2002, his son Matt signed on to assist with winemaking, and Matt's timing couldn't have been better: Production had doubled to more than 1,000 cases per year. He enrolled in the enology and viticulture program at Walla Walla Community College and was a member of the program's first graduating class. Today, Matt is Five Star's chief winemaker, and current production is around 5,000 cases. This has freed David to assume the duties of operations manager, marketing director, and chief bottle-washer.

Located at the Walla Walla Airport Complex, across from Eleganté Cellars, Five Star Cellars offers an inviting space to sample its ultrapremium wines: merlot, syrah, cabernet sauvignon as well as some serious red blends. Be sure to check out their "Quinque Astrum" (Latin for "five star") a super Tuscan blend with a sangiovese backbone. Matt and David have made significant improvements to the leased space. It's on "their nickel" so to speak — they didn't have to do it — but they chose to make the changes to improve the public's tasting experience. These improvements reflect their commitment to excellence. As part of this renovation, they've added a wood stove. Imagine visiting on a cold winter day with the stove blazing, keeping you toasty warm.

By christening their winery "Five Star," the Huses have set the bar high, but Five Star has proven worthy of its name.

FIVE STAR CELLARS
opened: 2000
winemaker(s): Matt Huse
location: 840 C Street, Walla Walla, WA 99362-7423
phone: 509-527-8400
web: www.fivestarcellars.com
e-mail: info@fivestarcellars.com
gift shop: Yes
tours: Yes
fee: Tasting fee applies
hours: Saturday 10–4, or by appointment
lat: 46.092448 **long:** -118.271723

DIRECTIONS: Five Star Cellars is located at the Walla Walla Regional Airport Complex. **From Walla Walla**, take Hwy 12 east about three miles. Take the Walla Walla Airport exit and go left (north) onto Airport Way for about one mile. Turn right onto Douglas Ave. Turn left onto C St. and continue to 840 C St. Five Star Cellars is on the right.

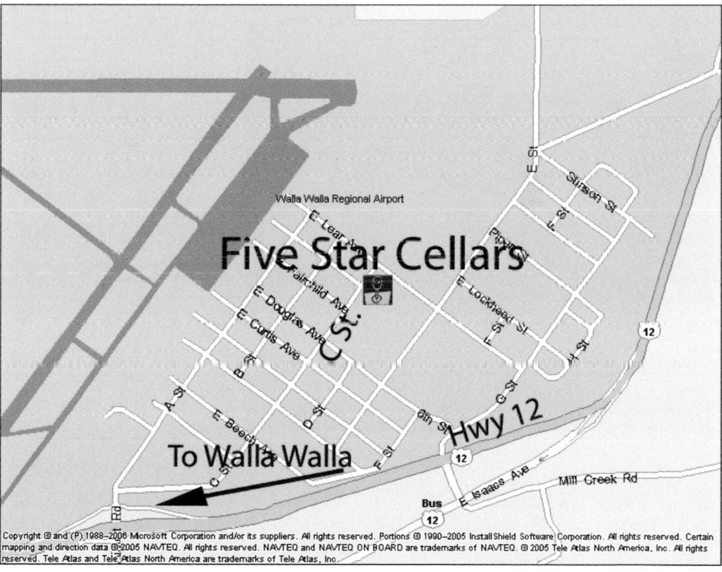

Mannina Cellars 7

To know Mannina Cellars is to appreciate the winegrowing family behind it — not just a lone winemaker, mind you, but an entire cast of family members, including a black Lab named Lucy. Although Don Redman is owner and winemaker, his wife, Nicole, and their three children are often found pruning the vines at their Cali Vineyard or assisting at their Walla Walla Airport winery. Don is ever grateful for his family's involvement and for his family heritage, so it's no accident that many Mannina Cellars wines bear the names of family members. There is the red blend "Cali," named after his grandmother Rose Cali, and "RoseAnne's Red," named for his mother. Even the winery's name, "Mannina," comes from Don's maternal grandmother, who emigrated from Italy. A photograph of Mannina graces the wall behind the tasting room.

Speaking of Cali, I would be remiss if I didn't disclose one of the reasons for my sojourn to Mannina Cellars. At $17 a bottle, this blend of primarily cabernet sauvignon and merlot is a bargain. At the very least, it is Mannina Cellars' own attempt at an economic stimulus package for the valley. (Even more palatable, Mannina Cellars' wine club members take an additional 15 percent off their purchase. So for about $175, they can cart a whole case of Walla Walla's finest to their car trunks. That's a steal.) When a particular wine grabs my palate, I start imagining certain food pairings with it, and the image that popped into my mind as I sipped the Cali was a glass of this dark ruby wine accompanying a rib-eye steak with a red wine reduction. Egads, I'm drooling.

As a side note, the other thing that drew my attention during my visit was the artwork of local artist Squire Broel on Mannina Cellars labels. Squire's watercolor of vineyard rows adorns the labels of the winery's merlot, cabernet sauvignon, "RoseAnne's Red" and sangiovese. For me, this imagery is a beautiful reminder that Don relies exclusively on Walla Walla Valley fruit, including that from such notable vineyards as Pepper Bridge, Seven Hills, and Les Collines. As Don's own, 28-acre Cali Vineyard matures, look for his increasing reliance on his own fruit.

Naming wines and vineyard after family members pays homage to the past. The sounds of laughing children coming from Mannina Cellars' barrel room spoke to the perfect present. With my clinking bottles of Cali in the back seat, I couldn't wait for the future — and one particular steak recipe.

Don Redman

MANNINA CELLARS
opened: 2006
winemaker(s): Don Redman
location: 760 C Street, Walla Walla, WA 99362
phone: 509-200-2366
web: www.manninacellars.com
e-mail: info@manninacellars.com
fee: Tasting fee may apply
hours: Friday 11:30–4:30 Saturday 11–4:30, or by appointment
lat: 46.0881651 **long:** -118.275991

DIRECTIONS: Mannina Cellars is located at the Walla Walla Regional Airport Complex. **From Walla Walla**, take Hwy 12 east about three miles. Take the Walla Walla Airport exit and go left (north) onto Airport Way for about one mile. Turn right onto Douglas Ave. Turn left onto C St. and continue to 760 C St. Mannina Cellars is on the right.

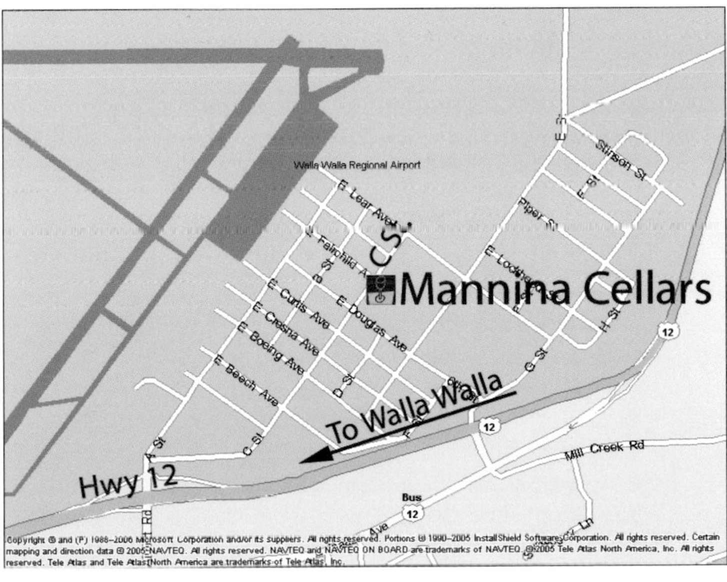

Tamarack Cellars 8

Ron Coleman has the nicest smile, and he's not fazed by visitors to this winery who turn up their noses at the thought of trying his chardonnay or wince when they sample his "Firehouse Red." He just smiles and conveys a "to each his or her own" attitude. Ironically, his *c'est la vie* approach wins a lot of converts. Behind his friendly demeanor is a quiet confidence honed by years of experience in the wine trade. With winemaking stints at Canoe Ridge and Waterbrook as well as working as a wine sales representative and sommelier, Ron's wine background runs deep. These past experiences and his creative talents converge with Tamarack Cellars.

Established in 1998 by Ron and his wife, Jamie, the winery is located in a restored World War II fire station and barracks at the Walla Walla Airport wine incubator complex. Ron is dedicated to making handcrafted wines using varieties from select vineyards in several Washington appellations, including Walla Walla Valley, Horse Heaven Hills, Rattlesnake Hills, Yakima Valley, and Red Mountain. By doing so, he can focus on a single-vineyard reserve wine or blend varieties from a number of different vineyards. He's like a stage director, and the play can take many twists.

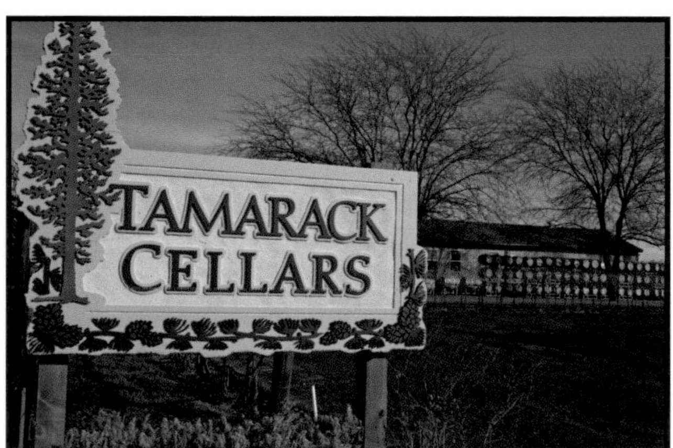

Tamarack Cellars' current production is approximately 12,000 cases a year, give or take a few pallets. His hugely popular "Firehouse Red" blends a number of black grape varieties that corresponds with the vintage year. For example, his 2008 Firehouse Red features eight grape varieties, including cabernet sauvignon, syrah, merlot, cabernet franc, and four others. It's a symphony of flavors with no one variety dominating the flavor profile. The 2009 will feature nine varieties, which ultimately begs the question: "Will the 2018 vintage highlight 18 varieties?" Well, why not!

If available for tasting, other got-to-try Tamarack wines are the sangiovese, merlot, syrah, cabernet franc, cabernet sauvignon, chardonnay, DuBrul Vineyard Reserve, Sagemoor Vineyard Reserve, and Seven Hills Vineyard Reserve. Ron's winemaking style is big and bold, yet very smooth and approachable — in a word, balanced.

The winery is named after the tamarack, a coniferous North American larch tree (*Larix laricina*) that has needles borne on short spur shoots. This WineTrail enthusiast forgot to ask Ron why he named his winery Tamarack Cellars, but keeping a little mystery in life is not such a bad thing. Besides, this gives other WineTrail explorers something to discover.

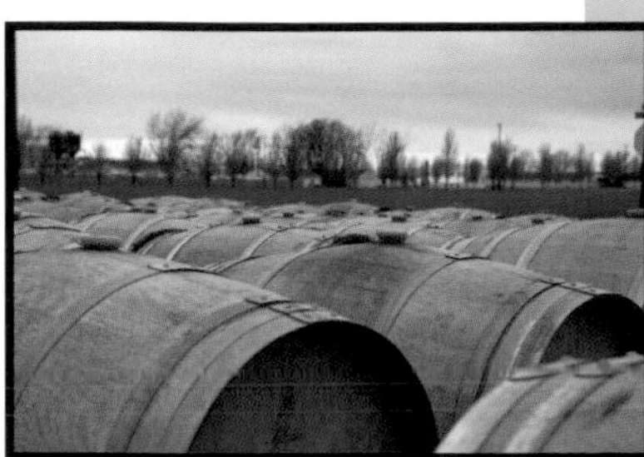

TAMARACK CELLARS
opened: 1998
winemaker(s): Ron Coleman
location: 700 C Street, Walla Walla, WA 99362
phone: 509-526-3533
web: www.tamarackcellars.com
e-mail: info@tamarackcellars.com
tours: Yes
fee: Tasting fee refundable with purchase
hours: Thursday and Friday 12–4, Saturday and Sunday 10–4, or by appointment (Winter hours: Saturday 10–4)
lat: 46.091608 **long:** -118.272498

DIRECTIONS: Tamarack Cellars is located at the Walla Walla Regional Airport Complex. **From Walla Walla**, take U.S. 12 east about three miles. Take the Walla Walla Airport exit and turn left (north) onto Airport Way and go about one mile. Turn right onto Douglas Ave. Turn left onto C St. and continue to 700 C St. Tamarack Cellars is on the right.

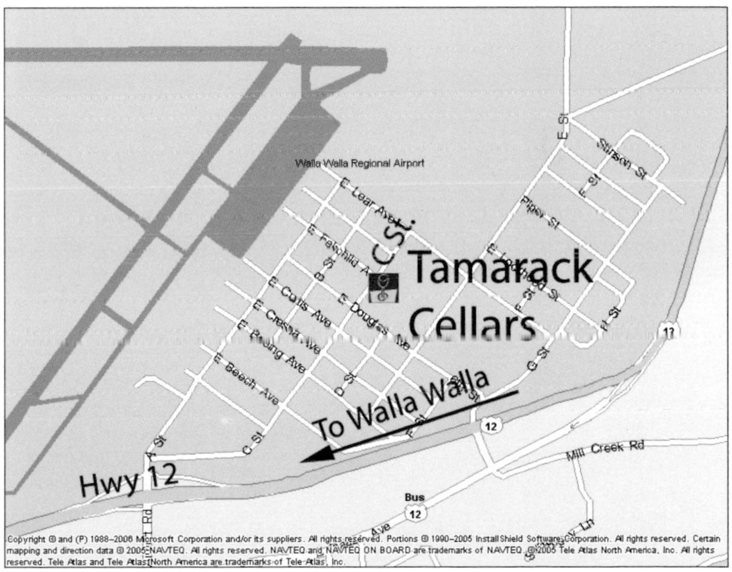

SYZYGY 9

OK, you're having a dream and you've been called upon to spell "syzygy" in a national spelling bee. Phew, you breathe a sigh of relief, because you are a big fan of SYZYGY! Moreover, as you spell out s-y-z-y-g-y, you recall that the word is defined as the alignment of earth, moon, and sun. Such was the inspiration of winemaker Zach Brettler when he launched SYZYGY in 2002 — the convergence of different Walla Walla and Columbia Valley vineyards and varieties to create the perfect blend of red wine. It's also in keeping with Zach's other passion — he's a astronomy hobbyist.

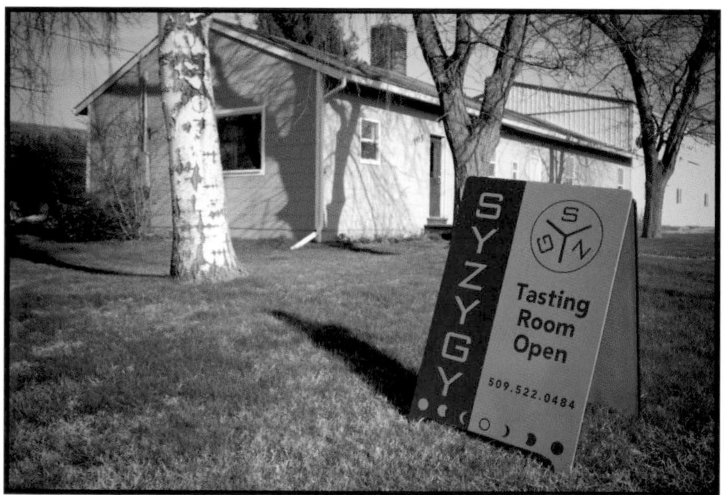

Zach gets his grapes from a who's who of Washington grape growers: Conner Lee, Minnick Hills, Sagemoor, Stone Valley, Spofford Station, and Seven Hills. Of note is the fact that he purchases his grapes by the acre and not by the ton. That's an unusual approach. By purchasing his grapes by the acre, Zach is clearly communicating his focus on high-quality grapes, sacrificing tonnage for quality. Grape growers "green prune" to leave fewer clusters on the vine, thus ensuring the remaining grapes get the vine's attention. Although this lowers the yield per acre, what remains are intensely flavored grapes.

SYZYGY's distinctive orange-and-blue bottle label may indicate that the wine inside is 100 percent syrah or 100 percent cabernet sauvignon, and that it is, but it's actually a blend of the same grape variety but from various vineyards. The goal is syzygy — an optimal blend of grapes from different sources to achieve just the right balance, taste, and finish. And it's more than a wine style that Zach brings to his craft; it's also a philosophy that speaks to a cosmic harmony of sorts. Something seems to be in alignment, because Zach's blends have gone on to receive high acclaim from wine connoisseurs. Check out his bold but oh-so-velvety red blend "Saros." The 2006 "Saros" achieved a 92 rating by none other than Robert Parker's *Wine Advocate.*

SYZYGY's tasting room/winery is located near the end of Boeing Avenue in a former military barracks. The original golden-colored hardwood floors are a distinctive complement to the orange walls. It gives the room an airy feel. It's a pleasurable space meant to be shared with friends, family, and lovers — it feels like syzygy.

SYZYGY
opened: 2002
winemaker(s): Zach Brettler
location: 405 East Boeing Avenue, Walla Walla, WA 99362
phone: 509-522-0484
web: www.syzygywines.com
e-mail: info@syzygywines.com
picnic area: Yes
tours: Yes
fee: Complimentary wine tasting
hours: March through December, Saturdays 11–4, or by appointment
lat: 46.087386 **long:** -118.274176

DIRECTIONS: SYZYGY is located at the Walla Walla Regional Airport Complex. **From Walla Walla**, take U.S. 12 east about three miles. Take the Walla Walla Airport exit and turn left (north) onto Airport Rd which becomes A St. Turn right onto E Boeing Ave. SYZYGY is on the left.

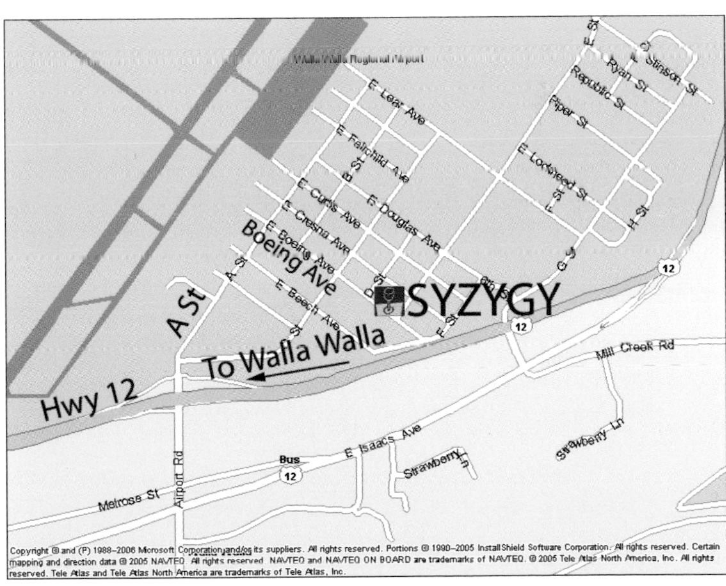

Buty Winery 10

The story goes that Frank Buty gave his future son-in-law, Caleb Foster, this warning: "Any man who marries one of my 'beauties' will become the beast." The beauty Frank was referring to was one of his three daughters, Nina Buty, but fortunately for everyone involved, Nina and Caleb didn't heed her dad's admonition. And behold, their marriage begot Buty Winery.

The winery wasn't born of a whim, however. Before launching Buty Winery in 2000, winemaker Caleb Foster cut his teeth as an apprentice at Woodward Canyon Winery, working for Rick Small; did a stint at Mount Baker Winery; and spent time overseas in New Zealand and South Africa, where he cultivated his predilection for blends. During this period, Caleb and Nina fine-tuned their own style of winemaking and eventually

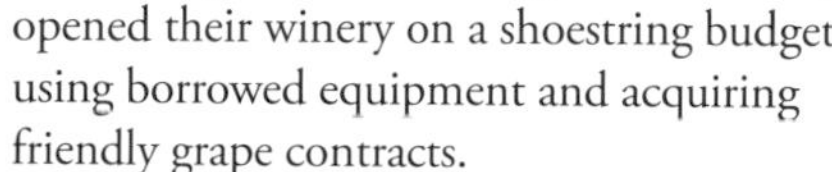

opened their winery on a shoestring budget, using borrowed equipment and acquiring friendly grape contracts.

Then, a loyal fan base grew, which translated into quick sales. This success occurred despite a relatively high price tag for some of their wines ($55 for a bottle of their Buty "Rediviva of the Stones" 2007) and the fact that a large chunk of their sales took place exclusively at the tasting room. With Buty's total production at approximately 3,500 cases, don't be surprised to see the words "sold out" associated with some of their releases.

Well aware that great wine starts in the vineyard, Caleb and Nina collaborate with a who's who of well-known growers, including Champoux, Lonesome Spring Ranch, Conner Lee, and Phinney Hill. However, in 2006 they realized a long-held dream of owning a 10-acre plot in the prized cobblestone-populated land located on the Oregon side of the Walla Walla Valley. The singular goal for this vineyard — planted in syrah, Mourvèdre, grenache, cabernet sauvignon, Marsanne, and roussanne — is to grow fruit for the production of their prized "Rediviva of the Stones" red blend.

Buty's portfolio includes chardonnay, red and white Bordeaux blends, and the aforementioned southern Rhône blend ("Rediviva"). Their bottles bear the distinctive "buty mark" logo on the label — a clever touch. Along with the Buty label, the couple now has a second — dubbed Beast — which offers wallet-friendlier prices yet delivers stunning fruit-forward flavors. As I sampled their delectable Beast-labeled "Rosé of the Stones," it hit me that Nina's dad's prophecy did come true — Buty and the Beast had a fairytale ending.

BUTY WINERY
opened: 2000
winemaker(s): Caleb Foster and Nina Buty Foster
location: 535 East Cessna Avenue,
Walla Walla, WA 99362-7412
phone: 509-527-0901
web: www.butywinery.com
e-mail: info@butywinery.com
fee: Tasting fee
hours: Daily 11–4, winter hours by appointment
lat: 46.087158 **long:** -118.271464

DIRECTIONS: Buty is located at the Walla Walla Regional Airport. **Eastbound on Hwy 12**, take the airport exit. Turn left onto Airport Way, which turns into A St. Turn right onto Cessna Ave., and follow it nearly to its end. Cross E St. and Buty is on your left.

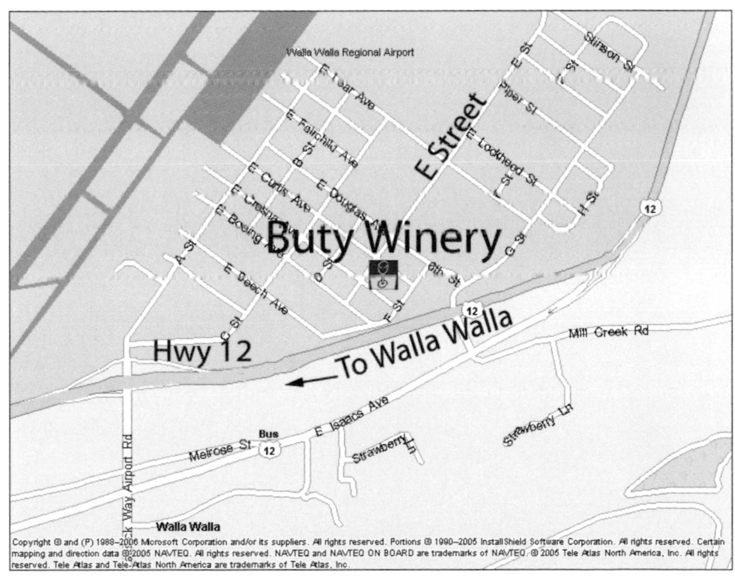

428 11

You could spend years learning about the art and science of winemaking, yet rare are the classes that teach the business side of owning a winery. Even if you were inclined to sign up for one, the fact is that most enology and viticulture programs offer little in the way of instruction on the financial aspects of winemaking.

Most wine-program graduates can wax eloquently about fermentation science, sensory evaluation, and canopy-management techniques, but ask them what it costs to plant an acre of cabernet or invite them to produce a three-year cash-flow analysis for start-up winery, and you are likely to get that desperate, deer-in-the-headlights look. The fact is if these grads had taken a business class focusing on the balance sheets — the profit and loss — of a winery, many would chuck that dream of going into the biz. It's a daunting, deep-pocket venture.

But that challenge didn't faze Jeff Sully, who is the owner/winemaker of Walla Walla Airport Complex's 428 Wines on weekends and an accountant during the week. I first met Jeff at the end of tax season in April, when he was busy working his "second harvest" *à la* IRS. He and his wife, Kim Sully, had the intestinal fortitude to relocate from California to Walla Walla to open a winery and pursue his accountant practice. Turns out, Jeff's résumé includes stints as the chief financial officer for a California winery, a consultant for the U.S. Department of Commerce, and various financial management positions in the Finger Lakes region of New York. When Jeff mentioned he would be teaching a business class at Walla Walla Community College's Institute for Enology and Viticulture, I winced, thinking that he might scare some students from pursuing their dream. But then I reconsidered: The fact that he has launched his own winery would give students some encouragement.

The 428 (read "four-two-eight") winery gets its name from the street address of Kim's childhood home. For most of us, the thought of our childhood home brings memories of joy and fun, and the Sullys wanted the customers of 428 to have those same feelings when experiencing their wines — most of them delectable red blends. In keeping with the street theme, Jeff's initial releases bear the name "Boulevard." At least he didn't call them "Cash Flow Red" or "Break Even Cuvée" — that would probably not have been a wise business decision.

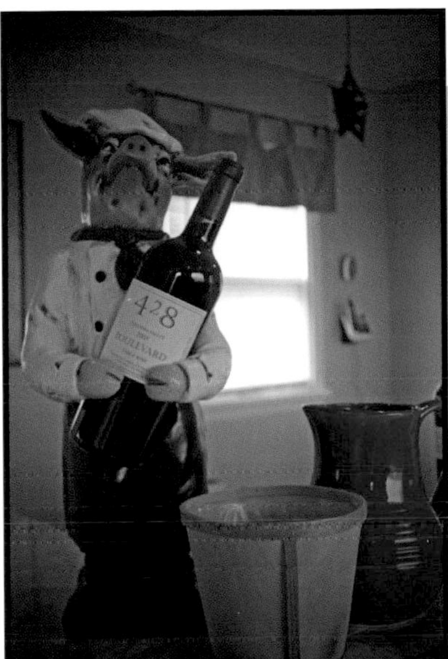

428
opened: 2007
winemaker(s): Jeff Sully
location: 675 E Street, Walla Walla, WA 99362
phone: 509-526-4259
web: www.428wines.com
e-mail: jeff@428wines.com
picnic area: Yes
fee: Tasting fee may apply
hours: Saturdays 11–5
lat: 46.089773 **long:** -118.27003

DIRECTIONS: 428 is located at the Walla Walla Regional Airport Complex. **From Walla Walla**, take U.S. 12 east about tree miles. Take the Walla Walla Airport exit and turn left (north) onto Airport Way for about one mile. Turn right onto Douglas Ave. Turn left onto E St. The winery is on the left.

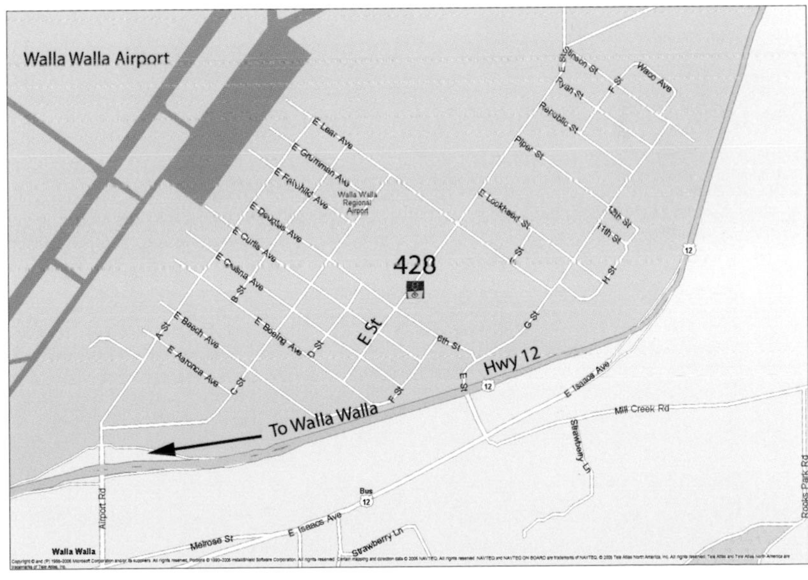

Kontos Cellars 12

Hot tubs and a seemingly genetic desire to make great wine began the journey for brothers Cameron and Chris Kontos. While stargazing from their family's hot tub on cold winter nights, the brothers talked of starting a winery. However, lest you think this was a pipe dream, please note that winemaking is in their blood. People familiar with the Walla Walla wine industry appreciate the premium wines of Fort Walla Walla Cellars, where the brothers' father, Cliff Kontos, is co-owner and winemaker. Yes, pedigree does have certain bennies, but you had better work hard, take risks and know what you are doing to be successful in the crowded field of vino in Walla Walla.

Located on "Incubator Block" (Piper Avenue) in the Walla Walla Regional Airport complex is the charming yellow structure that Kontos Cellars calls home — at least temporarily. The modern building stands in stark contrast to nearby World War II–constructed housing. As the "incubator" nickname implies, building leases here have a limited time span, six years to be exact.

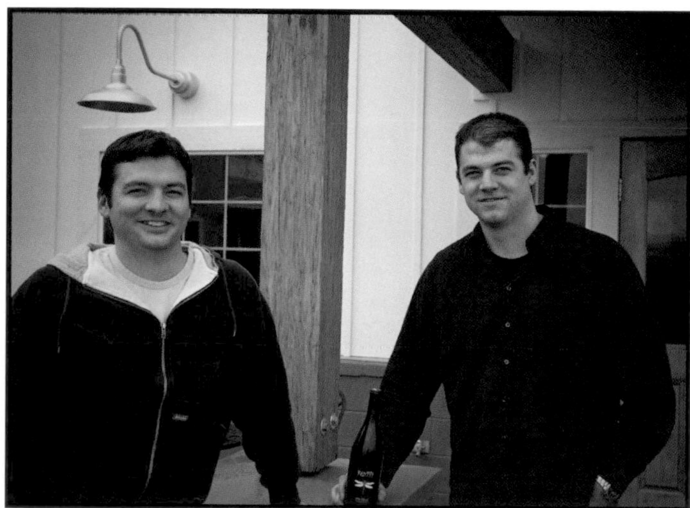

Chris and Cameron Kontos (l to r)

A distinctive identity is key for all new start-ups. To this end, the brothers fused their Greek-derived name (actually the name Kontos is the Americanized version of a much longer Greek name) with the Washington state official insect – the green darner dragonfly. As they were dreaming of launching the winery, the brothers would notice dragonflies landing on wine barrels or buzzing around their wheat field and saw this as good omen for Kontos Cellars. After all, a dragonfly's life is all about metamorphosis, and the brothers knew that they were about to embark on a life-changing adventure.

When it comes to winemaking, Cameron is in charge, and he had the good fortune to learn from one of the best winemakers of Walla Walla: Forgeron Cellars' Marie-Eve Gilla. For seven years, Cameron worked as Forgeron'sassistant winemaker learning from Marie-Eve the intricacies of grape and barrel selection, and a style of winemaking that results in wines that are somewhere between fruit-forward bombs and tannin-rich grippy libations. You can cellar these wines if desired or uncork them the evening you buy them. I know that, for me, one sip of his Alatus red blend had me reaching for my wallet. His style of winemaking resonates. After my introduction, Kontos Cellars wines weren't just Greek to me.

KONTOS CELLARS
opened: 2008
winemaker(s): Cameron and Chris Kontos
location: 594 Piper Avenue, Walla Walla, WA 99362
phone: 509-386-4471
web: www.kontoscellars.com
e-mail: info@kontoscellars.com
picnic area: Yes
wheelchair access: Yes
fee: Complimentary wine tasting
hours: Saturdays and Sundays 10–4
lat: 46.0919422 **long:** -118.26111

DIRECTIONS: Kontos Cellars is located at the Walla Walla Regional Airport Complex. **From Walla Walla**, take U.S. 12 east about 3.5 miles. Take G St./Interchange Rd exit to Walla Walla Airport and go left (north) on G St. Proceed about half a mile and turn left onto Piper Ave. The cellars is on the left.

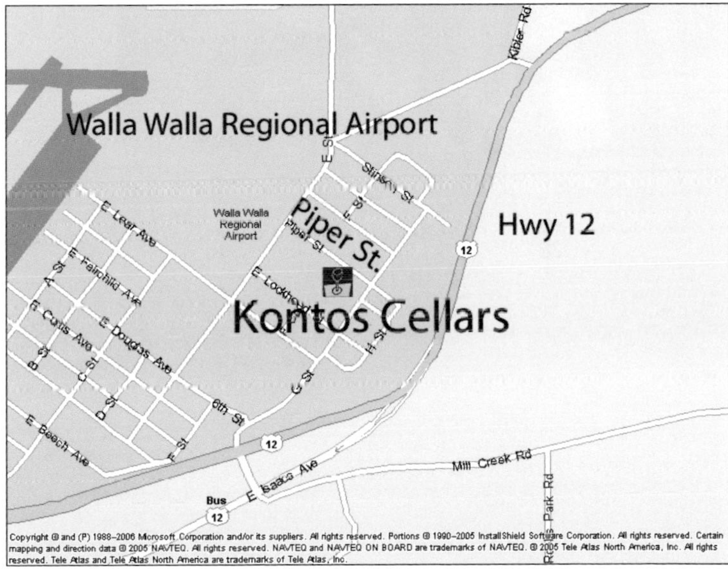

Lodmell Cellars 13

The dogs' names are Mazzy and Kimball, and although they were playing and romping around the winery during my visit, they kept a close eye on their owner, Andrew Lodmell. In his mid-40s, with a tanned, whisker-stubbled face shaded under a well-worn baseball cap, Andrew has the look of an Eastern Washington farmer. The blue-collar, Levi-jeans look belies the fact that this lean "dirt guy" grew up on Mercer Island, WA, where folks drive Mercedes, not John Deere. Andrew pointed out that Mazzy and Kimball were once feral vineyard dogs, and they're still most comfortable playing among the 30 acres of Lodmell Vineyards wine grapes, located near the Snake River, 30 miles northwest of Walla Walla.

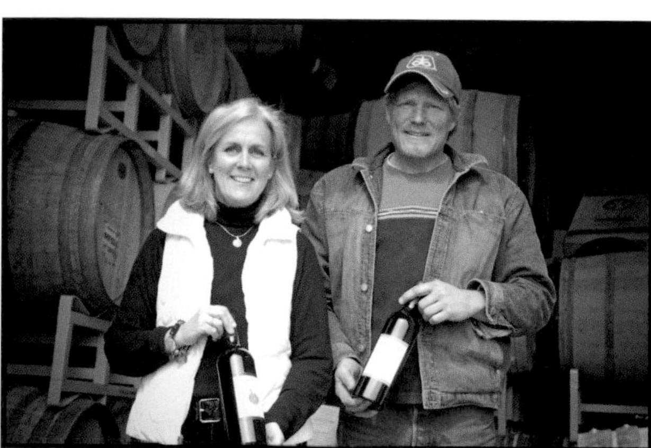
Kristie Lodmell Kirlin and Andrew Lodmell

A few minutes with Andrew reveals his love of the land, and like other farmers-turned-winemakers in the valley, he's a farmer first despite growing up in the shadow of Seattle and a winemaker second. A fourth-generation farmer, Andrew's great-grandfather established the family farm in the late 1800s. As it's often said, it all starts in the vineyard; you can't make good wine from bad grapes. Lodmell Vineyards' south-facing slope, high heat units, shallow soils, and arid conditions put plenty of stress on the grapes, and the result is intense flavor profiles. That's a good thing — a really good thing.

To allow Andrew the much-needed time to grow grapes, his sister Kristie Lodmell Kirin and her husband, Randy Kirin, focus on the business side of the winery. In addition to financing the operation, the Seattle-based couple (Kristie in particular) manages the tasting room, markets the wine, and handles the myriad piles of paperwork. There is a multitude of other business-related chores, and fortunately for everyone concerned, Kristie's sales management background serves Lodmell Cellars well. Check out Lodmell's elegant website, the eye-catching snake icon on its wine labels, and the image of the Norwegian flag on the sign above the winery's entrance, paying homage to the family's heritage.

Now in the third year of a six-year, nonrenewable lease at the Walla Walla Regional Airport wine incubator complex, the family is thinking about where to establish Lodmell Cellars' permanent home. The town of Dayton, the airport complex, and the vineyard site are all under consideration. Although the winery's future location is uncertain, there is one constant: Lodmell Vineyards. To borrow a quote from *Gone with the Wind*, "Land is the only thing in the world worth workin' for, worth fightin' for, worth dyin' for! Because it's the only thing that lasts."

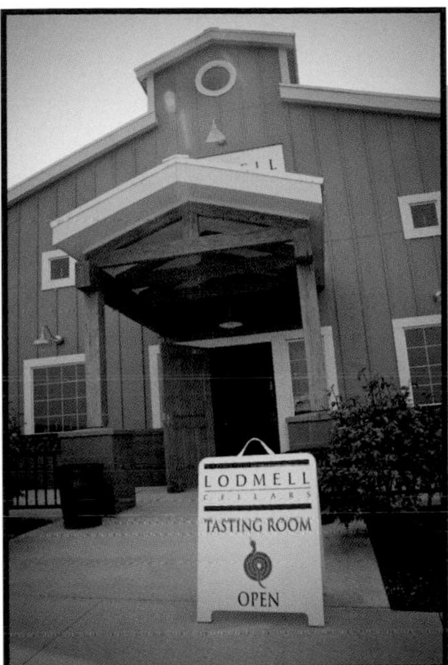

LODMELL CELLARS
opened: 2008
winemaker(s): Andrew Lodmell
location: 598 Piper Avenue, Walla Walla, WA 99362
phone: 509-525-1285
web: www.lodmellcellars.com
e-mail: info@lodmellcellars.com
picnic area: Yes
wheelchair access: Yes
fee: Complimentary wine tasting
hours: Saturday 11–5, or by appointment
lat: 46.091942 **long:** -118.261110

DIRECTIONS: Lodmell Cellars is located at the Walla Walla Regional Airport Complex. **From Walla Walla**, take Hwy 12 east about 3.5 miles. Take G St./Interchange Rd exit to Walla Walla Airport and turn left (north) on G St. Proceed about half a mile and turn left onto Piper Ave. The cellars is on the left.

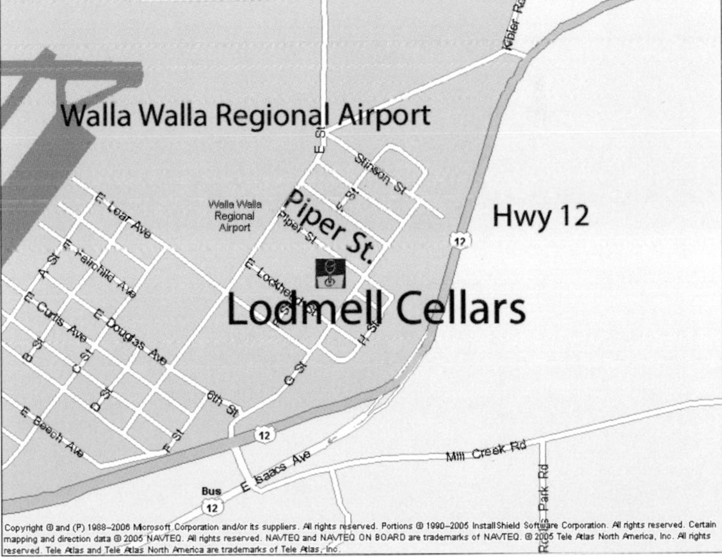

Adamant Cellars 14

Warning: By the time you read this, Adamant Cellars may have moved, Why? Because of its success. You see, at the time of this writing, Adamant Cellars was in the fourth year of its six-year lease at the "incubator complex" at the Walla Walla Regional Airport and Industrial Park. The winery has fledged and will need to leave the proverbial nest and fly on its own. It has mastered the art of winemaking and — just as important — succeeded in the business factor of the equation. Such is the fate of all successful start-up wineries that get their start in this stylish incubator compound. The owners of Adamant will now need to find new space for the next chapter of their evolution.

The husband-and-wife team of Devin and Debra Stinger are those owners. Devin manages the winemaking duties, from working with select growers in the Walla Walla AVA through vinification and bottling. He even takes care of the unglamorous paperwork duties demanded by ever-watching federal and state regulators and tax collectors. Meanwhile, Debra performs "everything else," which essentially means she's kept busy full-time managing the tasting room, marketing their wines, crushing grapes and mopping floors. It's hard work. Also noteworthy is the fact that Devin has a full-time job with Walla Walla–based Key Technology Inc. One wonders if, with two full-time jobs, this guy ever sleeps!

The couple began their winemaking adventure in 2000 in the basement of their Portland home, where they made their first wine. Using the name "Adamant" (a substance of impenetrable hardness, whose name shares the same etymology with the word "diamond"), the Stingers embarked on their winemaking business venture in late 2006, when they began leasing space in a bright red, state-of-the-art incubator building. They provided the winemaking equipment (tanks, pumps, and barrels) and long hours to create a style of wine in keeping with their own preferences — balanced, elegant, and approachable.

Look for Devin to continue to evolve his portfolio of wines. Now that he's established excellent wines relying on Walla Walla's "fruit salad" of varieties (cabernet sauvignon, merlot, syrah, sémillon, and sauvignon blanc), look for him to venture into Spanish-style wines with the release of tempranillo and albariño wines. There's even a tempranillo-based sparkling wine in the works, made using the traditional *méthode Champenoise* (Champagne method). Realizing they now have to fly on their own, the Stingers are aiming to soar.

ADAMANT CELLARS
opened: 2006
winemaker(s): Devin Stinger
location: 600 Piper Avenue, Walla Walla, WA 99362
phone: 509-529-4161
web: www.adamantcellars.com
e-mail: devin@adamantcellars.com
picnic area: Yes
wheelchair access: Yes
fee: Complimentary wine tasting
hours: Open most weekends 11:30–5; call ahead to confirm
lat: 46.092903 **long:** -118.263276

DIRECTIONS: Adamant Cellars is located at the Walla Walla Regional Airport Complex. **From Walla Walla**, take U.S. 12 east about 3.5 miles. Take G St./Interchange Rd exit to Walla Walla Airport and turn left (north) on G St. Proceed about half a mile before turning left onto Piper Ave. Look for the red colored "incubator" building on the left to find them.

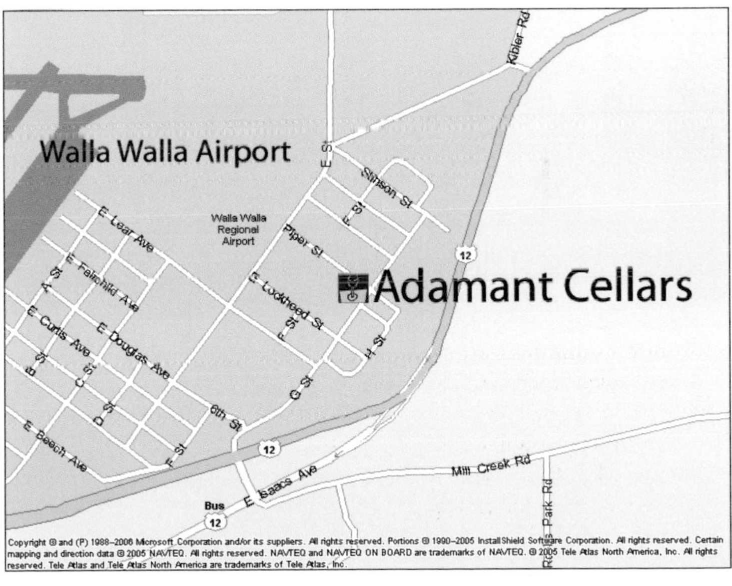

CAVU Cellars 15

Aviation enthusiasts will delight in discovering a winery bearing the name CAVU — an acronym for "ceiling and visibility unlimited." And how appropriate that CAVU Cellars is located at the Walla Walla Regional Airport's "incubator complex" on Piper Avenue. But it wasn't a case of kismet that brought CAVU to the complex. A flyover would reveal the location's ready access to the most treasured crop: its vineyards. On the ground, CAVU's efficiently designed 1,600-square-foot winemaking playground is the perfect space to make a dream a reality.

The winery's name pays homage to winemaker/owner Joel Waite's airline-pilot father, Jim Waite. It's befitting because Joel's parents (Jim and Karen Waite) are business partners and active participants in all aspects of the winery. The day of my visit found Joel and his dad racking barrels of wine in the production area. It was an unusually balmy January day, and the industrial-sized garage door was open, permitting easy access to the outside crush pad. The snow-covered Blue Mountains in the distance created an idyllic backdrop.

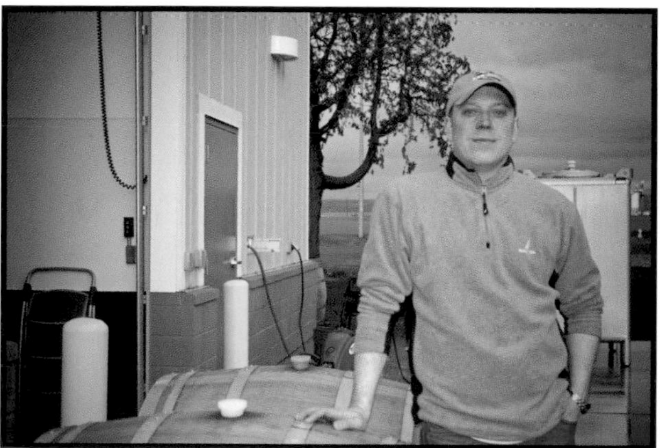
Joel Waite

Joel's winemaking style leans toward creating food-friendly wines and relies in part on atypical varieties such as barbera and Malbec. It turns out that his background includes considerable experience in the culinary arts as owner and chef of Catered Affairs, a Washington, D.C.–based enterprise that provided high-end private dinners. A later training stint at V. Sattui Winery, through the Napa Valley Cooking School, ignited his desire to pursue a winemaking career.

As Joel notes, it was during a trip to Walla Walla to attend a family wedding that he was struck with the notion of moving to the valley and immersing himself in winemaking and owning a winery. Once relocated, Joel traded his chef's apron for textbooks at Walla Walla Community College's respected Institute for Enology and Viticulture. Following some hands-on experience at Maryhill Winery, Joel opened CAVU Cellars' doors in the spring of 2009, together with Jim and Karen. Phew!

By sourcing his grapes from prestigious vineyards such as Les Collines Vineyard in Walla Walla Valley and Alder Ridge in Horse Heaven Hills, Joel is off to a great start. Of course, it doesn't hurt to have noted wine critic Stephen Tanzer say of Joel's 2008 CAVU Cellars Horse Heaven Hills Barbera, "I can't think of too many other West Coast barberas that actually taste like barbera." With clear skies ahead, CAVU Cellars is prepared for take-off with many vintages to come.

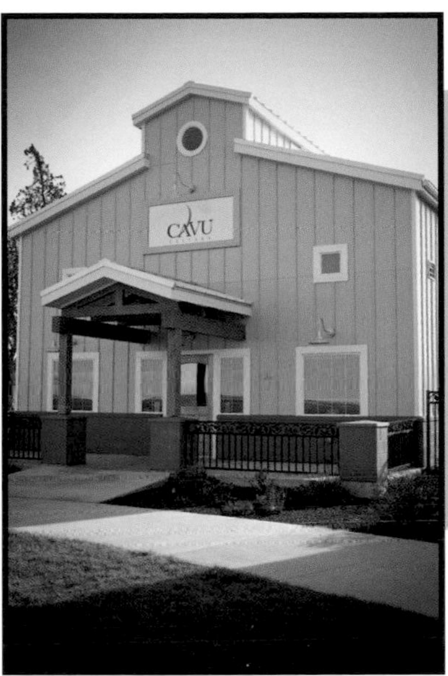

CAVU CELLARS
opened: 2009
winemaker(s): Joel Waite
location: 602 Piper Avenue, Walla Walla, WA 99362
phone: 509-540-6352
web: www.cavucellars.com
e-mail: info@cavucellars.com
picnic area: Yes
wheelchair access: Yes
fee: Complimentary wine tasting
hours: Saturdays and Sundays 11–5
lat: 46.091942 **long:** -118.261110

DIRECTIONS: Located within the Walla Walla Regional Airport Complex. **From Walla Walla**, take Hwy 12 east about 3.5 miles. Take G St./Interchange Rd exit to Walla Walla Airport and turn left (north) on G St. Proceed about half a mile then turn left onto Piper Ave. CAVU Cellars is on the left.

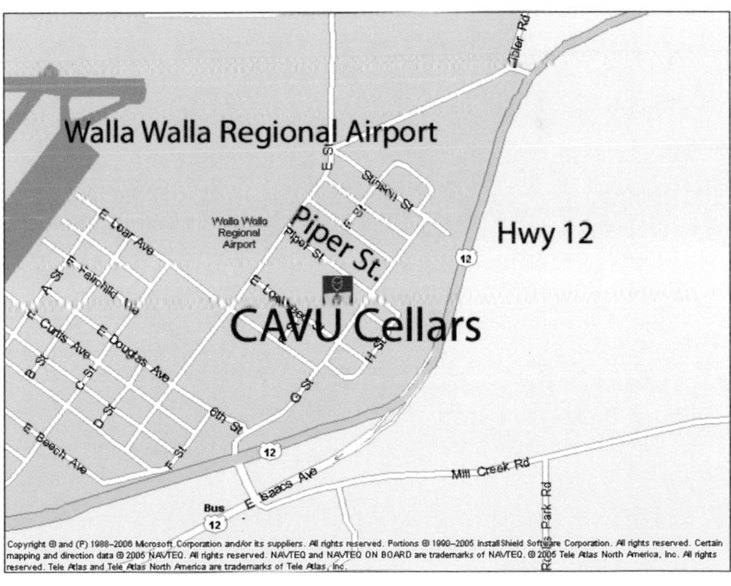

Ash Hollow Winery 16

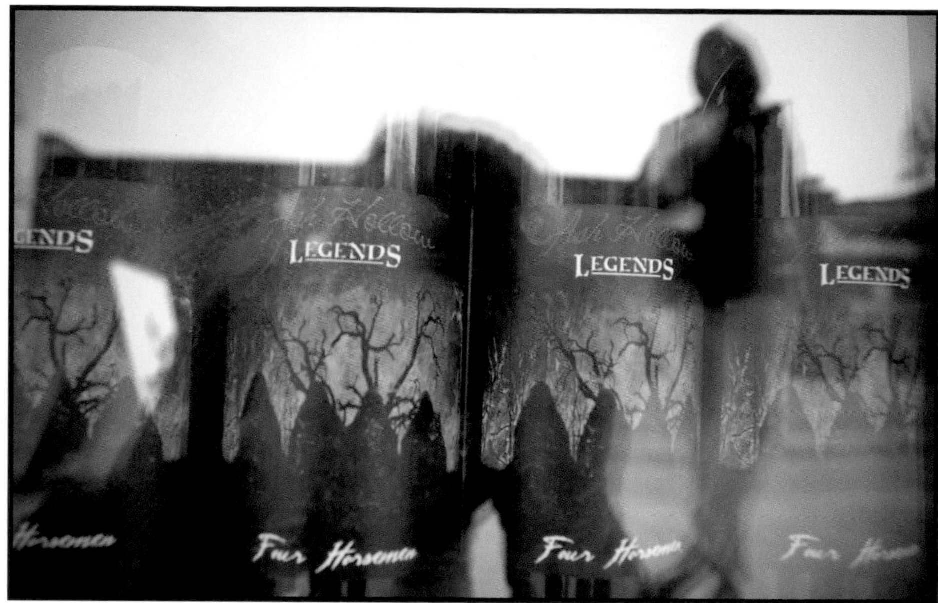

You know that old adage "The more things change, the more they remain the same." Well, that isn't the case at Ash Hollow Winery. True, the name is the same as the original winery, which began in 2002, but gone are John Turner (managing partner) and Steve Clifton (consultant winemaker and partner). Currently, John Turner is running for Walla Walla County sheriff, having returned from Iraq, where he was embedded with the U.S. military as a investigator for counterterrorism; and Steve Clifton is making wine in southern California. But that's another story....

When I asked our affable tasting-room host, "What about the Ash Hollow motto, 'Family, friends, food, fun, and great wine' — is that still in play?" She replied, "We're revisiting that line. The family-and-friends theme has become overused by other wineries and it doesn't differentiate us." While scribbling my notes, I glanced over at the new wine labels the winery is using for its Legends series of red blends: "Four Horsemen" and "Headless Red." These new labels are stunningly bold, in stark contrast to the rather staid and traditional Ash Hollow Winery labels, which bear the ink drawing of a lone tree. Turning the music down a bit, my youthful pourer explained, "We're about having fun, and the new wine labels reflect that."

I applaud the ownership group and managing partners (including the likes of Jay Tucker of Reininger Winery fame) for evolving the winery in this direction. Perhaps it was serendipity, but they managed to hire employees who possess turbo-charged creative drive, potentially positioning Ash Hollow to connect with the often-overlooked but fastest-growing demographic of wine drinkers — the 21- to 30-year-olds. Led by sales and marketing director Jennifer Gregory and talented winemaker Spencer Sievers, the winery's future looks anything but ashen.

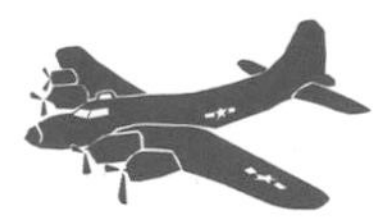

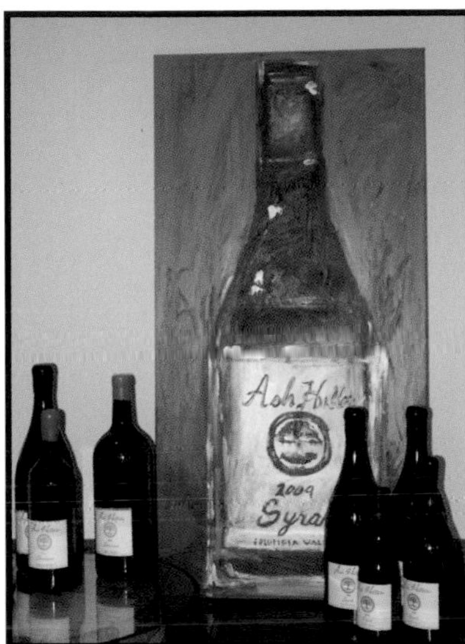

Art and fine wine converge at Ash Hallow

ASH HOLLOW WINERY
opened: 2002
winemaker(s): Spencer Sievers
location: 1460 F Street, Walla Walla Airport Complex, Walla Walla, WA 99362
phone: 509-529-7565
web: www.ashhollow.com
e-mail: info@ashhollow.com
wheelchair access: Yes
gift shop: Yes
tours: Yes
fee: Tasting fee applies refundable with purchase; no charge for wine club members
hours: Daily, call for hours
lat: 46.090310 **long:** -118.265623

DIRECTIONS: From downtown Walla Walla head east on U.S. Hwy 12 about three miles toward the Walla Walla Regional Airport. Past the main Airport exit then take the G St. exit. Turn right onto G St. Travel about a half mile and turn left at 13th St./Republic Ave. Take the first right onto F St. The tasting room is in the second group of buildings on the right.

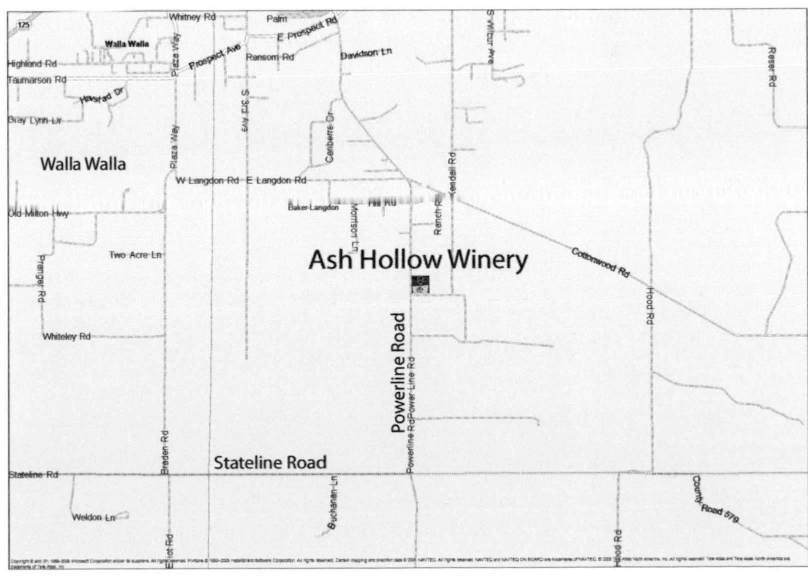

WineTrail East

Walla Walla East WineTrail

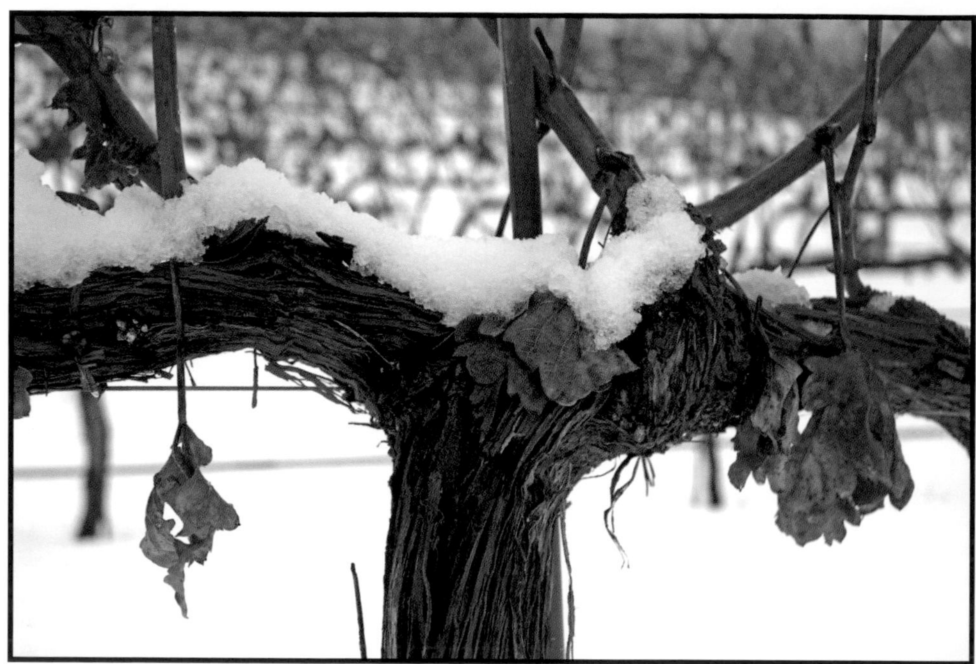

Although WineTrail East includes only a handful of wineries — College Cellars of Walla, K Vintners, Walla Walla Vintners and àMaurice — you're going to want to leave enough room in the car for a couple of cases of wine. Their wines are that good. WineTrail East is just the right trek for a wine-touring day trip. During most of the year, the area east of Walla Walla, with its rolling hills of wheat and lush green vineyards, is picture perfect.

Walla Walla WineTrail East

1 College Cellars of Walla Walla
2 K Vintners
3 àMaurice Cellars
4 Walla Walla Vintners

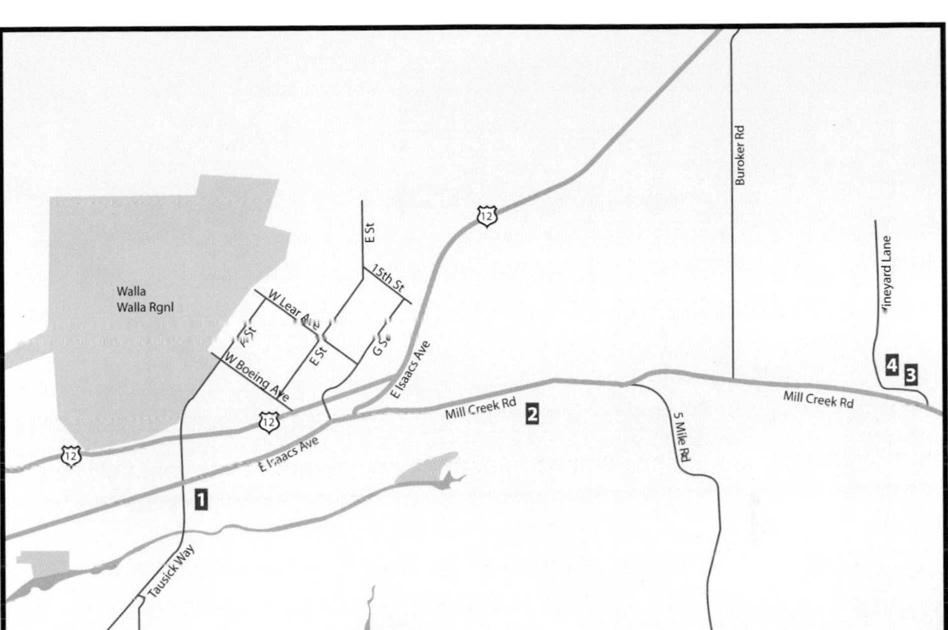

Region: **Walla Walla Wine Country**

# of tasting rooms on tour: **4**

Estimate # of days for tour: **1**

Getting around: **Car**

Key Events:

- ❑ **Events sponsored by Walla Walla Valley Wine Alliance: Spring Release Weekend (first full weekend of May); Balloon Stampede Weekend (second full weekend of May); Vintage Walla Walla (first full weekend of June); Entwine: An auction to support Walla Walla Arts, Wine, and Education (mid-October); and. Holiday Barrel Tasting (first full weekend of December). See winetrailsnw.com for details.**

Tips:

- ❑ **Restaurant suggestions: In Waitsburg — the Whoopemup Hollow Café or Jimgermanbar; In Dayton — Weinhard Café or the Patit Creek Restaurant.**
- ❑ **Consider using a limousine service (Black Tie Limo 509-525-8585, Blue Stocking Tours 509-522-4717, Sunset Coach Tours 509-303-0355, or Four Star Limousine Service 509-521-7849 are some of the many services to contact).**

Best:

- ❑ **Best Picnicking: àMaurice Cellars and Walla Walla Vinters**

Whoopemup Hollow Café

Waitsburg, a small town about 20 miles east of Walla Walla, is full of fun surprises. One of these surprises is Whoopemup Hollow Café. For the last five years, Whoopemup Hollow Café has been serving up some of the best Southern comfort food this side of the Mason-Dixon Line. In addition to offering great Southern food, the co-owners — chef Bryant Bader, pastry chef Valerie Mudry, and dining room manager Ross Stevenson — have created an upbeat, stylish café with a down-home atmosphere and a patio that is perfect for leisurely summer-evening dinners. The café's ambience encourages diners to leave their cares at the door and enjoy the warmth of Southern hospitality.

Photo by Alan Ayers

Photo by Alan Ayers

Many of the menu items change according to what fresh local produce is in season. Be assured, however, that you will always find the café's most popular dishes on the menu, such as filé gumbo, Bry's famous jambalaya, and spicy cornmeal fried catfish. How do you choose what wine to pair with these deliciously spicy dishes? Ross suggests that you shouldn't take the pairings too seriously. Instead, experience the food, sip a wonderful wine from the diverse wine list, and just have fun. Be sure to save room for one of Valerie's mouth-watering desserts; the local favorite is Aunt Luella's

Photo by Alan Ayers

chocolate Coca-Cola cake. I don't know who Aunt Luella was, but she sure knew how to make a great chocolate cake.

All in all, Whoopemup Hollow Café will make your drive to Waitsburg worthwhile. Ross agrees and says, "Come ready to have a good time and focus on the people you are with and the food."

Photo by Alan Ayers

120 Main Street
Waitsburg, WA 99361
509-337-9000
whoopemuphollowcafe.com

Jimgermanbar

Jimgermanbar is another great reason to drive the 20 miles from Walla Walla to Waitsburg. Jimgermanbar is considered an oasis by many, because here, cocktails, not wine, reign supreme. We are talking about hand-crafted, one-of-a-kind cocktails created personally by Jim German, owner and mixologist extraordinaire.

Jim takes cocktails very seriously. His creations are works of art, meant to be sipped and savored either by themselves or paired with one or more of the tasty "Etruscan snacks" prepared by Jim's very talented wife, Claire.

Photo by Alan Ayers

Jim also takes the notion of the "cocktail hour" seriously. His bar is truly a place to unwind, so once you arrive, take Jim's advice and "relax, enjoy, and just slow down."

119 Main Street
Waitsburg, WA 99361
509-337-6001
jimgermanbar.com

College Cellars of Walla Walla 1

"What do you hope to do with your degree?" I asked as my pourer offered me a sample of cabernet sauvignon. She was a second-year student at the Institute for Enology and Viticulture at Walla Walla Community College and with graduation on the horizon, she had some choices to make. I suspect she will have many opportunities to choose from.

When you visit Walla Walla's wineries, I encourage you to make a point of chatting with the tasting room staff and discovering their backgrounds. Chances are that many pourers you encounter are students at the institute. In addition, many other members of local winemaking staffs are graduates of the program, including Matt Huse of Five Star Cellars, Ryan Raber of Castillo de Feliciana Vineyard and Winery, and Denise Slattery and Steve Michener, who began Trio Vintners, to name a few. East of the college is Walla Walla Vintners, created by Dr. Myles J. Anderson, a founder of the Institute for Enology and Viticulture.

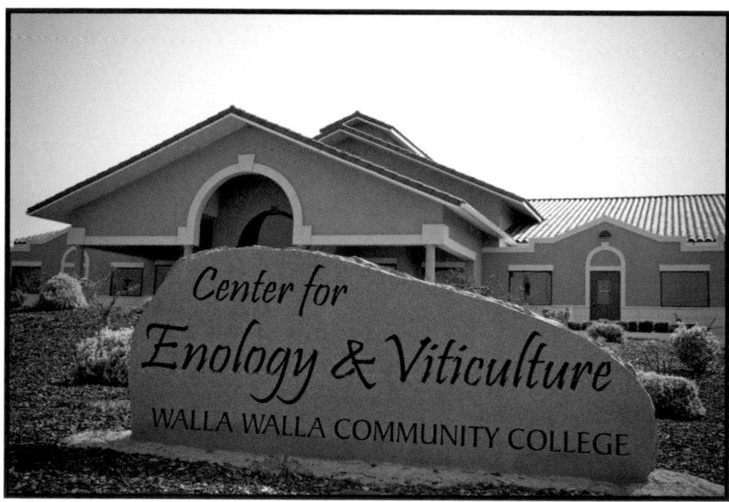

Open to the public only on Friday afternoons, College Cellars of Walla Walla offers students of all ages and backgrounds an intensive hands-on experience in crafting wines, with most of their first year devoted to fieldwork in the vineyards. During their second year, students round out their education with additional exposure to the science associated with winemaking. One-quarter of the students come from outside the state of Washington, and many end up finding work in Walla Walla, attracted to its small-town feel and the opportunity to apply their freshly gained knowledge.

During my visit at College Cellars, I particularly enjoyed my sample of "Governor's White," a Bordeaux blend of sémillon and sauvignon blanc, in part because the grapes came from the college's Stan Clarke Teaching Vineyard. Stan Clarke was a founding member of the viticulture program and a key instructor at the school before his premature death in 2007. Despite his busy schedule, he spent considerable time with me during the research of my first book, *WineTrails of Washington*. I owe him much. As I swirled and sipped, I couldn't help but glance heavenward in appreciation.

COLLEGE CELLARS OF WALLA WALLA
opened: 2003
winemaker(s): Michael Moyer and students
location: 500 Tausick Way,
Walla Walla, WA 99362-9270
phone: 509-524-5170
web: www.collegecellarsofwallawalla.com
e-mail: info@collegecellars.com
weddings: Yes
tours: Yes
fee: Complimentary wine tasting
hours: Fridays 1–5, or by appointment
lat: 46.068313 **long:** -118.292938

DIRECTIONS: From downtown Walla Walla, head east on E Poplar St. Go about 0.3 miles. Bear right (east) onto Alder St. and proceed 1.8 miles. Road changes name to Tausick Way. College Cellars is on your right at the corner of Tausick Way and Isaacs Ave.

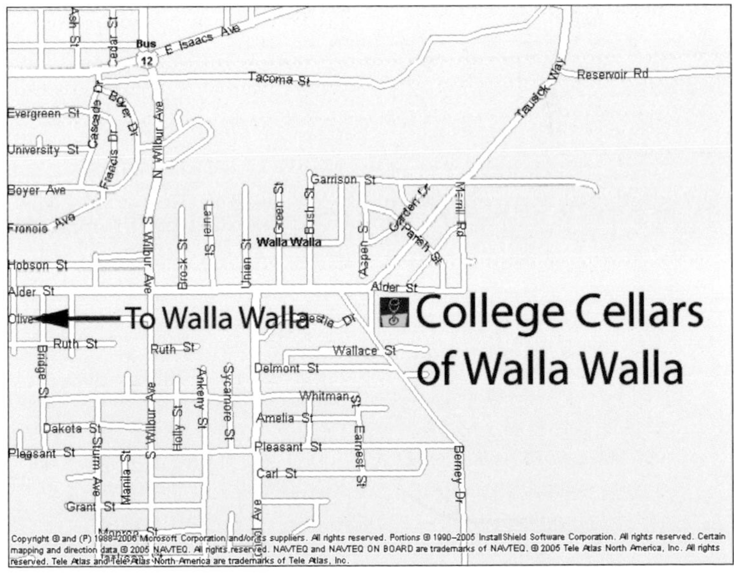

K Vintners 2

Call him an edgy rock 'n' roll aficionado, an any-reason-to-ride motorcyclist, or a wine-loving freak — just don't call him lucky, because it's not by luck that Charles Smith has succeeded in the wine business. We're not talking about successful small-lot wine production. No, we're talking over-the-top production under such labels as K Vintners, Charles Smith and The Magnificent Wine Company. To succeed, you must have a good product, yes. Equally important, however, is a business vision and the wherewithal to market your product — which Charles has in spades. His rare combination of amazing palate fused with focused energy has garnered the man and his wines a cult-like following.

Charles is on a quest to create exceptional syrah as well as other varieties that express the *terroir* of Columbia Valley and Walla Walla Valley. The syrah grape happens to find Washington very hospitable, thriving in places like Walla Walla and Wahluke Slope, where Charles acquires his fruit. His 2005 Old Bones Syrah received a 99 point rating from none other than Robert M. Parker's *Wine Advocate*. In 2009, *Food & Wine* magazine awarded Charles the prestigious "Winemaker of the Year" award. I'd say his quest has been fulfilled.

Originally from northern California, Charles managed rock 'n' roll bands in Scandinavia for 11 years before moving back to the U.S. and launching K Vintners. He also is the creator and winemaker for The Magnificent Wine Company, whose bottles sport his boldly lettered label "House Wine" (see Walla Walla Wine Works). The wines themselves go easy on the wallet, with price points in the teens. Another point in their favor: They are ready to drink with an evening's meal, and truth be told, that is why most Americans buy wine — for the dinner table, not for the cellar.

The K Vintners winery and main tasting room are located a few miles east of Walla Walla on Mill Creek Road. (A satellite tasting room downtown is planned, but had not yet opened at press time.) Unless your eyes happen to be glued to the Blue Mountains ahead of you, you can't miss the giant K looming in front of the small vineyard and a big, old farmhouse, a massive tree ensconced next to it. Once you arrive, be prepared to party. This isn't one of those genteel, reverential, church-quiet establishments; it's a house of kick-ass wines. Party on, dudes!

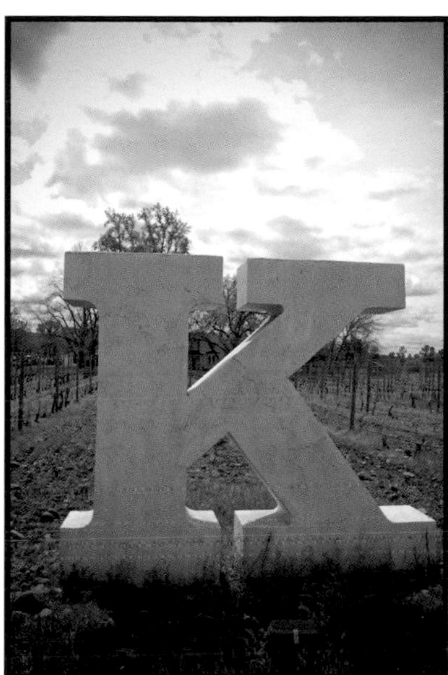

K VINTNERS
opened: 2001
winemaker(s): Charles Smith
location: 820 Mill Creek Road, Walla Walla, WA 99362-8415
phone: 509-526-5230
web: www.kvintners.com
e-mail: charles@kvintners.com
picnic area: Yes
tours: Yes
fee: Tasting fee may apply
hours: Friday 12–5; Saturday 10–5; and Sunday 10–2 beginning in spring; Closed in winter
lat: 46.086685 **long:** -118.2495

DIRECTIONS: From downtown Walla Walla, take U.S. 12 east 4.3 miles and turn right onto Interchange Rd, which becomes Mill Creek Rd. About half a mile down and on the right look for the large block white K sculpture.

Alternatively, take E Rose Ave. east about half a mile. Bear right onto E Isaacs Ave. and continue for about four miles. Turn right onto Mill Creek Rd and find K Vintners on the right at 820 Mill Creek Rd.

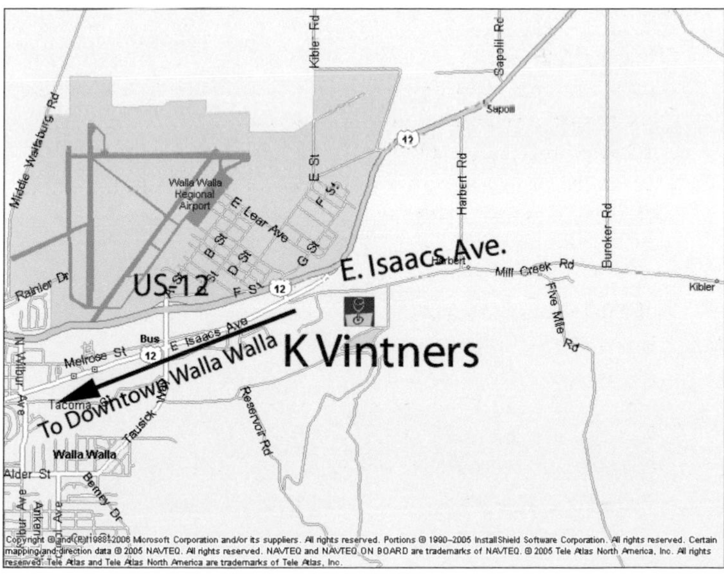

àMaurice Cellars 3

Malbec originated in France where it is one of the five great grapes of the Bordeaux region. In France, Malbec is often blended with other Bordeaux varieties such as cabernet sauvignon or merlot to create some of the world's great classic wines. However, Argentina now takes center stage in the production of Malbec, a full-bodied varietal with dark fruit flavors and a long-lasting finish.

After working the fall harvest at Paul Hobbs' celebrated Viña Cobos winery in Argentina's Mendoza wine-growing region, àMaurice winemaker/partner Anna Schafer knows a thing or two about Malbec. From vineyard to crush to vinification, she has developed a fine understanding of when to pick, what oak to use and how long the wine should age in the barrel. It's little wonder that many a WineTrail fan comes to àMaurice Cellars to experience (and buy) Anna's latest Malbec release, perhaps indulging just outside the winery/tasting room where a wrought-iron table and comfy chairs beckon visitors to relax.

Although àMaurice isn't the only winery in the valley to produce this varietal, it certainly enjoys a reputation for creating top-notch Malbec, and this may be what attracts most visitors to àMaurice. But Anna's other creations also shine; critically acclaimed syrah, viognier, chardonnay and a Bordeaux blend that honors a different Northwest artist each year serve to showcase the talents of this dual-hemisphere winemaker. One particular example is the rich yet smooth 2006 red blend "The Tsutakawa," which captured my palate for one exquisite moment.

The Schafer family, including parents Tom and Kathleen Schafer, planted 13 acres of *Vitis vinifera* grapes in the Mill Creek area east of Walla Walla in 2006. At 1,200 feet and with good air drainage, the location is reminiscent of Mendoza's high-altitude vineyards. Now that the vineyards are mature, the family adheres to sustainable methods in maintaining them. The Schafers are charter members of Vinea, an alliance of Walla Walla wineries and vineyards that follow strict guidelines for sustainable viticulture.

The notion of sustainable crops is nothing new to the Schafers, given their family heritage. Tom's father, Maurice Schafer, was responsible for developing a self-sustaining 20,000-acre evergreen tree farm. Because of Maurice's vision, and his kindness toward others, the Schafers paid homage to him by naming the winery after him; in the French language, à Maurice means "to Maurice."

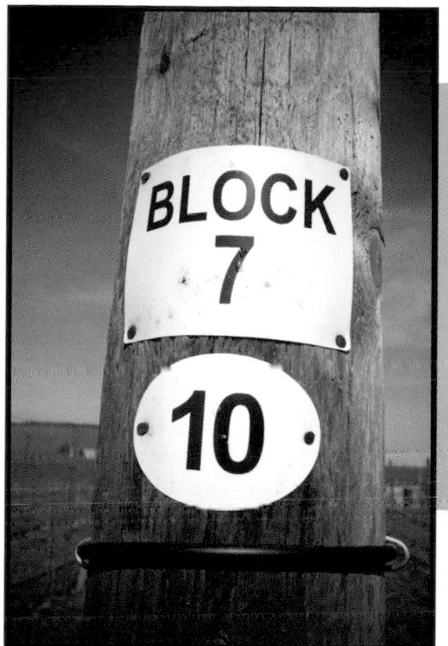

ÀMAURICE CELLARS
opened: 2006
winemaker(s): Anna Schafer
location: 178 Vineyard Lane, Walla Walla, WA 99362
phone: 509-522-5444
web: www.amaurice.com
e-mail: info@amaurice.com
picnic area: Yes
wheelchair access: Yes
fee: Complimentary wine tasting
hours: Saturdays 10:30–4:30, or by appointment
lat: 46.086677 **long:** -118.201349

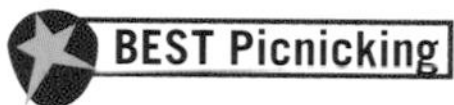

DIRECTIONS: From downtown Walla Walla take U.S. 12 about three miles to the Rooks Park exit. Cross Isaacs Ave. onto Mill Creek Rd. The winery is 3.2 miles past Isaacs Ave. Take a left onto Vineyard Lane and you will find àMaurice on the right. Walla Walla Vintners is located next to the property.

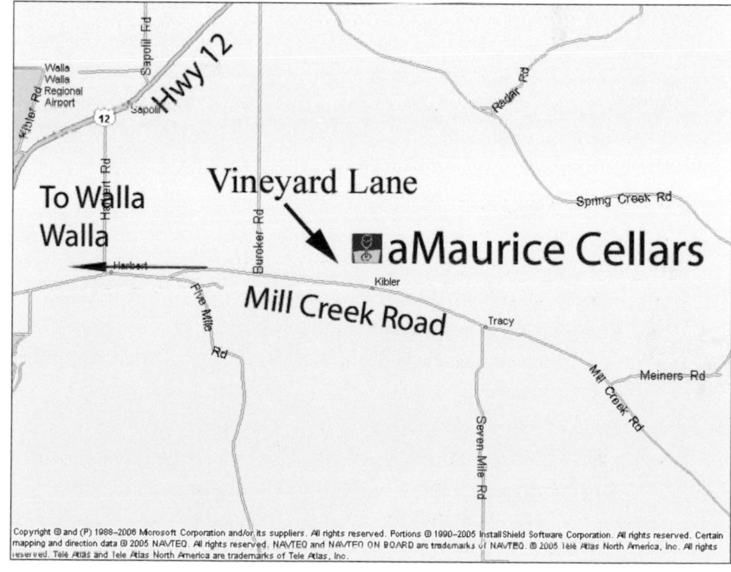

Walla Walla Vintners 4

Started by Dr. Myles Anderson and Gordon Venneri, Walla Walla Vintners was a "hobby business" that morphed into a very successful venture. Both men come from well-ordered, structured backgrounds. Myles Anderson was the founding director of Walla Walla Community College's Institute for Enology and Viticulture. Gordon is a retired accountant and a retired agent for Knights of Columbus Insurance. You would expect, with these backgrounds, that the two men would operate from a detailed business plan, complete with financial projections that would warm a banker's heart. Nope, no plan. Nada. Zilch.

Before launching Walla Walla Vintners in 1995 (and becoming the eighth bonded winery in Walla Walla Valley), Myles and Gordon experimented. The winery grew out of a labor of love for handcrafting premium wine. It also grew out of much failure. Here's what they say on their website: "As winemakers we made home-crafted wines for over 10 years before we considered making commercial wine. This was all done in our backyard using borrowed, makeshift equipment and for a while, a small apple press. …We experimented with oak chips, used oak barrels, beer kegs, food-grade plastic buckets, plastic apple juice containers, Coca-Cola syrup stainless steel containers, and glass carboys. The yeast and chemicals came from a local drug store that specialized in stocking such items for beer and winemakers." That is passion!

Walla Walla Vinters' winery cat Nellie

Myles and Gordon have also gained a reputation for being exceptionally generous with their time, expertise, and winemaking equipment. They provide the training ground for the enology and viticulture program's interns, educate other would-be winemakers, and lend their production facility and equipment to start-ups such as nearby àMaurice Winery. Their winemaker, William vonMetzger, graduated from the enology and viticulture program.

However, Miles and Gordon's real claim to fame is their wine — premium red wine. The buzz surrounding the release of their 2003 sangiovese was loud, and the wine earned top honors at the Seattle Wine Awards. Their other reds, including cabernet sauvignon, cabernet franc, and a red-blend cuvée, have also garnered high marks.

WALLA WALLA VINTNERS
opened: 1999
winemaker(s): William vonMetzger, Myles Anderson and Gordon Venneri
location: 225 Vineyard Lane, Walla Walla, WA 99362
phone: 509-525-4724
web: www.wallawallavintners.com
e-mail: info@wallawallavintners.com
picnic area: Yes
tours: Yes
fee: Complimentary wine tasting
hours: Friday 1–5; Saturday 10:30–4:30; Monday through Thursday by appointment; closed Sunday
lat: 46.086543 **long:** -118.201977

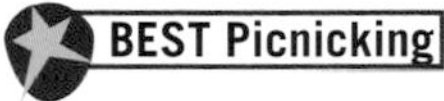

DIRECTIONS: From downtown Walla Walla take Hwy 12 about three miles to the Rooks Park exit. Cross Isaacs Ave. onto Mill Creek Rd. The winery is 3.2 miles past the Isaacs Ave intersection. Walla Walla Vintners is on the left in the distinctive red barn. àMaurice Cellars is just next door.

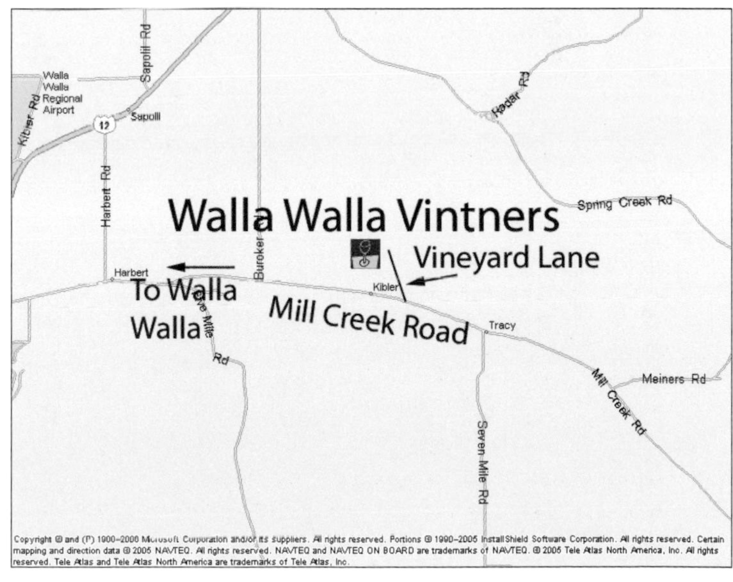

WineTrail South

Walla Walla South WineTrail

Many WineTrail enthusiasts head to the southern outskirts of Walla Walla, where excellent wineries abound. With about 20 wineries to taste your way through, you'll want to budget several days for this WineTrail.

For winery tourists who enjoy bicycling, the gentle hills of WineTrail South will get the heart pumping and work up an appetite. Whether you are in a car, on a bike, or sampling premier wines at one of the tasting rooms, the views of the Blue Mountains' foothills in the distance and rows of cabernet sauvignon grapes provide a terrific backdrop. Be sure to pack a picnic. Along this WineTrail , you will experience one of Washington's top wine-country resorts, picturesque vineyards, great people, and some intense reds.

Walla Walla WineTrail South

1 Basel Cellars Estate Winery
2 Zerba Cellars
3 Watermill Winery & Blue Mountain Cider Company
4 Amavi Cellars
5 Beresan Winery
6 Balboa Winery
7 Saviah Cellars
8 Waters Winery
9 Va Piano Vineyards
10 Northstar Winery
11 Pepper Bridge Winery
12 Castillo de Feliciana Vineyard and Winery
13 Dusted Valley Vintners
14 Isenhower Cellars
15 Rulo Winery
16 Tertulia Cellars
17 Trust Cellars
18 Gifford Hirlinger Winery
19 JLC Winery / Spofford Station

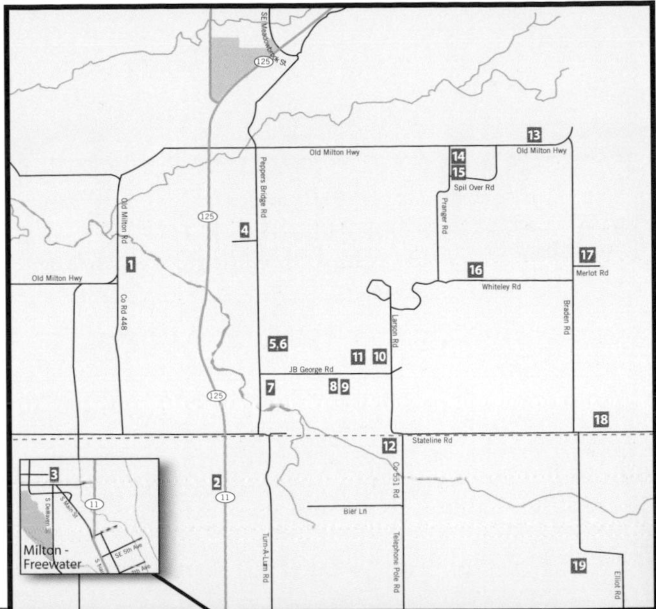

Region: **Walla Walla Wine Country**

# of tasting rooms on tour: **19**

Estimate # of days for tour: **2 to 3**

Getting around: **Car or bike**

Key Events:
- ❑ **Events sponsored by Walla Walla Valley Wine Alliance: Spring Release Weekend (first full weekend of May); Balloon Stampede Weekend (second full weekend of May); Vintage Walla Walla (first full weekend of June); Entwine: An auction to support Walla Walla Arts, Wine, and Education (mid-October); and Holiday Barrel Tasting (first full weekend of December). See winetrailsnw.com for details.**

Tips:
- ❑ **Consider using a limousine service (Black Tie Limo 509 525-8585, Blue Stocking Tours 509-522-4717, Sunset Coach Tours 509-303-0355, or Four Star Limousine Service 509-521-7849) are some of the many services to contact.**

Best:
- ❑ **Best Destination: Basel Cellars Estate Winery**
- ❑ **Best Views: Amavi Cellars, Basel Cellars Estate Winery, Northstar Winery, Pepper Bridge Winery, Castillo de Feliciana Vineyard and Winery, Tertulia Cellars, Trust Cellars, JLC Winery**
- ❑ **Best Picnicking: Amavi Cellars, Northstar Winery, Pepper Bridge Winery, Castillo de Feliciana Vineyard and Winery, Tertulia Cellars, Waters Winery, Va Piano Vineyeards, Dusted Valley Vintners, Gifford Hirlinger Winery**
- ❑ **Best Gift Shop: Northstar Winery**
- ❑ **Best Eats: Northstar Winery**

The Whitehouse-Crawford Restaurant

When you enter the understated yet elegant dining room of the Whitehouse-Crawford Restaurant, situated in a historic landmark building, you sense that you are about to enjoy a very special meal. You won't be disappointed. Whether you choose to eat in the dining room or in the bar, the food will be delicious.

Photo by Alan Ayers

Sonia Schmitt, co-owner, and Jamie Guerin, chef and co-owner, are passionate about using only the freshest ingredients. They have spent 10 years training, mentoring, and establishing close working relationships with local purveyors. As a result, the menu, which changes weekly, features dishes that showcase the abundant local ingredients offered by these purveyors.

Whitehouse-Crawford also pays tribute to the excellent wines produced in Walla Walla. It has one of the area's largest selections of local wines, which pair wonderfully with the menu items. The staff is knowledgeable and always ready to offer wine-pairing suggestions. Fabulous matches include L'Ecole Nº 41 Chenin Blanc to accompany the roasted carrot and beet salad; the 2000 Cayuse Camaspelo to pair with the roasted duck breast; and the 1998 L'Ecole Nº 41 Apogee to sip with Whitehouse-Crawford's famous burger.

Photo by Alan Ayers

All of Whitehouse-Crawford's focus is on Walla Walla, from its historic building to its extensive collection of local wines to the freshest local ingredients possible. In short, Whitehouse-Crawford offers a unique Walla Walla dining experience not found anywhere else.

55 West Cherry Street
Walla Walla, WA 99362
509-525-2222
whitehousecrawford.com

Photo by Alan Ayers

Picnicking à la Walla Walla

From spring through fall, Walla Walla abounds in dining alfresco. With plenty of in-town parks including delightful Pioneer Park to the nearby Bennington Lake Recreation Area, your biggest challenge will be to decide where to picnic. However, for my money, I'd toss my blanket and unpack my basket at a winery — especially a winery south of town with views of vineyards and surrounding mountains.

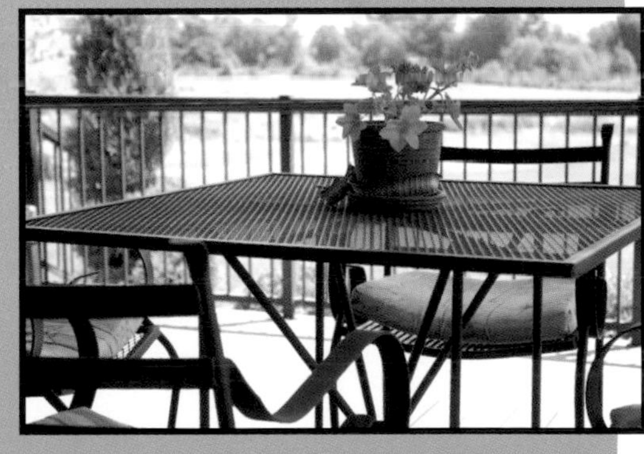

In town, WineTrail trekkers will find plenty of options for packing the picnic basket. You can pick up a large thin-crusted pizza from Sweet Basil Pizzeria or a delectable "supersubmarine" sandwich from a local institution, Tony's Sub Shop on Isaacs. Salumiere Cesario on North 2nd Avenue offers one-stop convenience for artisan meats and cheeses, and fresh made sandwiches. Get takeout from Olive Market Place & Café and be sure to include one of their fresh-baked cookies that can easily feed a family of four. Cheers!

Basel Cellars Estate Winery 1

One word: "Wow."

Basel Cellars Estate Winery first bursted on the wine-tour scene in 2005 and 2006 when *Seattle magazine* bestowed on it the title of "Best Destination Winery." And it deserves those props. Situated on 87 acres high on a bluff just south of town, the winery proffers not just fine wine, but luxury accommodations, including spacious meeting rooms, a gourmet kitchen for private dinners, hot tubs, a sauna, an outdoor pool with poolside cabana and much more. This is where well-heeled companies hold corporate retreats and loving partners get away from it all to create lasting memories. The winery's spacious 13,800-square-foot lodge is a fusion of elegant artisanship and rustic timbers, and if the hand-carved entrance doors don't grab you, the views of the valley and the surrounding Blue Mountains surely will. Guests are welcome to walk through the nearby vineyards and see firsthand the source of Basel Cellars' premium wines.

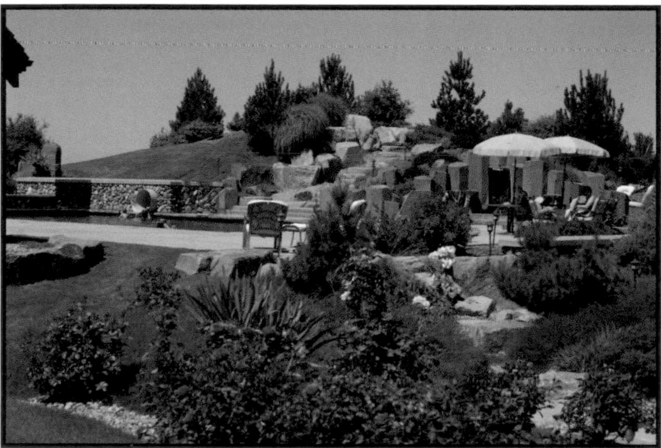

Pool at Basel Cellars

Founded in 2002, Basel Cellars Estate Winery is the brainchild of Greg and Becky Basel and their business partner, Steve Hanson. At the heart of their vision is the wine itself, which features grapes harvested from the Basels' environmentally friendly local vineyard, Pheasant Run Vineyard, as well as other local and Columbia Valley vineyards. Basel Cellars' winemaking takes place in a 9,600-square-foot subterranean facility. Yes, Basel Cellars has amazing winemaking digs and indeed, it uses the finest fruit, but perhaps the most vital ingredient is passion. It is the Basels' celebrated son, Justin, who provides this ingredient in abundance as winemaker of this grand estate.

A visit to Basel Cellars will first take you through a secured, gated entrance at the top of the bluff where the deluxe complex is located. You'll want to allow plenty of time to enjoy Basel Cellars' stellar line-up of wines: chardonnay, a Bordeaux white blend of semillon and sauvignon blanc called "Forget-Me-Not", reserve cabernet sauvignon, syrah, merlot, claret, and another red blend with the great name of "Merriment." You will also want to poke around the estate grounds, at least as far as the public is allowed off-leash.

There are many a reward to take away from a visit to Basel Cellars Estate, including an indelible appreciation of Washington's top winery destination — and a case of "Merriment" comfortably ensconced on your back seat (to be cellared for a fortnight).

BASEL CELLARS ESTATE WINERY
opened: 2002
winemaker(s): Justin Basel
location: 2901 Old Milton Highway, Walla Walla, WA 99362-7156
phone: 509-522-0200
web: www.baselcellars.com
e-mail: info@baselcellars.com
picnic area: Yes
wheelchair access: Yes
weddings: Yes
gift shop: Yes
tours: Yes
fee: Tasting fee refundable with purchase
hours: Daily 10–4
lat: 46.013094 **long:** -118.401088

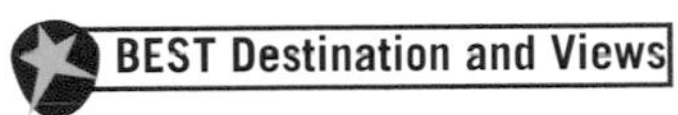

DIRECTIONS: From downtown Walla Walla take Hwy 125 south toward Milton-Freewater. Turn right onto Old Milton Hwy. Basel Cellars Estate Winery is located 0.8 miles further on your left.

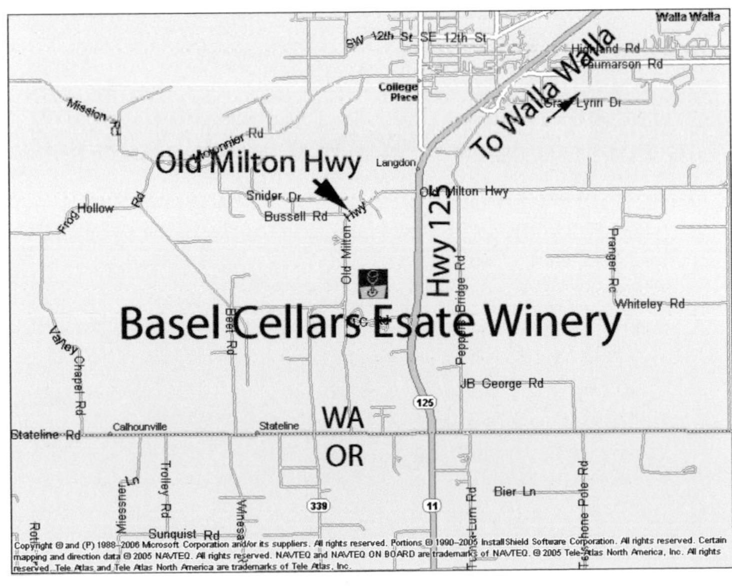

Zerba Cellars 2

Prior to launching their winery, Cecil and Marilyn Zerba had a successful nursery business that served the Walla Walla Valley. However, their love of wine and the economics of growing premium cabernet sauvignon and other varieties convinced the couple to plant grapes in three vineyards: Dad's Place, Cockburn Hills, and Winesap Road. In 2004, Cecil and Marilyn opened Zerba Cellars with their estate-bottled 2002 wines. It was a slow start — their 2004 release checked in at a paltry 200 cases. But production is on a roll now, with more than 6,000 cases released in 2008. This growth and other recent accolades have confirmed Cecil's mantra, "It's about the vines in the wines."

When I first met Marilyn at the tasting room, I made the same mistake that nine out of 10 visitors make. Dyslexia must have hit me, because I referred to her winery as "Zebra Cellars." The confusion is due, in part, to a drawing of a zebra prominently displayed on the label of Zerba's "Wild Z" red table wine. Marilyn cxplained that the zebra-adorned label was "tongue in cheek," because so many people make the mistake of referring to the Zerbas' winery as Zebra Cellars. I wasn't the first, and I won't be the last.

The winery's log-cabin-inspired tasting room was built with western juniper from central Oregon. This knotty tree consumes 40 to 50 gallons of water per day; consequently, vegetation is scarce surrounding a western juniper. The trees used to build the tasting room laid on the forest floor for years, allowing worms to attack and eat their way between bark and wood. The results are amazing patterns etched in the wood; as you sample Zerba's finest, study the wood to see nature's artwork. No two patterns are the same — just like the distinctive reds and whites of Zerba Cellars.

One of the real joys visitors experience at Zerba is its tasting extravaganza — especially if they are fans of Walla Walla's big reds. Anticipate tastes of cabernet sauvignon, merlot, cabernet franc, Malbec, sangiovese, chardonnay, viognier, semillon, port, and red and white blends. With this bounty, it's little wonder that the zebra on Zerba's Wild Z label is smiling.

ZERBA CELLARS
opened: 2004
winemaker(s): Cecil Zerba
location: 85530 Highway 11, Milton-Freewater, OR 97862
phone: 541-938-9463
web: www.zerbacellars.com
e-mail: info@zerbacellars.com
picnic area: Yes
fee: Tasting fee refundable with purchase
hours: Daily 12–5
lat: 45.922764 **long:** -118.381564
satellite location: 14525 148th Avenue NE, Apple Farm Village, Woodinville, WA 98072
satellite hours: Thursday through Sunday 12–6

DIRECTIONS: From Walla Walla take Hwy 125 south. After you cross the State Line Rd, Hwy 125 becomes Hwy 11 in Oregon. When you cross State Line Rd, stay right, and Zerba Cellars is one block south on the right-hand side.

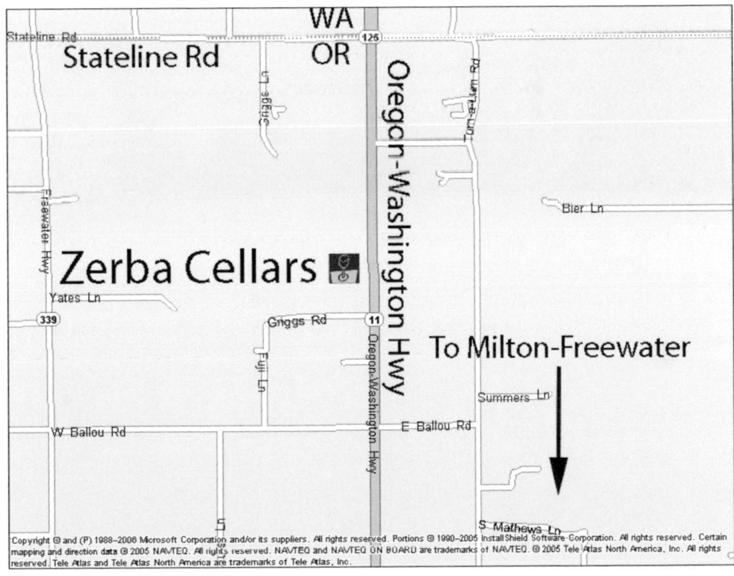

Watermill Winery & Blue Mountain Cider Company 3

Just like the old Doublemint gum jingle "Double your pleasure, Double your fun …," Watermill Winery & Blue Mountain Cider Company offers twice the tasting pleasure with two tasting rooms in one. Here, you can savor noble wine varietals while also sampling refreshing hard cider. It's all under one roof in a renovated tasting room, complete with a private dining area and a full-service kitchen.

Watermill Winery is located just 10 miles south of Walla Walla in the historic town of Milton-Freewater. The tasting room is actually a diminutive structure near the front of the property with the many-storied Watermill Building dominating the property in the back. With plenty of space for wine production and storage, capacity is clearly not an issue here.

Perhaps the Brown family, who owns the winery and cider house, will elect to ramp up production in the future, but right now they seem content to rack up awards. Their 2005 "Midnight Red" Walla Walla Valley Bordeaux blend took home the double gold from the 2008 San Francisco Wine Competition. I took one sip and a sale was made. Their 2005 reserve syrah also received 90 points from *Wine Enthusiast.*

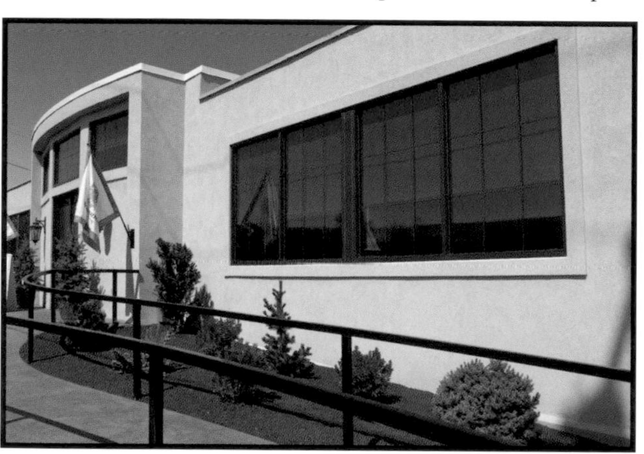

Watermill Winery's future looks promising, because it has the three essential ingredients for success: exceptional vineyards, advanced winemaking equipment and facilities, and a skilled and experienced winemaker, Richard Funk (of nearby Saviah Cellars). But perhaps the most important ingredient is this family's sense of unity, and their devotion to the land and history of this unique part of the Walla Walla Valley. You feel this passion at the winery. The Browns also have a strong sense of responsibility toward the environment, paying strict attention to eco-friendly, organic practices in managing Anna Marie Vineyard, McClellan Estate Vineyard, and Watermill Estate Vineyard.

The Blue Mountain cidery was a surprise find when I visited on a hot August day. Though a hardship to walk the 6 feet from the wine-tasting bar to the cider-tasting bar, I somehow managed. The hard cider has less alcohol than its wine counterpart, but certainly delivers on taste and refreshment. It's perfect by itself or paired with a summer salad or barbecue. My favorite was the bubbly cherry apple hard cider, created from a blending of five types of local apples with a splash of tart cherry freshness. A sip of this and I was reaching for my wallet a second time!

WATERMILL WINERY & BLUE MOUNTAIN CIDER COMPANY
opened: 2005
winemaker(s): Richard Funk
location: 235 East Broadway Avenue, Milton-Freewater, OR 97862
phone: 541-938-5575
web: www.watermillwinery.com
e-mail: info@watermillwinery.com
picnic area: Yes
wheelchair access: Yes
fee: Complimentary wine tasting
hours: Monday through Saturday 11–4, or by appointment
lat: 45.93724 **long:** -118.392709

DIRECTIONS: From Walla Walla take SR-125 [S. 9th Ave.] 5.2 miles and enter Oregon. Keep straight onto SR-11 [Oregon-Washington Hwy] for 4.4 miles. Turn right (west) onto E. Broadway Ave. and go .2 miles to the Watermill Winery & Blue Mountain Cider Company.

From Pendleton take SR-11 [Oregon-Washington Hwy] 27.6 miles north to Milton-Freewater. Bear left (northwest) onto SR-11 [S. Main S.], keep straight onto S Main St for .4 miles, and arrive at 235 E. Broadway Ave.

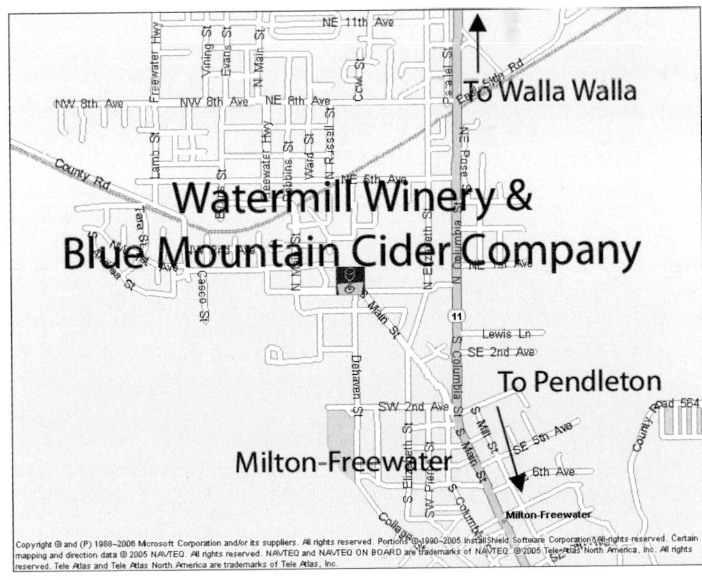

Amavi Cellars 4

Talk about night and day. The change from Amavi Cellars' reconstructed log cabin on 13th Avenue near downtown Walla Walla to its newly built contemporary digs south of Walla Walla is nothing short of spectacular. Perched on a hilltop off Pepper Bridge Road, the gleaming new tasting room has that stop-your-car, break-out-your-camera impact. At least it did for me, prompting me to fish for my Nikon in the back seat.

Inside the tasting room, visitors have a full frontal view of Pepper Bridge Winery, Amavi Cellars' sister winery, situated on a hilltop a little way in the distance. The view from a floor-to-ceiling wall of windows takes in the famous Pepper Bridge Vineyard (the source, along with Les Collines and Seven Hills Vineyards, of Amavi's wine grapes) at a slightly higher elevation than the valley floor. Doors lead to a spacious outside deck, where I spied several visitors soaking in the view with freshly opened bottles of Amavi Cellars' wine. As I took more photos from the deck, I had that "five S's of wine tasting" mantra going through my mind: seeing, swirling, smelling, sipping (or swallowing), and savoring.

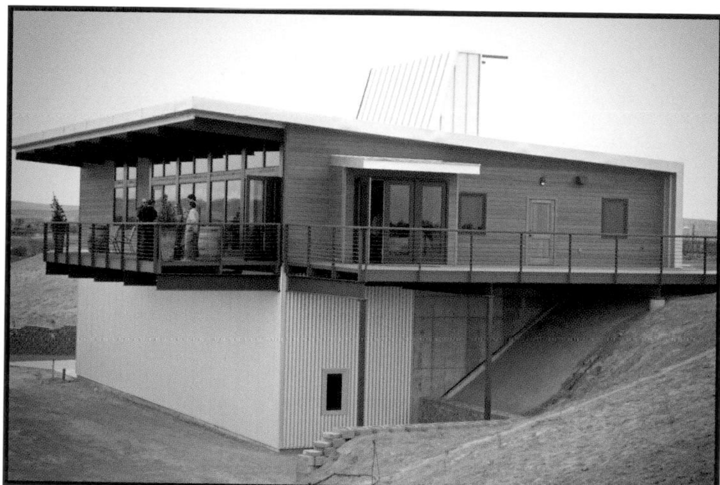

Back inside, Ray Goff (co-owner of Pepper Bridge Winery and Amavi Cellars) poured me a sample of their 2007 estate syrah, and I made a conscious decision to slow down and exercise the five S's. With a lean, athletic physique and sporting a Mad Hatter's hat, Ray gave me a generous pour and explained in his folksy Montana way that Amavi wines are one of the super values in the valley. Priced at less than $30, the creations of winemaker Jean-François Pellet are fruit-forward and ready to enjoy with an evening's meal.

Recalling the five S's of wine tasting, I gave my glass a few brisk swirls before sticking my nose inside the glass to smell the 100 percent syrah. There followed a full mouth onslaught (no wimpy sip this time) with agitated swishing to all parts of the palate, followed by an audible gulp. Now came the savoring part, during which, with a satisfied grin, I looked up to see Ray's expectant eyes on me. That's when I exclaimed in a very un–Robert M. Parker–like way, "Wow, that's really good stuff!" I decided then and there that I should adopt my own personal *six* S's of wine tasting mantra: seeing, swirling, smelling, sipping (or swallowing), savoring, and *silence* … well at least enough silence to carefully consider the next words out of my mouth.

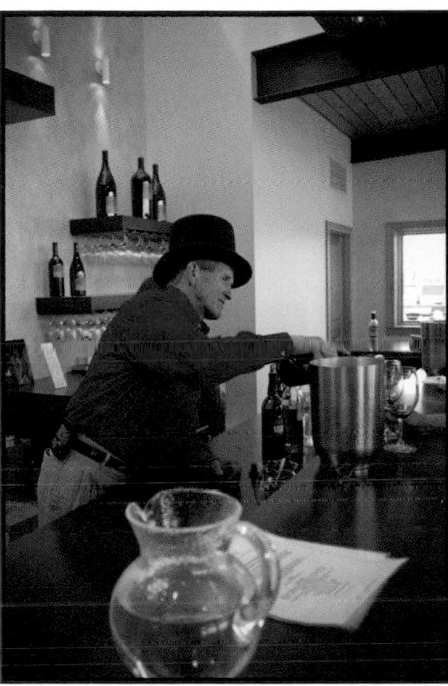

Ray Goff

AMAVI CELLARS
opened: 2001
winemaker(s): Jean-François Pellet
location: 3796 Peppers Bridge Road, Walla Walla, WA 99362-1769
phone: 509-525-3541
web: www.amavicellars.com
e-mail: info@amavicellars.com
picnic area: Yes
wheelchair access: Yes
tours: Yes
fee: Complimentary wine tasting
hours: Daily 11–5, or by appointment
lat: 46.0241781 **long:** -118.3836383
satellite location: 14810 NE 145th Street; Building A-3, Woodinville, WA 98072
satellite hours: Monday through Sunday 11–5

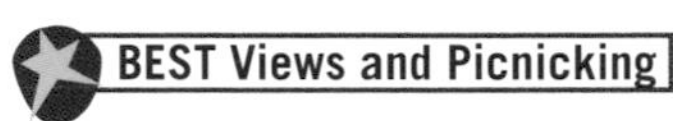

DIRECTIONS: From Walla Walla, travel south for approximately three miles on Hwy 125. Turn left at the intersection of Hwy 125 and Old Milton Hwy. Turn right onto Peppers Bridge Rd. Amavi Cellars is located on the right about a quarter of a mile from the turn.

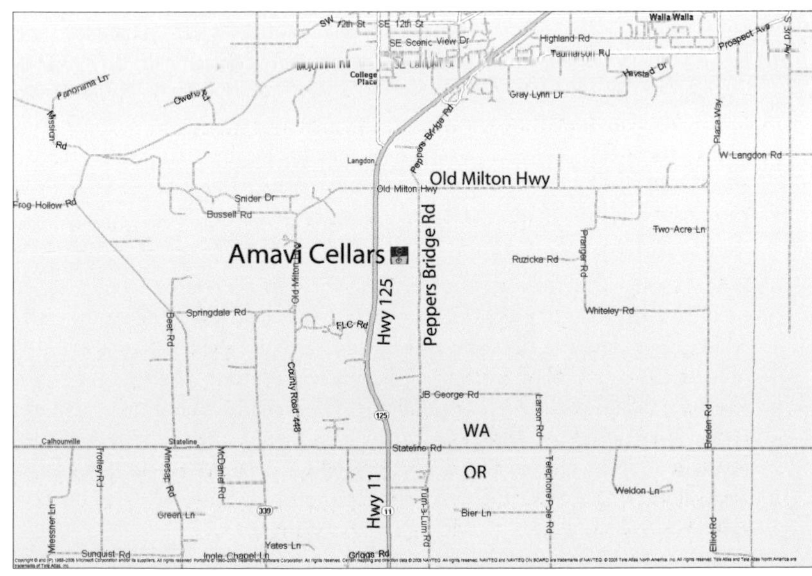

Beresan Winery 5

Located about four miles south of Walla Walla, Beresan Winery occupies a lovingly restored 1926 red barn. The barn is a distinctive landmark and one of our favorite stops along Walla Walla WineTrail South. Tom and Debbie Waliser, owners of Beresan Winery, meticulously renovated the old barn to serve the dual purpose of making and tasting wine. When you walk into the barn's tasting room, at its south end, you are struck by the attention to detail. The barn's high ceilings, rustic colors, quality woodwork, and turn-of-the-century furnishings create an ambiance that speaks volumes about the Walisers' passion for making great wine.

By the way, the greeting committee of tail-wagging, friendly dogs is composed of strays that have found a home at Beresan Winery. They are just a few members of the menagerie of animals at this former horse farm, as you will discover.

Tom Waliser is a quintessential "wine grower." He manages his own 20-plus acres of estate vineyards — Yellow Jacket Vineyard, Beresan Estate Vineyard, and Waliser Vineyard — the source for Beresan Winery's estate wines. He's also the vineyard manager for some of the region's most prestigious vineyards, including Pepper Bridge Vineyard, Seven Hills West, Candy Mountain Vineyard (love that name) and Mirage Vineyard. Evidently, farming is in Tom's genes. The Waliser family history includes many generations of farmers whose origins go back to the Beresan area of the Ukraine. Eventually, these farmers made their way to Walla Walla, where the family's farming expertise continues.

However, growing premium wine grapes is one thing. Converting the fruit to fine wine is another. For this, Tom turned to another Tom — Tom Glase, who also makes wine under his own wine label, Balboa. Together, the two Toms collaborate from vineyard to bottle to produce a portfolio of predominantly red estate wines, including syrah, merlot, cabernet sauvignon, carménère, and several red blends. Among the red blends is a 50/50 blend of merlot and cabernet franc bearing the name of "Viuda Negra" (Spanish for "black widow"). **WineTrail Note:** Make a point of asking Debbie about the story behind the name "Viuda Negra." To date, we know of no plans to create a wine with the name "Tom Squared," but it would be fitting given the two Toms' critically acclaimed achievements. Regardless of the name, all Beresan wines reflect the intense flavors and character of its estate vineyards.

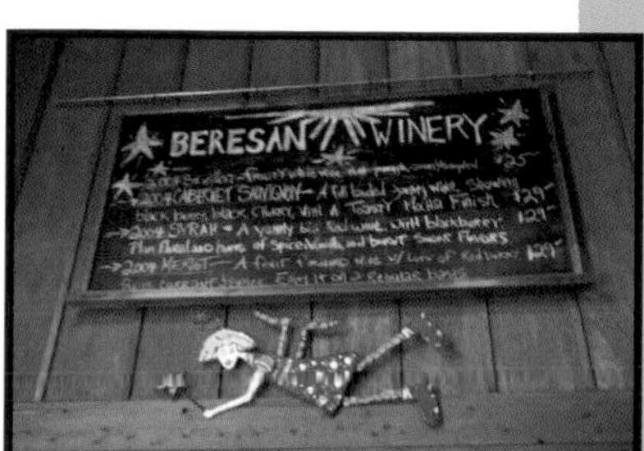

BERESAN WINERY
opened: 2003
winemaker(s): Tom Glase
location: 4169 Pepper Bridge Road, Walla Walla, WA 99362-7135
phone: 509-522-2395
web: www.beresanwines.com
e-mail: info@beresanwines.com
picnic area: Yes
tours: Yes
fee: Complimentary wine tasting
hours: Fridays 12–5 and Saturdays 11–4, or by appointment
lat: 46.031921 **long:** -118.37886

DIRECTIONS: From Walla Walla, travel south for approximately three miles on Hwy 125. Turn left at the intersection of Hwy 125 and Old Milton Hwy. Turn right onto Peppers Bridge Rd. Beresan Wines is located at the corner of JB George Rd and Peppers Bridge Rd.

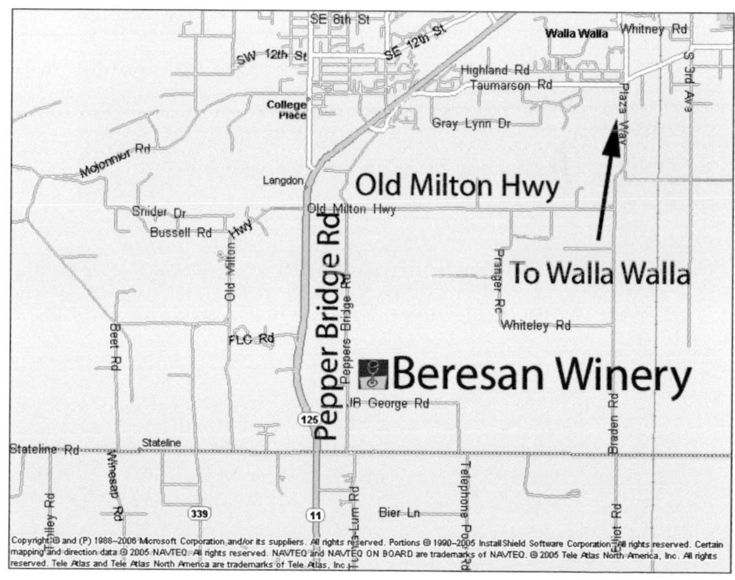

Balboa Winery 6

"Hey, what happened to the screw caps?" I asked, eyeing the bottle closure for a Balboa bottle of wine. In response, our tasting-room host said, "We went with a more environmentally sound closure. A conglomerate cork that uses sustainable cork products that are biodegradable." I should have seen this coming. After all, Balboa is known for its environmentally sound practices. From the vineyards it chooses to work with to its decision not to use decorative foil around bottle necks, Balboa Winery is all about sustainability. Guiding this endeavor is owner, winemaker and "go green" advocate Tom Glase.

There's a certain breed of person who feels compelled to roll the dice and leave the comforts of home to resettle in a new place. These are adventurous souls, willing to take a risk and try something new. Tom is just such a person, giving up a comfortable existence on Bainbridge Island and moving to Walla Walla in 1997. Tom was volunteering at Walla Walla's L'Ecole N° 41 Winery when its owner/winemaker, Martin Clubb, asked him if he knew of anyone available to work at the winery. In fact, Tom did know of someone — himself. However, there was one slight problem: Tom had just accepted a position as a loan officer with a local bank and was expected to report to work the next Monday morning. It took about two minutes of soul searching before Tom had decided what his course of action would be. On Monday, he called the bank and informed management that he wouldn't be taking the job.

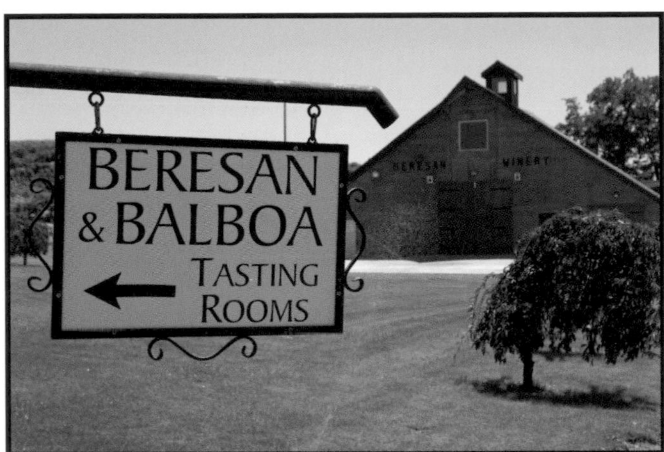

There followed a three-year stint at L'Ecole N° 41, during which Tom learned to make wine — very good wine. He then left L'Ecole N° 41 to become winemaker for Tom Waliser at Beresan Winery. With a winemaking facility and premium grapes at his disposal, it wasn't long before Tom had created his own wine under the Balboa label. With fruit sourced from vineyards managed by Waliser's Premiere Vineyard Management company, Tom focuses on single-vineyard wines such as Mirage Vineyard Syrah, Pepper Bridge Syrah and Mirage Vineyard "Cat's Meow" (I love that name almost as much as I relish the blend).

If you are looking for good-value wines, consider Balboa Winery's merlot. At only $18 a bottle, you can opt for the top sirloin instead of the hamburger special. Now that's sustainability of the economic kind!

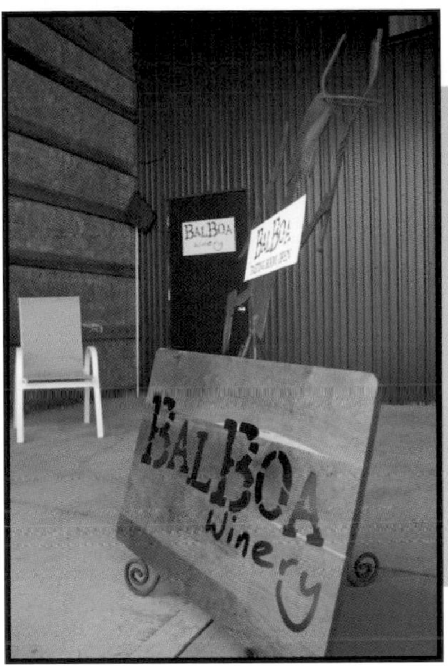

BALBOA WINERY
opened: 2006
winemaker(s): Tom Glase
location: 4169 Peppers Bridge Road, Walla Walla, WA 99362
phone: 509-301-6932
web: www.balboawinery.com
e-mail: info@balboawinery.com
picnic area: Yes
fee: Tasting fee may apply
hours: Open most weekends — call ahead
lat: 46.031921 **long:** -118.37886
satellite location: 7 South 4th, Walla Walla, WA 99362
satellite hours: Thursday through Sunday 11–4

DIRECTIONS: From Walla Walla, travel south for approximately three miles on Hwy 125. Turn left at the intersection of Hwy 125 and Old Milton Hwy. Turn right onto Peppers Bridge Rd. Balboa Winery is located at the corner of JB George Rd and Peppers Bridge Rd co-located at Beresan Winery.

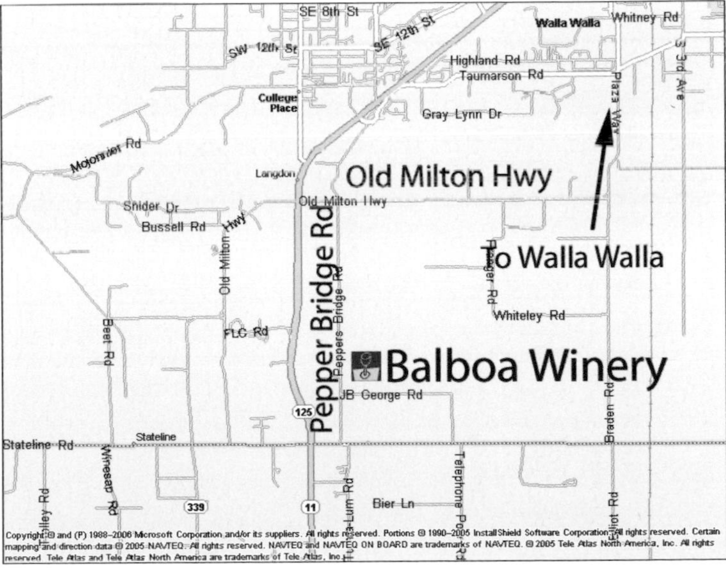

Saviah Cellars 7

Saviah Cellars celebrates tradition. Perhaps that is why an old wine press rests in its tasting room/winery located just south of Walla Walla. Reflecting winery owners Richard and Anita Funk's roots in Montana, the wines have names that pay tribute to their heritage: a white wine called "Star Meadows" is the location of the original family homestead; its "Une Vallée" red wine derives its name from their current family homestead; and its "Big Sky" *cuvée* gets its name from…well, you guessed it, Montana's official nickname. The Funks also produce a delicious blend of Columbia Valley merlot and cabernet sauvignon that they have dubbed "The Jack," named in honor of Anita's grandfather. The Saviah name itself comes from Anita's side of the family — it was her grandmother's middle name.

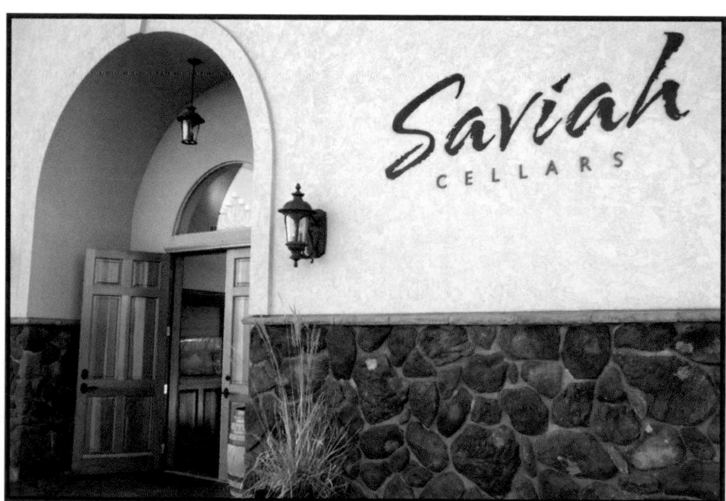

Richard and Anita moved from Montana in 1991 and, armed with a background in environmental science, Richard focused on water-quality programs. His work with the Walla Walla Health Department brought him in close contact with many of the local winemakers. He also found time to get his fingernails dirty by analyzing the soil around the valley. It wasn't long before the artistic side of winemaking captured his scientific mind. In 2000, his father and mother, Mike and Kay Funk, joined forces with Richard and Anita and launched Saviah Cellars.

With all winemaking, you have the rhythm of cycles, from harvest through crush, fermenting, and bottling. States Richard, "The winemaker's cycle repeats itself over and over, year after year. Always the same and always different ... and the winemaker is always hopeful." It's all about appreciating these cycles and understanding your role in them, whether it is making premium wine or keeping the family legacy alive. Saviah Cellars excels at both, and when you sample its "Une Vallée" red, you will come to understand that a lot more than chemistry and microbiology goes into creating this wine. It's a fusion of traditional values and good science.

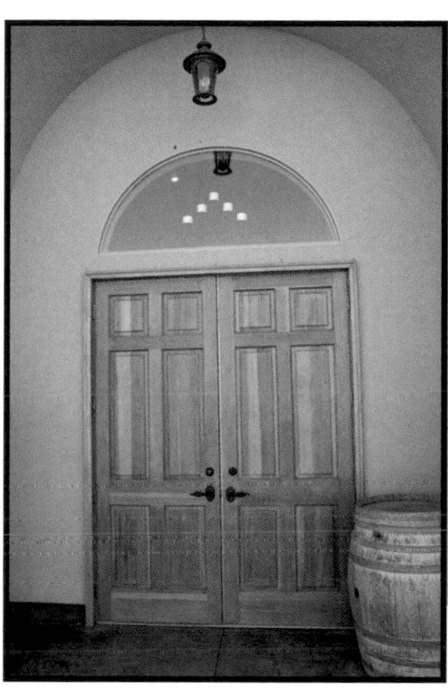

SAVIAH CELLARS
opened: 2000
winemaker(s): Richard Funk
location: 1979 JB George Road, Walla Walla, WA 99362
phone: 509-522-2181
web: www.saviahcellars.com
e-mail: info@saviahcellars.com
picnic area: Yes
tours: Yes
fee: Tasting fee
hours: Sunday through Thursday 11–5, Friday through Saturday 10–5
lat: 46.005412 **long:** -118.380841

DIRECTIONS: From Walla Walla, travel south for approximately three miles on Hwy 125. Turn left at the intersection of Hwy 125 and Old Milton Hwy. Turn right onto Peppers Bridge Rd. Saviah Cellars is located at the corner of JB George Rd and Peppers Bridge Rd.

When coming from the west on U.S. 12, go past Whitman Mission and turn right onto Last Chance Rd. Turn left onto Whitman Rd, and right on S College Ave. Continue to SR 125 (south) and turn right. Turn left at the first light you come to, Old Milton Hwy. Take a right onto Peppers Bridge Rd. Saviah Cellars is at the corner of Peppers Bridge Rd and JB George Rd.

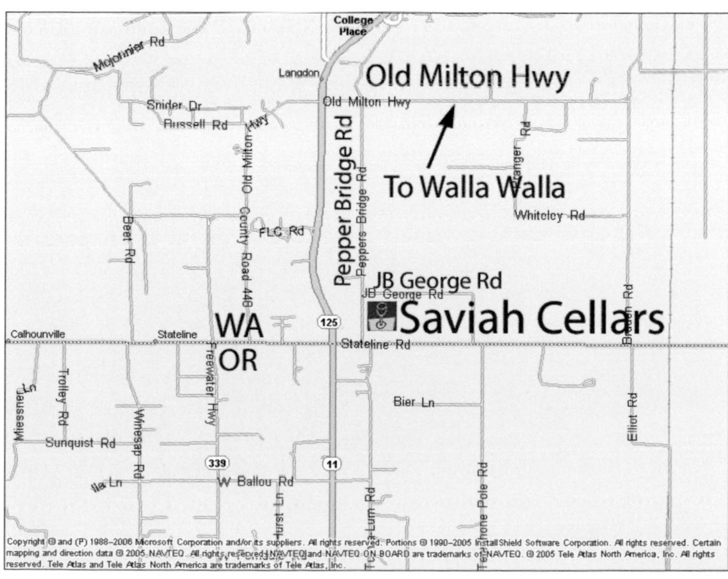

Waters Winery 8

When I first visited Waters Winery's tasting room in 2006, a sign on the door greeted visitors with "Sold Out — See You Next Vintage." The space was a postage-stamp-size room at the Train Depot building in downtown Walla Walla. Even though founder Jason Huntley and winemaker Jamie Brown were producing fewer than 1,000 cases of wine, I figured that these native Walla Wallans must have been doing something right.

Fast-forward to a few years later and now their tasting room has morphed into a beautiful state-of-the-art winemaking and tasting facility south of town on J.B. George Road. To say that Waters Winery has arrived is an understatement. As I snapped pictures from the hillside above the winery portion of the contemporary-style complex, it hit me that I was witnessing Jason's evolving strategy. In 2006, I got a glimpse of the newborn winery. Now, in 2010, I see a winery in its adolescent period. And I feel confident that a visit in 2014 will reveal the next stage — a maturing winery with estate vineyards at full production and an even larger community of loyal fans.

At the heart of Waters Winery's collection of wines is syrah. However, you won't find a blend of syrah from various vineyards in the Columbia Valley. Rather, you'll discover vineyard-designated syrah from Leonetti Cellar's Loess Vineyard, Pepper Bridge Vineyard, or the winery's own estate vineyard, Forgotten Hills. Why is this? I suspect it's because syrah is such a *terroir* expressive grape it allows Waters Winery to showcase a multitude of flavor profiles. This characteristic also permits winemaker Jamie Brown to create different styles of syrah, such as that made by fermenting the syrah with a small percentage of viognier, as it's done in the northern Rhône.

As I studied the calligraphy on the Waters label, wondering how the hell anyone could write so beautifully, the pourer reminded me that Waters Winery is behind the production of two other brands. In a brilliant move, Jason teamed with Gramercy Cellars' Greg Harrington to create their exclusive 100-case 21 Grams cabernet sauvignon as well as wallet-friendly Substance wines. With its periodic-table theme, Substance would allow me to easily "tweet" 140 characters of praise — if I had time to tweet. Waters wines, 21 Grams, and Substance are all reminders that the Washington wine scene is forever evolving. I could particularly appreciate this progress on this latest visit, with nary a "sold out" sign in sight.

WATERS WINERY
opened: 2006
winemaker(s): Jamie Brown
location: 1825 JB George Road, Walla Walla, WA 99362
phone: 509-525-1590
web: www.waterswinery.com
e-mail: via website
picnic area: Yes
wheelchair access: Yes
fee: Tasting fee may apply
hours: Friday and Saturday 10–5, or by appointment
lat: 46.005429 **long:** -118.374453

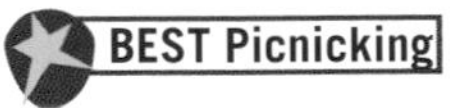

DIRECTIONS: From downtown Walla Walla follow Rose St. to 9th St. and turn left — 9th St. becomes Hwy 125. Turn left on Old Milton Hwy and take the first right onto Peppers Bridge Rd. Drive about a half mile and turn left onto JB George Rd. Continue about 3/4 of a mile and turn right into Waters Winery. Follow the driveway through the vineyard to the winery and tasting room.

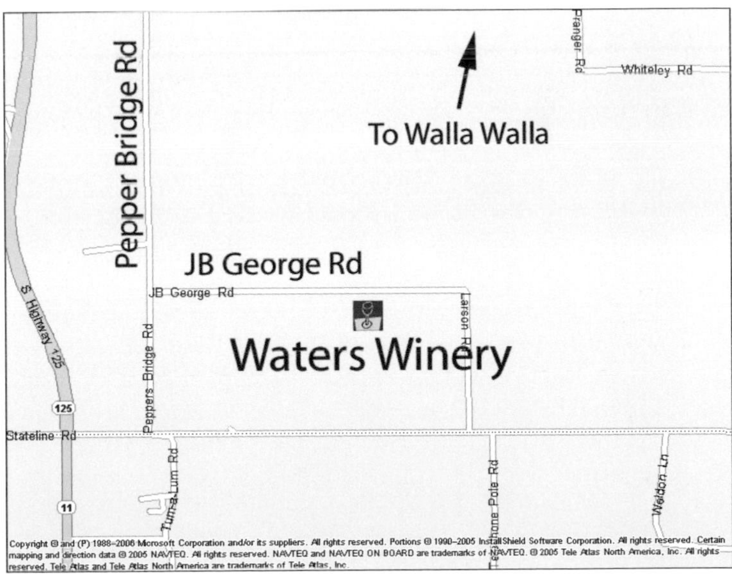

Va Piano Vineyards 9

Imagine drinking superb wine and contributing to a good cause while under the roof of a Tuscan-inspired estate. You can, simply by experiencing Va Piano Vineyards. Upon buying a bottle of Va Piano's "Bruno's Blend" at the vineyards, a portion of your purchase goes to a charitable organization, such as an African-based charity that supports children orphaned by AIDS. But how does a medium-priced wine get the name of "Bruno," and why an African-based charity?

The answers have their roots in the mid-'90s, when Va Piano's proprietor and winemaker, Justin Wylie, attended Gonzaga University's Florence campus during his senior year. There, Justin met and befriended the Rev. Bruno Segatta, a Catholic priest and assistant dean of the Florence program. Bruno, as students and friends alike know him, is also an avid painter and ardent contributor to a variety of charities for developing countries. Routinely, he contributes half the proceeds of his art sales to such causes. Thus, when Justin and his wife, Liz, sought to name their wine, it seemed right to name it "Bruno's Blend" and feature Bruno's artwork on the label. What's more, the idea of contributing toward one of Bruno's charities was only fitting.

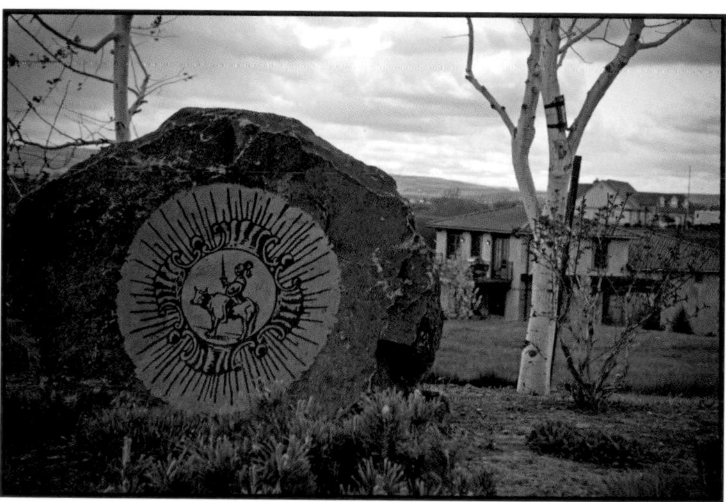

The 7,500-square-foot, Tuscan-inspired winery and tasting room features timber-beamed ceilings, a red-tile roof, earth-toned stucco, and distressed alder doors. The colors, textures, and quality of materials hark back to Justin's time in Tuscany. Inside the tasting room, Bruno's artwork graces Va Piano's walls, and the décor's warm earth tones and the staff's relaxed style make you feel right at home. It is the perfect setting in which to experience "Bruno's Blend" as well as Va Piano's other wines: a citrusy, crisp sauvignon blanc; a full-bodied, intensely flavored syrah; and a complex, multilayered cabernet sauvignon. However, to savor the moment (and the wine), you need to keep Va Piano Vineyards' motto in mind: *Chi va piano, va sano e va lantano*, which translates to "He who goes slowly, goes safely and goes far." Thus the name "Va Piano," or "go slowly," reminds us to swirl, observe the dark red color, take in the aroma, and concentrate on some amazing tastes.

VA PIANO VINEYARDS
opened: 2003
winemaker(s): Justin Wylie
location: 1793 JB George Road, Walla Walla, WA 99362
phone: 509-529-0900
web: www.vapianovineyards.com
e-mail: info@vapianovineyards.com
picnic area: Yes
gift shop: Yes
fee: Tasting fee refundable with purchase
hours: Friday and Saturday 11–5, or by appointment
lat: 46.005432 **long:** -118.373125

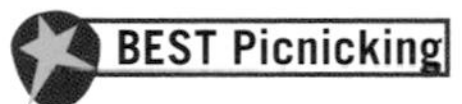

DIRECTIONS: **From Walla Walla**, travel south for approximately three miles on Hwy 125. Turn left at the intersection of Hwy 125 and Old Milton Hwy. Turn right onto Peppers Bridge Rd. Turn left onto JB George Rd and go about half a mile. Va Piano Vineyards is on the right.

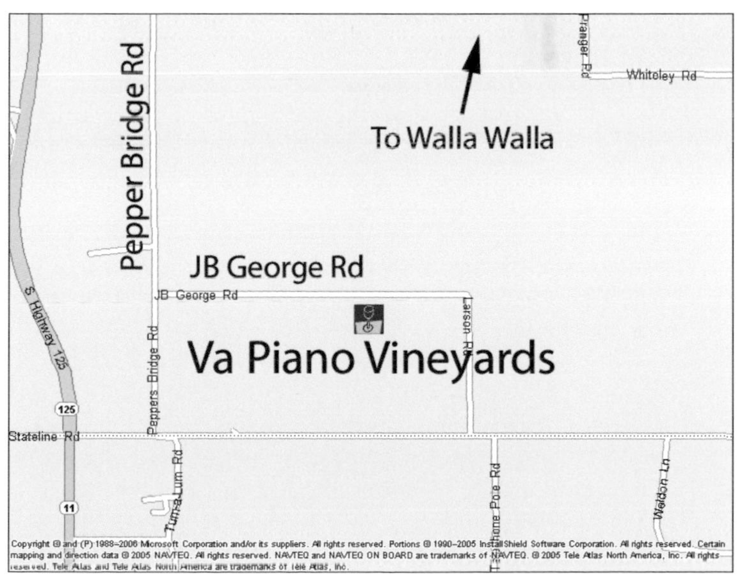

Northstar Winery 10

Northstar's focus is on merlot. Not just your garden-variety merlot, but ultrapremium merlot sourced from the best vineyards in Washington using their finest grapes. Merlot, a black-skinned grape that originated in France back in the 1700s, is often called Bordeaux's other red-wine grape, cabernet sauvignon being the signature grape of the region. However, here's a little secret that tends to raises an eyebrow or two: The number-one grape produced in Bordeaux is merlot, not cabernet sauvignon.

Sporting tinted glasses and a hair style reminiscent of U2's Bono, winemaker David "Merf" Merfeld meets the challenge of blending the best-of-the-best merlot grapes with other Bordeaux-derived varieties, including cabernet sauvignon, petit verdot, and cabernet franc, to produce 90+ point award winners. Words such as "intense," "muscular," "chocolate," and "licorice" come to mind when I taste Northstar's prized merlots. It's all in the blending, and Merf draws upon what he dubs a "spice rack" of varieties to create merlot-based wines. "Declassified" wines bearing the Stella Maris label are sold at more wallet-friendly prices. Northstar's lone white wine, a semillon affectionately known to locals as "Stella," bears the Stella Blanca label.

Located just south of Walla Walla, within a stone's throw of Pepper Bridge Winery and Tertulia Cellars, Northstar offers a commanding view of the distant Blue Mountains. These mountains provide most of the water for the valley's 1,200 acres of *Vitis vinifera*, including the 14 acres of grapes growing next to the winery (take a wild guess at the variety). Ste. Michelle Wine Estates, the parent company of Northstar, is all about elegance, and this is in evidence in Northstar's stylish tasting room and state-of-the-art production facility. The commodious tasting room offers plenty of space to mingle with side doors leading outside to a spacious patio, where live music often fills the air during event weekends.

Be sure to ask a staff person if you can take a peek at Northstar's production area. From a side door, you look down into the winemaking area. By most standards, the facility is huge, with mammoth stainless steel tanks lining the walls like sentinel soldiers. From this vantage point, it's easy to imagine Merf and his production team blending great wines from their industrial-size spice racks. It's also kept as spotless and well organized as a hospital operating room. Why, you could eat off the floor…but don't. They'd have to "cut you off" back in the tasting room.

NORTHSTAR WINERY
opened: 1992
winemaker(s): David 'Merf' Merfeld
location: 1736 JB George Road, Walla Walla, WA 99362
phone: 509-525-6100
web: www.northstarmerlot.com
e-mail: info@northstarmerlot.com
picnic area: Yes
gift shop: Yes
tours: Yes
fee: Tasting fee; 10% discount on purchase
hours: Monday through Saturday 10 4, Sunday 11–4, or by appointment
lat: 46.005707 **long:** -118.370804

BEST Gift Shop, Views, Picnicking and Eats

DIRECTIONS: From downtown Walla Walla, take SR-125 (south) [S 9th Ave.] for about four miles. Turn left onto Old Milton Hwy and continue for about half a mile. Turn right onto Pepper Bridge Rd and drive one mile. Turn left at JB George Rd then drive about 0.5 miles. At the end of the road, turn left onto limited access road. Drive through grapevine-lined lane and turn right at first driveway to Northstar Winery.

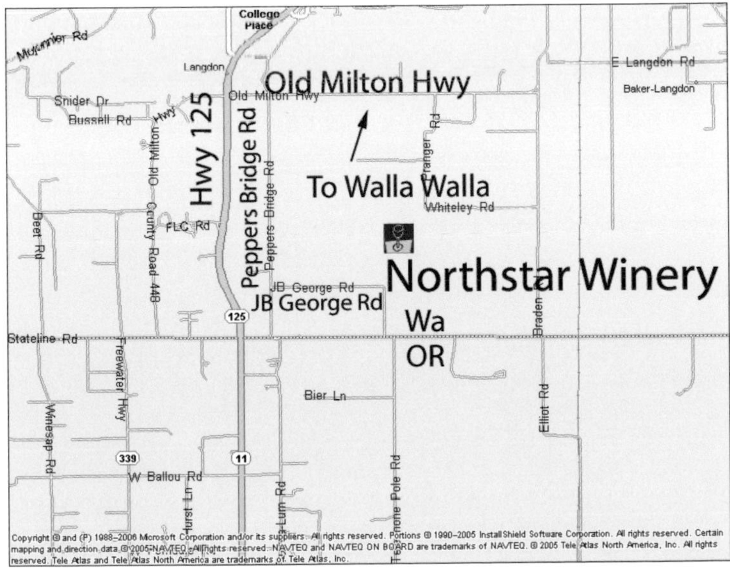

Pepper Bridge Winery 11

As you approach Pepper Bridge Winery, you are likely to spot a Swiss flag flying above this handsome tri-level estate and winery. No, you haven't left the U.S.; the flag honors the home country of Pepper Bridge winemaker Jean-François Pellet. It was in Switzerland that Jean-François honed his winemaking skills, beginning at his family's winery/vineyard and later working in Spain.

The wonderful thing about Pepper Bridge is the team of people who have come together to create an integrated winery, working cohesively from "grape buds to bottle." This team is composed of managing partners, viticulturists, winemakers, marketing and sales staff, and tasting-room hosts. Whomever you visit with, you are struck by their professionalism and dedication to Pepper Bridge Winery. You come to understand that the winery is more than the personality of one individual — it is about an organization.

The winery/tasting room sits on a hill on the southern edge of Walla Walla, with Northstar Winery within view to the northeast. The hill provides a panoramic vista of the Blue Mountains, but the location was chosen to take advantage of gravity's force. The three-story production facility allows harvested grapes to gently flow from top to bottom, from destemming to fermentation. It is this design and attention to detail that is responsible for Pepper Bridge's award-winning 100 percent Walla Walla estate merlots and cabernet sauvignons.

Pepper Bridge's quaint tasting room, which sits next to the production facility, possesses a charming "French country" feel inside and out. The absence of a gift shop is intentional — the wine is center stage here. At $8, the tasting fee here is a bit steep, but it goes toward any purchases made. Tasting-room manager Lisa Schmidt can speak in-depth about Pepper Bridge wines, as well as Walla Walla winemaking in general, having spent most of her life in Walla Walla Valley.

WineTrails Northwest rarely advocates joining a particular winery's wine club, but we make an exception with the Pepper Bridge Vine Club. Using an innovative approach, Pepper Bridge Winery sells vines to its Vine Club members at the cost of $150 per year. For that fee, members receive a bottle of wine, a certificate of ownership, and a "hands-on" day in the Pepper Bridge Vineyard, where they learn pruning, thinning, and harvesting techniques. What's more, your name is prominently displayed on your vine. Now that's a different kind of wine club…*vive la différence*!

PEPPER BRIDGE WINERY
opened: 2000
winemaker(s): Jean-Francois Pellet
location: 1704 JB George Road,
Walla Walla, WA 99362
phone: 509-525-6502
web: www.pepperbridge.com
e-mail: info@pepperbridge.com
picnic area: Yes
tours: Yes
fee: Tasting fee refundable with purchase
hours: Daily 10–4
lat: 46.005711 **long:** -118.369476
satellite location: 14810 NE 145th Street; Building A-3, Hollywood Schoolhouse, Woodinville, WA 98072
satellite hours: Monday through Sunday 11–5

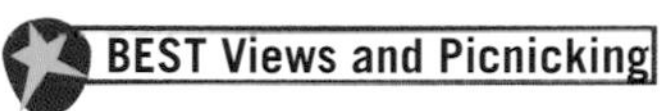

DIRECTIONS: From downtown Walla Walla, take SR-125 (south) [S 9th Ave.] for about 4 miles. Turn left onto Old Milton Hwy and continue for about half a mile. Turn right onto Peppers Bridge Rd and drive one mile. Turn left at JB George Rd and drive about .5 miles. At the end of the road, turn left onto limited access road. Drive through grapevine-lined lane and continue straight to Pepper Bridge Winery.

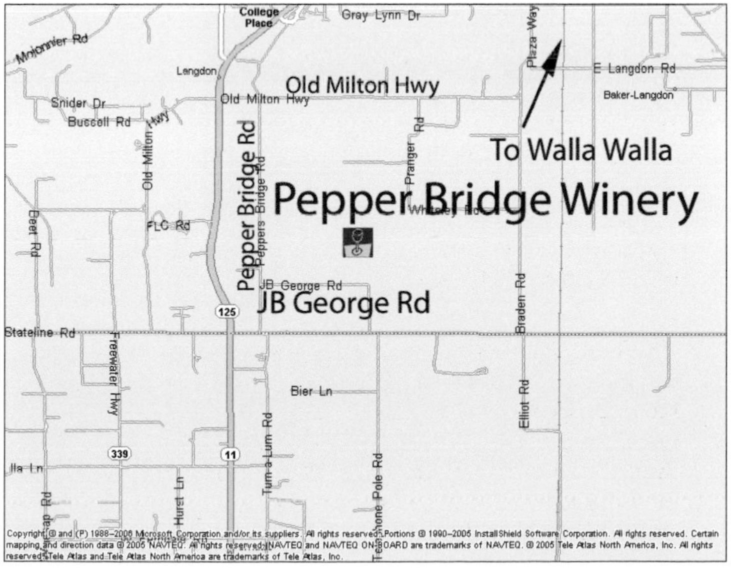

Castillo de Feliciana Vineyard and Winery 12

Rarely does the WineTrail Guy gush over a particular winery. After all, my motto is to leave it up to my readers to discover their own preferences. However, in the case of upstart Castillo de Feliciana Vineyard and Winery, I will make an exception to the rule and strongly recommend that you allow time for this gem. Here's why.

First, owners Sam and Deborah Castillo made one brilliant move in getting their new winery off the ground. They hired young winemaker Ryan Raber. It wasn't by accident or a chance meeting at a Walla Walla soiree that they glommed onto Ryan. Rather, they all share a common place of origin — the lovely hamlet of Duvall, Washington, outside of Seattle. It was there that Sam Castillo established his dental practice and became affectionately known to locals as "Dr. Sam." The Castillos knew Ryan had graduated near the top of his class from Walla Walla Community College's Institute for Enology and Viticulture program in 2005. And they appreciated all the medals and awards his wines received when he was chief winemaker for Tertulia Cellars. But more than that, I suspect it was his youthful energy and good character that won their hearts.

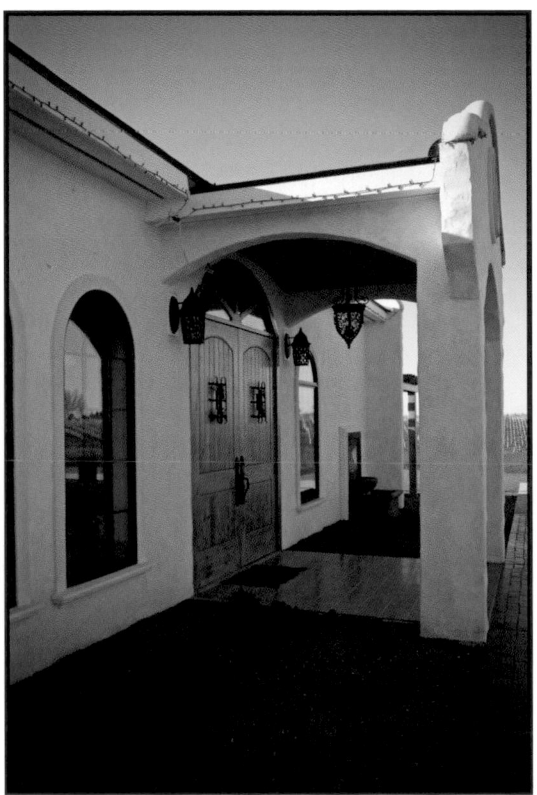

The winery itself lies just over the state line south of Walla Walla and features a Mediterranean style that brings to mind the red-tile-roofed abodes in southern Spain overlooking the blue Atlantic. In this case, however, the view from the house features a maturing vineyard surrounding the property. In keeping with the Castillos' Spanish heritage, their wines lean toward the varieties of the Iberian Peninsula with wines such as tempranillo, albariño, and red blends made in a style suggestive of Spain's Priorat region and comprising a healthy dose of grenache (*garnacha*).

Let me suggest that you make Castillo de Feliciana the last stop on your day's tour. Just outside the tasting room are an open fire pit, inviting chairs, and a view of the Blue Mountains in the distance, reminding one of the mountains found in Spain's Rioja region. Sitting there, soaking in the moment and sampling their tempranillo, I found myself wanting to suggest to Sam or Deb that they start serving paella — it would be the ultimate dish to pair with this wine!

CASTILLO DE FELICIANA VINEYARD AND WINERY
opened: 2009
winemaker(s): Ryan Raber
location: 85728 Telephone Pole Road, Milton-Freewater, OR 97862
phone: 541-558-3656
web: www.castillodefeliciana.com
e-mail: info@castillodefeliciana.com
picnic area: Yes
wheelchair access: Yes
weddings: Yes
tours: Yes
fee: Tasting fee refundable with purchase
hours: Friday, Saturday and Sunday 11–5
lat: 45.994770 **long:** -118.366502

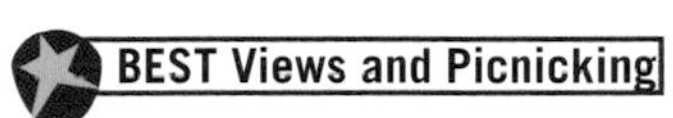

DIRECTIONS: From downtown Walla Walla (2nd Ave.) go west on W Poplar St for a half mile. Turn left onto SR-125 [S 9th Ave.] and proceed 5.2 miles. Turn left onto Stateline Rd and travel one mile. Turn right onto Telephone Pole Rd and arrive at 85728 Telephone Pole Rd.

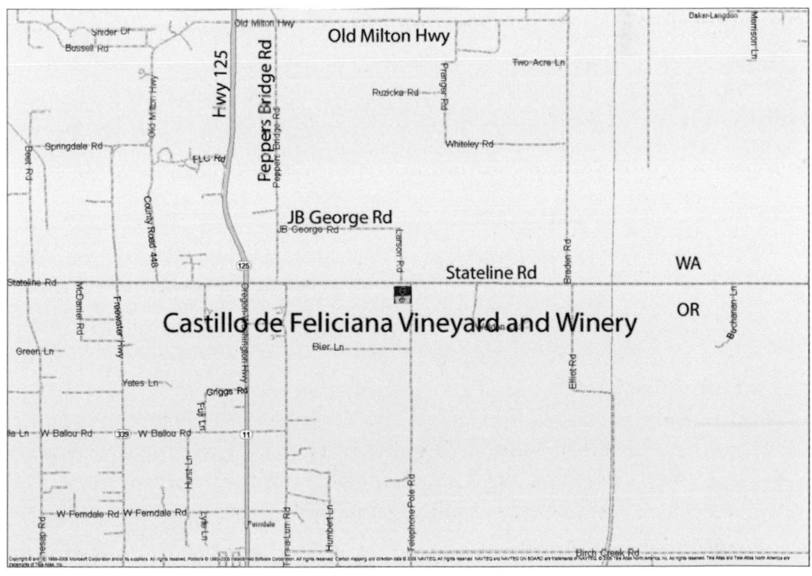

Dusted Valley Vintners 13

Named by *Wine Press Northwest* as 2010 Washington Winery of the Year, Dusted Valley Vintners is the story of two families from Wisconsin — the Johnsons and the Braunels. In 2003, they moved to Walla Walla, driven by a love affair with Northwest wines. Chad Johnson's background includes a degree in food science; Corey Braunel grew up on a ginseng farm in northern Wisconsin. In addition to sharing a passion for making wine, it turns out that Chad and Corey also share a familial connection. Chad is married to Janet, and Corey is married to her sister Cindy.

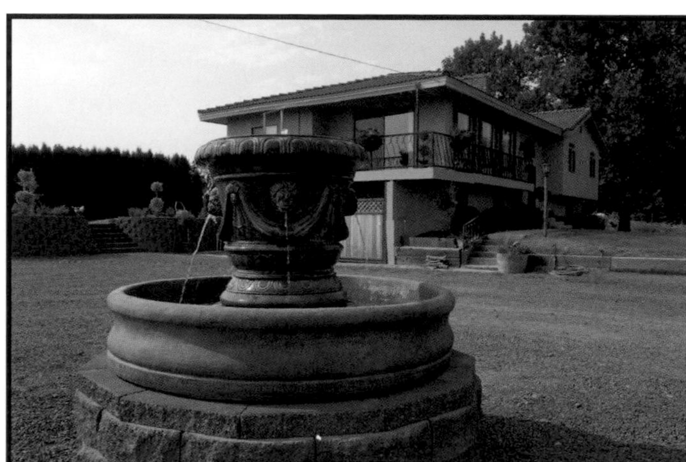

Given their Badger background, it may come as no surprise that Corey and Chad use white oak (*Quercus alba*; aka American oak) from Wisconsin to barrel-age some of their wines. Although other well-established wineries outside Walla Walla rely on American oak (e.g., the renowned Silver Oak Winery in California uses American oak exclusively), it is rare to find a winery in the valley venturing beyond the standard French oak. But Corey and Chad must be on to something with this American oak thing. Their 2006 Reserve Cabernet Sauvignon, which features oak from Wisconsin, grabbed a gold medal at the 2009 Seattle Wine Awards, leading many to speculate that the exceptionally tightly grained American oak imparts unique flavors to the Walla Walla reds.

In addition to the winery, the families own 90 acres of vineyards in the Walla Walla Valley, giving them control over their growing portfolio of wines, from bud break to bottling. The fact that the 90 acres of vineyards are scattered among four different locations provides distinct flavor profiles for their fundamental ingredient — the grapes.

With a wide assortment of Dusted Valley Vintners wines to sample — including my personal favorite, the "Stained Tooth" syrah — you'll want to budget plenty of time to taste. If time permits, you can retreat to the outside patio and enjoy a bottle of wine with the Blue Mountains in the background. No worries if you forgot your corkscrew. This is a cork-free zone. Chad and Corey elected to go with a screw-cap closure on all their wines for quality purposes. As the fun-loving brothers-in-law like to say, "Crack that cap and enjoy a bottle of Dusted Valley wine." However, if you find yourself imbibing their wine sans food, there is one edible you may wish you had packed. Yep, you guessed it, Wisconsin cheese.

DUSTED VALLEY VINTNERS
opened: 2003
winemaker(s): Chad Johnson and Corey Braunel
location: 1248 Old Milton Highway, Walla Walla, WA 99362-8174
phone: 509-525-1337
web: www.dustedvalley.com
e-mail: info@dustedvalley.com
picnic area: Yes
tours: Yes
fee: Tasting fee refundable with purchase
hours: Friday and Monday 1–5; Saturday 11–5; Sunday 12–5, or by appointment
lat: 46.024052 **long:** -118.350308
satellite location: 14465 Woodinville Redmond Rd. NE, Woodinville, WA 98072
satellite hours: Daily 12–5

DIRECTIONS: From downtown Walla Walla, take SR-125 (south) [S 9th Ave.] for about four miles. Turn left onto Old Milton Hwy and arrive at 1248 Old Milton Hwy — Dusted Valley Vintners is on the left.

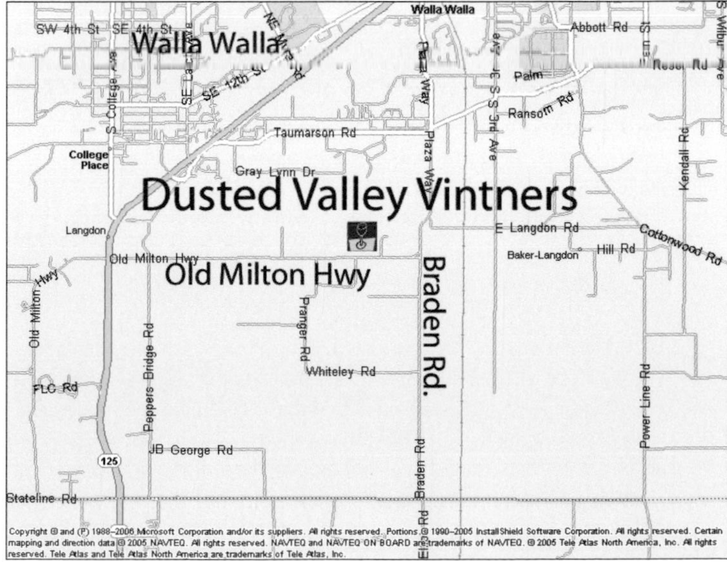

Isenhower Cellars 14

"Go, Butler!" exclaimed Olivia, one of the Isenhowers' three daughters. The little blond-haired girl was dressed in a Butler Bulldog cheerleading outfit and she, along with friends and family, was gearing up for the 2010 Final Four match-up with Michigan State. It turns out that her mom, Denise Isenhower, graduated from Butler University, hence the Bulldog shout-out.

While Olivia doodled with crayons, her dad, Brett Isenhower, described the family's 1998 move from Colorado to make wine, equating it to "diving head first into shallow water." But the couple came armed with backgrounds in chemistry (both Denise and Brett were pharmacists) as well as Brett's successful business experience in concocting homemade beer. An exhaustive review of wine-growing areas (Brett is very analytical) found Walla Walla to be more than just a dot on the map. As Brett put it, "Walla Walla is the most attractive town in Eastern Washington," referring not just to its climate and soil, but to the town's general culture, architecture and school system. At that, Olivia rattled off something in Spanish, to which 40-something Brett smiled and explained that she attends a bilingual grade school. Proof positive that they had chosen wisely.

With more than 10 years of winemaking experience, Brett continues to evolve — and experiment with — his chosen craft. His current releases feature Bordeaux and Rhône varietal wines that grow exceptionally well in the Columbia Valley. Many of his wines have been christened after flowers, for example, "Wild Alfalfa" (syrah), "Batchelor's Button" (cabernet sauvignon), and "Red Paintbrush" (Bordeaux blend). However, there's nothing "garden variety" about these wines. Grabbing my attention was the wonderfully balanced white Rhône blend of roussanne and viognier called "Snapdragon," bearing a stunning label. Brett proudly pointed out that the label is the creation of local artist Squire Broel.

Now, with a second tasting room in Woodinville, which requires weekend jaunts to the west side of the state, and 3.9 acres of Malbec to tend in their own Indie Vineyard just outside the winery/tasting room, the Isenhowers' lives are in overdrive. But they do have one vital quality that fuels them: their passion. That energy combined with their exceptional wines is a formula for success. It explains why they are not willing to be content with their current achievements, but are forever tweaking, experimenting and evolving their winery to achieve further success. Speaking of which, Butler won!

Brett Isenhower

ISENHOWER CELLARS
opened: 1998
winemaker(s): Brett Isenhower
location: 3471 Pranger Road, Walla Walla, WA 99362-7307
phone: 509-526-7896
web: www.isenhowercellars.com
e-mail: info@isenhowercellars.com
wheelchair access: Yes
gift shop: Yes
tours: Yes
fee: Tasting fee refundable with purchase
hours: Monday through Friday 10–4, Saturdays 10:30–5
lat: 46.022913 **long:** -118.360427
satellite location: 15007 Woodinville-Redmond Road, Woodinville, WA 98057
satellite hours: Friday through Sunday 12–5

DIRECTIONS: From downtown Walla Walla, take SR-125 (south) [S 9th Ave.] for about four miles. Turn left onto Old Milton Hwy and continue for about 0.75 miles. Turn right onto Pranger Rd. Isenhower Winery is immediately to your left.

When coming from the west on US-12, go past Whitman Mission and turn right onto Last Chance Rd. Turn left onto Whitman Rd, and right on S College Ave. Continue to SR 125 (south) and turn right. Turn left at the first traffic light you come to at Old Milton Hwy. Isenhower Cellars is on your right, on the corner of Old Milton Hwy and Pranger Rd.

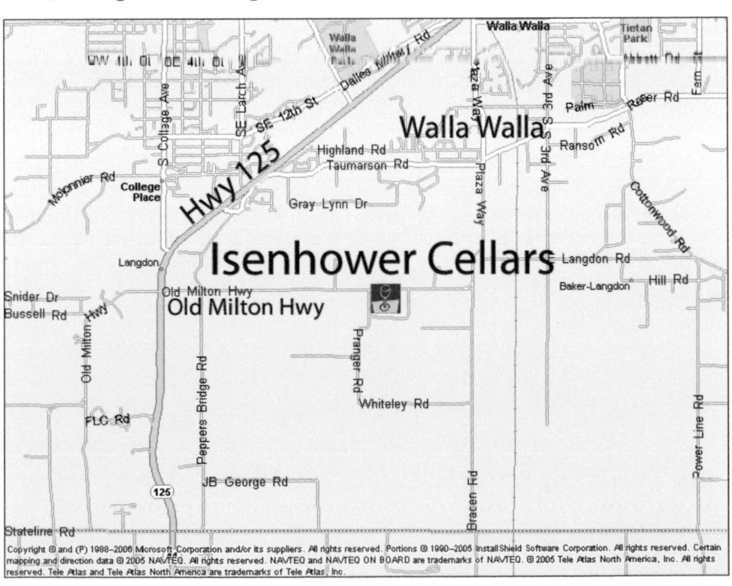

Rulo Winery 15

The sign above the front door states: "Relive a memory; realize a dream." Realizing a dream, though, often requires hard work and some serious intestinal fortitude. Such is the case for Rulo Winery owners Kurt and Vicki Schlicker, who launched their winery in 2000. By day, Kurt shares an anesthesia practice and is typically on duty at Providence St. Mary Medical Center in Walla Walla. Come fall, however, his and Vicki's attention turns to crush: the 24/7 rush to harvest, crush, destem, ferment, and press their grapes. At crush, Kurt's focus switches from gases that are inhaled to gas that's released by fermenting grapes, CO2, along with ethyl alcohol — a different form of anesthetic.

Unlike many of its big-bucks winery neighbors, Rulo Winery embodies America's heritage of hard-working, do-it-yourself individuals. You won't find tasting room staff bedecked in logo-emblazoned casual wear here. Instead, you find Kurt and Vicki working the tasting room, pouring and explaining their winemaking process to loyal fans and newly converted Rulo disciples. Even though the winery is typically open on Saturdays, it's best to call ahead before dropping in.

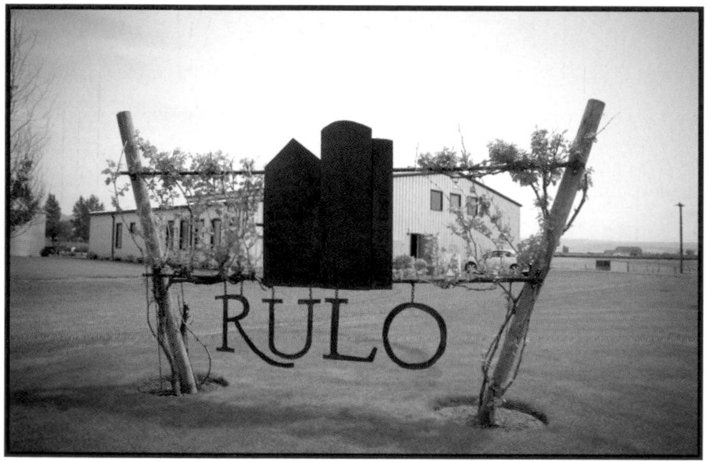

As you sample your way through the Schlickers' wonderfully delicious portfolio of reds, whites, and rosés, note the vineyards Rulo Winery gets its grapes from. They are among the who's who of Columbia Valley grape growers. These growers are scattered across a wide expanse of land. This means he must put many miles on his vehicle, checking out his blocks of grapes, talking to the growers about matters of irrigation and pest control, and determining when to pick.

The name "Rulo" harks to the Schlickers' family farm, located close to the Rulo grain elevator on the Washington side of the state line. That grain elevator was the inspiration for Rulo's nice logo: a simple line drawing of the elevator's silos. There are many grain-elevator stations strewn about the valley, and each one has a name. Locals know your location by your proximity to the nearest grain elevator. Kurt and Vicki refer to this as "farmer GPS." Like other community members, the Schlickers embody a work ethic that is so much a part of our heritage. As I exited through the door, I again looked up at the sign posted above it and thought of another quotation, an anonymous scribbler's words of wisdom I once read, that would be every bit as apropos for Rulo Winery: "There is no elevator to success. You have to take the stairs."

Kurt Schlicker

RULO WINERY
opened: 2000
winemaker(s): Kurt J. Schlicker
location: 3525 Pranger Road, Walla Walla, WA 99362
phone: 509-525-RULO
web: www.rulowinery.com
e-mail: schlick@pocketinet.com
wheelchair access: Yes
tours: Yes
fee: Tasting fee may apply
hours: Typically open Saturdays 12–3; call ahead
lat: 46.022375 **long:** -118.360433

DIRECTIONS: From downtown Walla Walla, take SR-125 (south) [S 9th Ave.] for about four miles. Turn left onto Old Milton Hwy and continue for about .75 miles. Turn right onto Pranger Rd. Rulo Winery is on the left past Isenhower Winery.

Coming from the west on U.S. 12, continue past Whitman Mission and turn right onto Last Chance Rd. Turn left onto Whitman Rd, and right on S College Ave. Turn right at SR 125 (south). Turn left at the first traffic light you encounter (Old Milton Hwy). Turn right onto Pranger Rd. and find Rulo Winery on your left.

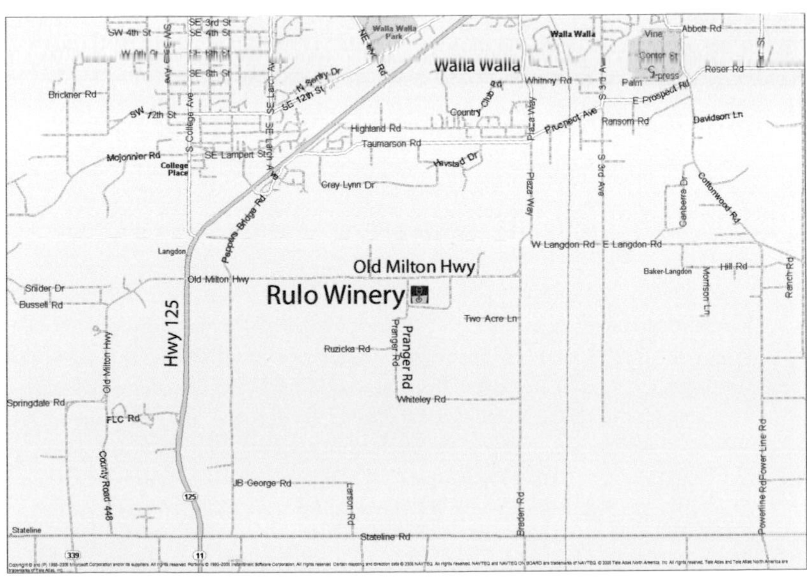

Tertulia Cellars 16

Tertulia — a word of Spanish origin describing a social gathering with literary or artistic overtones, especially in Iberia or Latin America. — Wikipedia.com

Stevie Johnson, sales and marketing director for Tertulia Cellars, pointed to its new wine label and asked, "What do you think?" My eyes focused on the prominent circle of children holding hands, and I was happy to see Tertulia's signature "circle of friends" logo still on the label. The illustration symbolizes a friendly gathering reminiscent of a neighborhood block party involving potluck food and lots to drink. The fact that the boys have two legs each and the girls have only one apiece adds to the quirky charm of the label.

Jim O'Connell, the Arizona-based owner of Tertulia Cellars, envisioned the creation of a winery that serves as a place of "social gathering of friends" — and that vision is realized in this architecturally pleasing space (which includes state-of-the-art winemaking equipment, including an indoor crush pad). The facility and tasting room are downright beautiful, and the Mediterranean orange and red colors only add to the venue's warmth. Moreover, although it was winter during my visit, I could easily imagine the outdoor patio filled with folks enjoying a summer evening, complete with good food, background music, and Tertulia Cellars wine to enjoy.

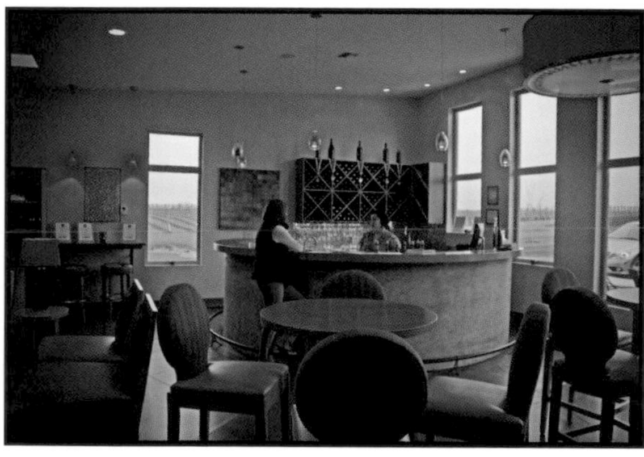

The dazzling wines I sampled during my visit are of a decided southern Rhône persuasion, with viognier, syrah, grenache, and Mourvèdre varietals on offer. The harmonious, full-bodied Les Collines syrah (I relish that midpalate taste explosion followed by a long finish) had me reading the label's fine print to appreciate this wine's pedigree. But there are also wonderfully rich Bordeaux varietals, including a sumptuous cabernet sauvignon. This wine would be perfect paired right away with that evening's whisky burgers or left to age for years in your basement cellar.

New winemaker Quentin Mylet has the enviable challenge of producing more than 4,000 cases of wine per year for the growing number of Tertulia Cellars' fans. Armed with an enology and viticulture degree from nearby Walla Walla Community College (he was the recipient of the Leonetti, the Dr. Walter J. Clore and the John Farmer scholarships), Quentin is expected to rely more on Tertulia Cellars' estate fruit to craft an increasing mix of Rhône-style wines. I'm sure that to celebrate the release of his wines, there will be a gathering each spring in Walla Walla, complete with laughter, food, and wine — a tertulia in the truest sense.

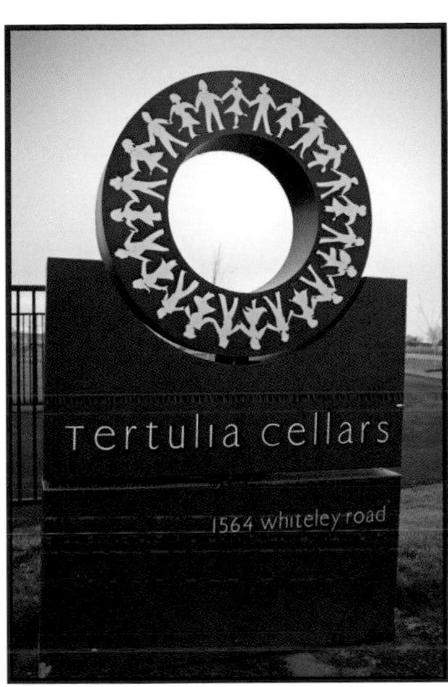

TERTULIA CELLARS
opened: 2007
winemaker(s): Quentin Mylet
location: 1564 Whiteley Road, Walla Walla, WA 99362
phone: 509-525-5700
web: www.tertuliacellars.com
e-mail: info@tertuliacellars.com
picnic area: Yes
wheelchair access: Yes
fee: Tasting fee refundable with purchase
hours: Thursday through Saturday 11–6, Sunday 11–5, or by appointment
lat: 46.013132 **long:** -118.357582

DIRECTIONS: From downtown Walla Walla, take S 2nd Ave. south to W Poplar St. and turn right. Go 0.5 miles to SR 125 (S 9th Ave.) and proceed 0.7 miles. Turn left (east) onto Plaza Way and travel 1.6 miles. Bear right (southwest) onto Braden Rd and proceed one mile. Turn right (west) onto Whiteley Rd and continue 0.2 miles to the winery.

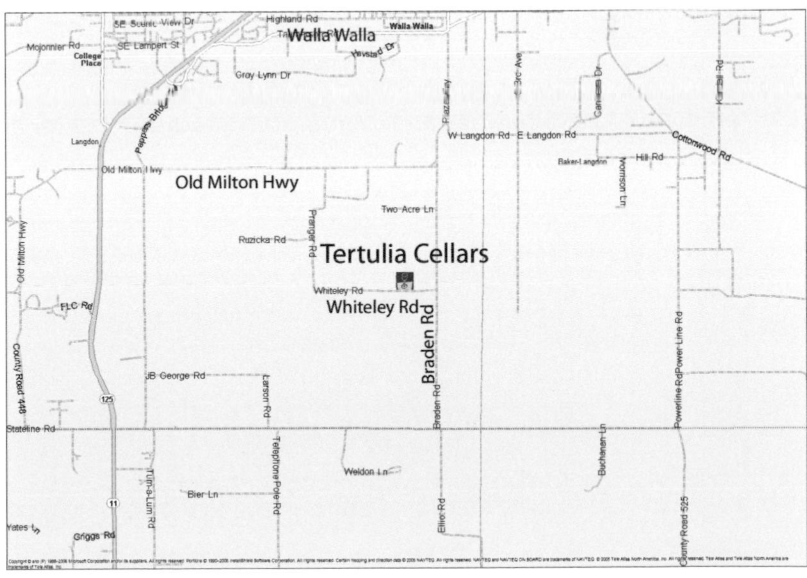

Trust Cellars 17

Steve Brooks has the best address in the valley — 1050 Merlot Drive — yet he doesn't make that particular varietal. How Steve, owner and one-man-band winemaker for Trust Cellars happened upon this address would make a Hollywood hit. Working in Atlanta for 19 years at CNN as a TV producer brought Steve little joy. At the age of 40, he had proven to himself and others that he had mastered his job, but the gloom of the news business and the constant travel were taking a toll. He sought a career that would allow him to spend more time with his two young girls and give him and his wife Lori, a television director also working at CNN, an opportunity to exercise their passion for food and wine. After all, this couple would plan tummy-tantalizing vacation itineraries focusing on the restaurants and foods they wanted to experience.

Steve Brooks

Steve knew he wanted to make wine, and by announcing to his coworkers and friends that he was quitting his executive job to become a winemaker, he was forced to make good on his promise. So in late 2001, spurred by a review of the American wine scene that included a *New York Times* article highlighting the winemaking virtues of Walla Walla, Steve and family packed their Volvo and headed west.

A visit to his Merlot Drive tasting room and winery finds a very relaxed Steve Brooks. Atlanta is now clearly in his rearview mirror, and he is happy with his decision to switch careers. Upon arrival, he discovered a community of winemakers willing to help by lending advice and equipment. He enrolled in the local Walla Walla Community College Institute for Enology and Viticulture and learned from the best. Not having the deep pockets to buy his own vineyards, Steve developed collaborative relationships with the region's premium grape growers. He notes that in exchange for him picking up the lunch tab, a local winemaker he admires told him the secrets of making rosé. Today, the only problem with Trust Cellars' cabernet franc rosé is that it sells out too quickly!

Uprooting your family from Atlanta, moving them to Walla Walla, and launching a new career takes a lot of guts. To do it, Steve had to place his trust in his family, his friends, and, ultimately, the one person he knows best — himself.

TRUST CELLARS
opened: 2007
winemaker(s): Steve Brooks
location: 1050 Merlot Drive, Walla Walla, WA 99362
phone: 509-529-4511
web: www.trustcellars.com
e-mail: steve@trustcellars.com
picnic area: Yes
fee: Tasting fee applies
hours: Thursday through Friday 11–4, Saturday 11–5, Sunday 11–4
lat: 46.063304 **long:** -118.335067

DIRECTIONS: From downtown Walla Walla, head southeast on S 5th Ave. toward W Alder St. Take a right onto W Alder St. and go 0.3 miles. Turn left at S 9th Ave. then continue 0.8 miles. Turn left at Plaza Way and go 1.6 miles to Braden Rd. Proceed 0.3 miles and turn left on Merlot Dr. at the winery's sign.

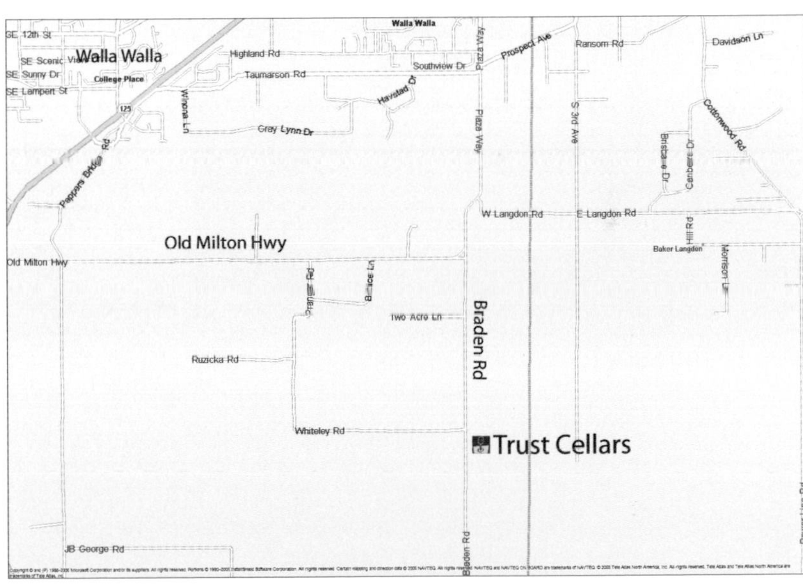

Gifford Hirlinger Winery 18

Located on Stateline Road on the south side of Walla Walla, Gifford Hirlinger Winery is literally a stone's throw — or a mere lob — from Oregon. Housed in an ultramodern building, the winery is the domain of to winemaker and co-owner Mike Berghan. The architecture is stunning and offers ample patio space to enjoy a bottle of wine with a front-row seat for viewing Mike's now-matured vineyard.

This is a family affair, complete with Mike's parents, his wife, Melissa, and assorted laughing children pitching in to assist. Resident border collies Chewy and Charlie also contribute to the process. I suspect that, besides looking adorable, the dogs keep the local deer from munching on the ripening grapes.

In early 2000, Mike made his mark on the Walla Walla wine scene with a red blend he appropriately named "Stateline Red," a Bordeaux marriage of estate cabernet and merlot. Berghan Vineyard also produces cabernet sauvignon, tempranillo, merlot, Malbec, petit verdot, and pinot gris. This is a hands-on operation: The Berghans' fingernails become brown from the soil, green from pruning, and purple from the crush. They've come to know the Walla Walla *terroir* intimately.

Visitors can choose from a variety of wines — primarily reds — to swirl and sip, but personally, I went straight for Mike's cabernet sauvignon, because I believe it showcases Walla Walla Valley black fruit so nicely. Rich, dark cherry flavors, tobacco notes, and hints of licorice with an exceptional finish are what I took away from this wine. Smacking my lips, I looked around for anything "grill worthy" to pair with this bold but tannin-tamed wine. Charlie and Chewy cocked their heads in curiosity at my strange gesture of appreciation.

Originally from Sandpoint, Idaho, Mike became incredibly bored while chasing the American dream at Smith Barney in San Francisco. He did what many of us only daydream of doing: He quit his high-paying job to get his hands dirty (literally) working for a vineyard management company in California. Eventually, he landed in Walla Walla, but that wasn't by chance; his ancestors homesteaded in the Walla Walla Valley. In fact, the name Gifford Hirlinger (GH for short) derives from his not-too-distant relatives. Yes, it's true that the name twists the tongue a bit, but my opinion of GH wines is not at all difficult to pronounce: liquid decadence.

Mike Berghan with Frank.

GIFFORD HIRLINGER WINERY
opened: 2001
winemaker(s): Mike Berghan
location: 1450 Stateline Road, Walla Walla, WA 99362
phone: 509-529-2075
web: www.giffordhirlinger.com
e-mail: wine@GiffordHirlinger.com
picnic area: Yes
fee: Tasting fee may apply
hours: Friday through Sunday 11–5, or by appointment
lat: 46.000845 **long:** -118.362626
satellite location: 14469 Woodinville-Redmond Road, Woodinville, WA 98072
satellite hours: Thursday through Monday 12–5

DIRECTIONS: From downtown Walla Walla, take SR 125 (south) [S 9th Ave.] for about four miles. Turn left onto Old Milton Hwy and continue for about one mile. Turn right onto Braden Rd and travel about 1.5 miles to Stateline Rd. Turn left and Gifford Hirlinger is found immediately on your left.

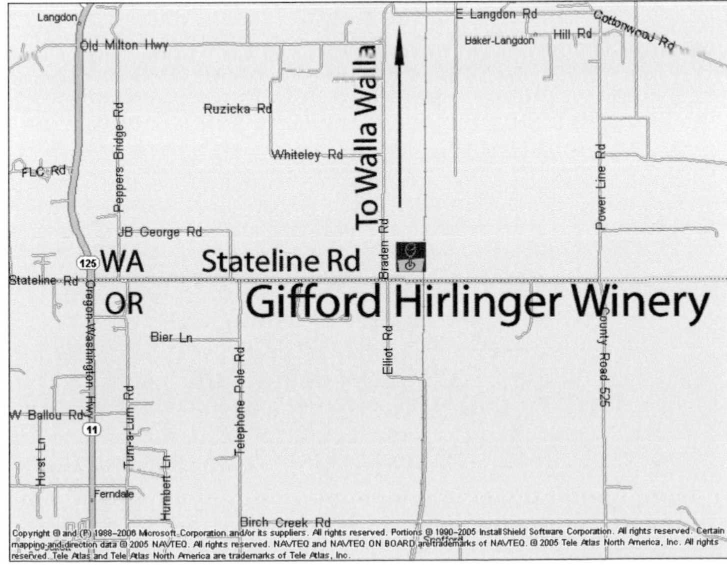

JLC Winery / Spofford Station 19

Cow tipping just got easier.

Back in 2005, the owner and winemaker of JLC Winery, Lynne Chamberlain, came up with a novel idea for recycling her spent cabernet and merlot grape skins (known as pomace). She began feeding these leftovers to her Angus cows at her Spofford Station farm. It turns out the cattle loved it, and Lynne noticed that the cattle not only gained weight but also seemed a little drowsy. The former 26brix restaurant in Walla Walla discovered Lynne's beef and soon began offering a $14 "Cow-bernet" burger. A herd of national media got wind of the story, and soon print publications such as *USA Today* and television news stations reported on the tale of the tipsy beef.

To appreciate JLC Winery is to know that Lynne Chamberlain is a farm girl at heart. Following a prolonged sojourn in Washington, D.C., she returned home to her family's 500-acre farm, located on the Oregon side of the Walla Walla Valley. It's where she grew up and it also is home to her celebrated 40-acre Spofford Station Vineyard. Along with the grapes, other crops such as mint and wheat are grown at the station. You might even find a few cases of uncorked Angus milling around.

WineTrail Note: The word "station" refers to locations where trains would stop and load farm produce for transport. Known as "stations" on the Oregon side, they are referred to as "grain elevators" in Washington. Built in the 1800s, the "grain train" still makes daily stops at the stations to load soft white wheat for transport to Portland and eventually on to markets in Asia.

JLC produces premium red wines, including Lynne's exclusive Spofford Station estate syrah and merlot wines. The label of her popular red table wine "Palette" features an angel enjoying her "angels' share" of wine. The original painting used for the label sold for $3,500 in a Portland benefit auction in 2006. As their own Angels Share Club member pamphlet explains, "In the days of old, before science grabbed attention, the winemaker left the cellar at evensong. His cellar rats continued to care for the precious elixirs as he rested. On returning, he noted that the juice in the barrel had been lowered. 'You have stolen my precious nectar!' The reply, 'No master, a mere sip is promised the Angels.' What is now called evaporation was known as 'Angels' Share.'"

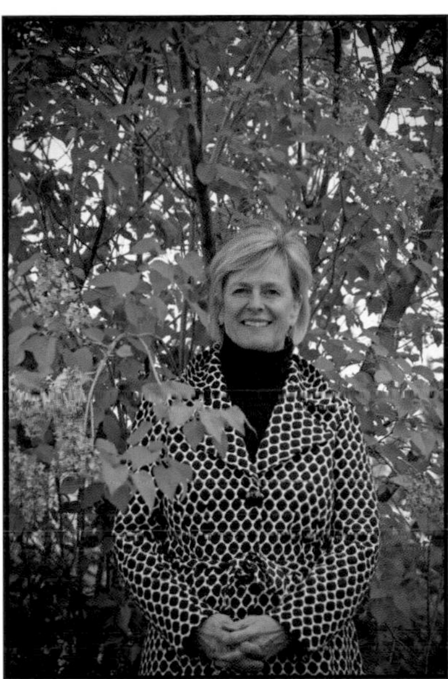
Lynne Chamberlain

JLC WINERY / SPOFFORD STATION
opened: 2002
winemaker(s): Lynne Chamberlain
location: 85131 Elliot Road,
Milton-Freewater, OR 97862
phone: 509-529-1398
web: www.jlcwinery.com
e-mail: info@jlcwinery.com
fee: Tasting fee refundable with purchase
hours: Friday 12–4, Saturday 11–4, or by appointment
lat: 45.9868881 **long:** -118.3405039

DIRECTIONS: From downtown Walla Walla take W Poplar St. west for 0.5 miles. Turn left (south) onto SR-125 [S 9th Ave.] and go 5.2 miles. Enter Oregon and keep straight on SR 11 for 1.8 miles. Turn left onto E Crocket Rd and go 0.2 miles. Turn left (north) onto Tum-a-Lum Rd for 0.1 miles. Turn right (East) onto Birch Creek Rd and drive 0.4 miles. Bear left (south) and continue of Birch Creek Rd for an additional 1.2 miles (the road will make several turns). At Elliot Rd turn left, the winery is about a quarter of a mile on the right.

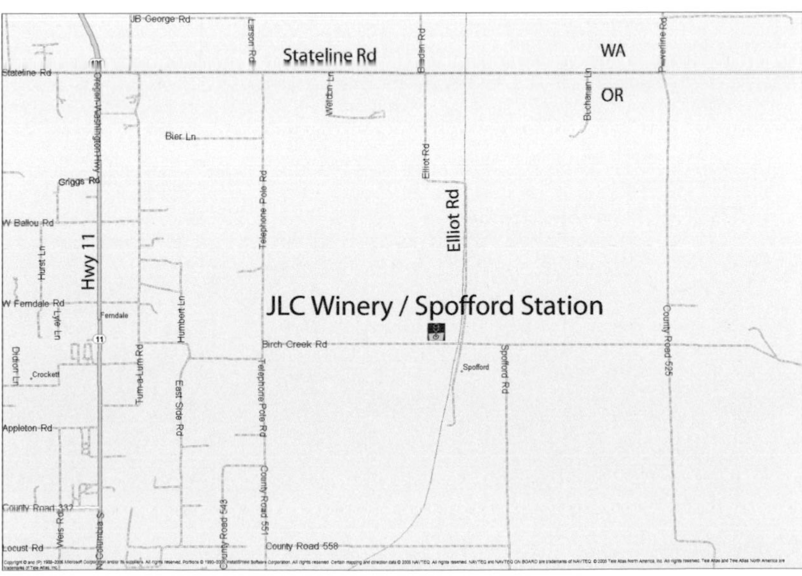

By-Appointment-Only

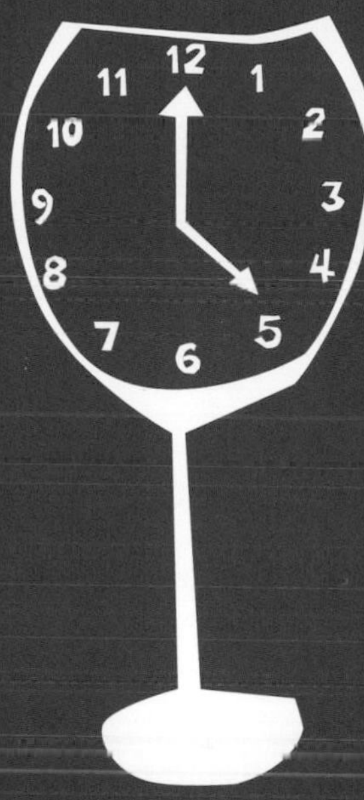

By-Appointment-Only Wineries WineTrail

Abeja

Throughout Walla Walla Valley, there are a number of wineries that are not open to the public but do welcome visitors who make an appointment. For experienced wine tourists, these wineries are a joy to visit. Why? Because you will have a slice of time to spend one-on-one with the winemaker, time to ask questions about their winemaking style, how they got their start, and the challenges they face. Often you'll be invited beyond the tasting room to sample wine right out of the barrel or tramp through the vineyard and get a free lesson in viticulture.

Call well in advance, though. Occasionally you can luck out with the "I'm just outside your gates and wondering if you are open" phone call, but in most cases, these wineries will need advance warning. By doing so, your reward will be one memorable experience. Cheers!

By-Appointment-Only Wineries

1 Abeja
2 Cadaretta
3 Couvillion Winery
4 Dumas Station Wines
5 Ensemble Cellars
6 Garrison Creek Cellars
7 Gramercy Cellars
8 Long Shadows Vintners
9 Patrick M. Paul Vineyards
10 Revelry Vintners
11 Robison Ranch Cellars
12 Tru Cellars
13 Tranche Cellars

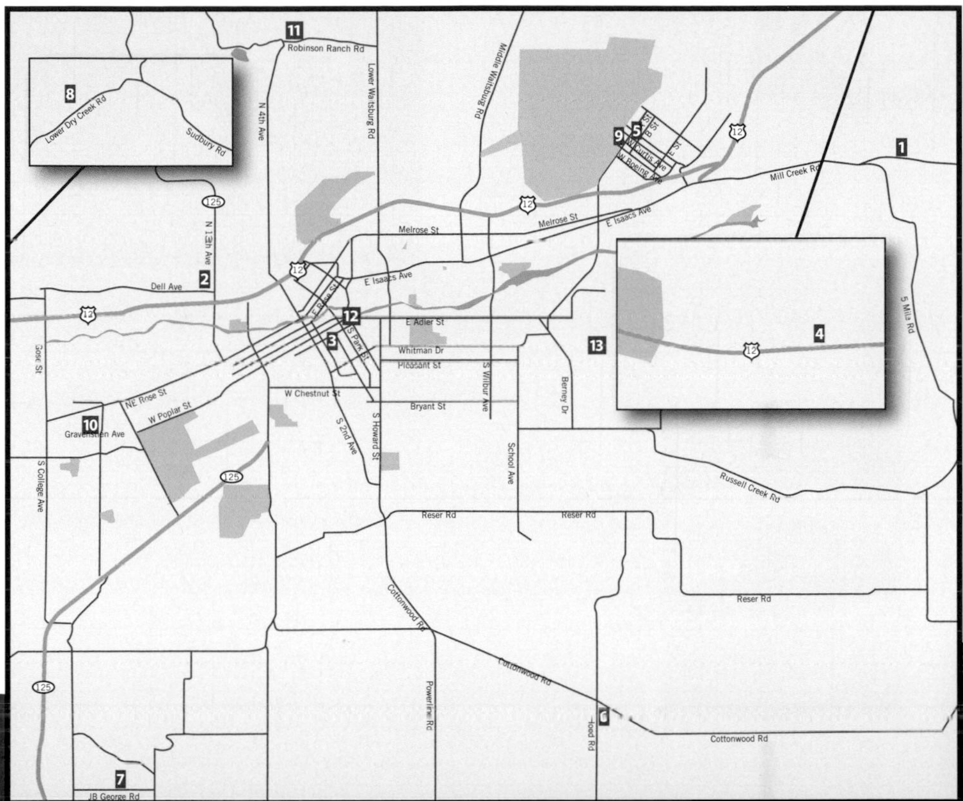

Region: **Walla Walla Wine Country**

# of tasting rooms on tour: **13**

Estimate # of days for tour: **2 to 3**

Getting around: **Car**

Best:
- ❑ **Eats: Abeja**
- ❑ **Lodging: Abeja**
- ❑ **Picnicking: Abeja, Garrison Creek Cellars and Gramercy Cellars**
- ❑ **Views: Abeja and Garrison Creek Cellars**

The Marc

Photo by Alan Ayers

The Marcus Whitman Hotel has been watching over Walla Walla and welcoming guests for more than 80 years. It was a special place to visit during its early days, and that special quality continues today.

The true spirit of the Marcus Whitman Hotel shines in its award-winning restaurant, The Marc. Whether celebrating an important event or just looking for a fine meal, The Marc, with its classic atmosphere and fresh flowers, offers the perfect setting for enjoying the restaurant's seasonal specialties.

Photo by Alan Ayers

Bear Ullman, executive chef, and Erik Johnson, restaurant chef, obviously take pride in the relationships that have been established with the Walla Walla agricultural community. These relationships are at the core of the restaurant's specialties. Dinner selections always include an enticing variety of meat and seafood dishes as well as vegetarian choices. There is, indeed, something for almost everybody.

Photo by Alan Ayers

As with the dining menu, wine selections change with the season. Although the wait-staff is well versed in pairing wines with the various seasonal dishes, the menu also includes a suggested wine pairing for each of the entrées. The perfect ending to a meal at The Marc is one, or more, of the homemade desserts featured on the menu.

The sign outside The Marc reads: "Indulge. Enjoy. Linger," and this is exactly what one should do at this venerable establishment.

Photo by Alan Ayers

Marcus Whitman Hotel
6 West Rose Street, Walla Walla, WA 99362
509-525-2200
marcuswhitmanhotel.com

The Vineyard Lounge

Photo by Alan Ayers

From 4 p.m. until closing, the Vineyard Lounge at the Marcus Whitman Hotel is a popular gathering spot for both tourists and locals. Its central location makes it a great place to stop after a day of tasting wine, after work, or for a relaxing evening.

The drink menu offers a wide variety of cocktails as well as a wonderful selection of local wines. Your beverage of choice can be enjoyed with appetizers, flatbread, sushi, or meals from the lounge's extensive bar menu.

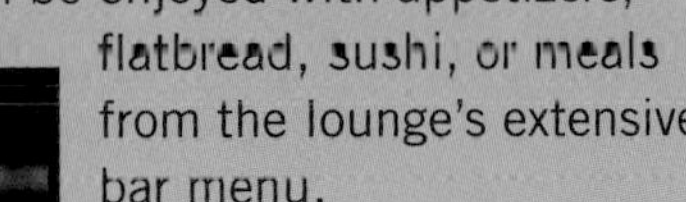

Photo by Alan Ayers

In the winter, snagging one of the comfy seats by the fireplace is a real coup. In the summer, lingering over a drink and food at one of the sidewalk tables is an enjoyable way to end the day.

Marcus Whitman Hotel
6 West Rose Street, Walla Walla, WA 99362
509-525-2200
marcuswhitmanhotel.com

Abeja 1

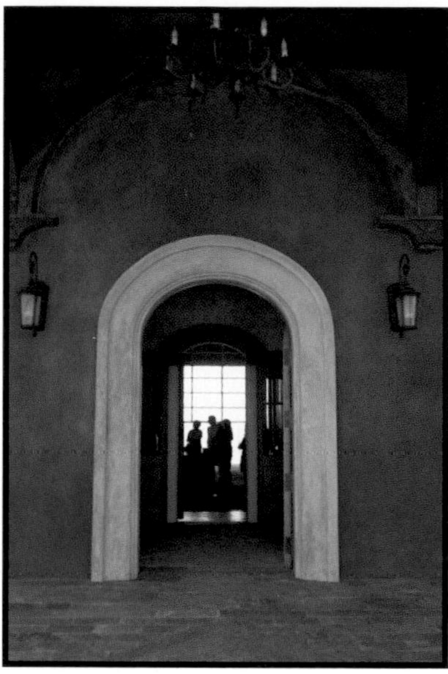

ABEJA
opened: 2000
winemaker(s): John Abbott
location: 2014 Mill Creek Road, Walla Walla, WA 99362-8424
phone: Winery 509-526-7400
web: www.abeja.net
e-mail: info@abeja.net
wheelchair access: Yes
tours: Yes
fee: As part of guest fee
hours: Available for guests at check-in
lat: 46.088354 **long:** -118.225922

www.winetrailsnw.com/wineries/abeja

Cadaretta 2

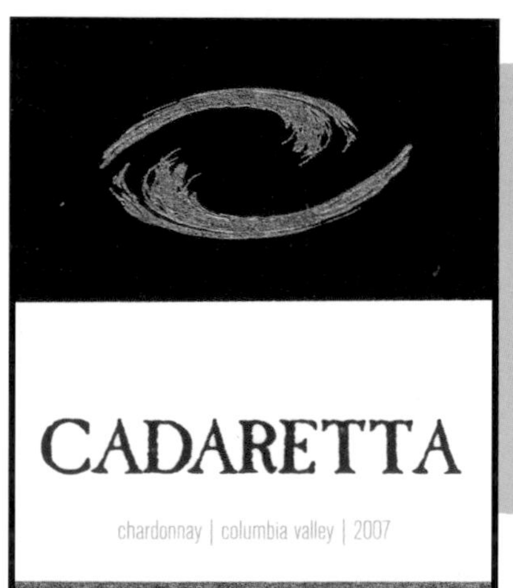

CADARETTA
opened: 2005
winemaker(s): Virginie Bourgue
location: 1120 Dell Avenue, Suite B, Walla Walla, WA 99632
phone: 509-591-0324
web: www.cadaretta.com
e-mail: rick@cadaretta.com
fee: NA
hours: NA
lat: 46.0711642 **long:** -118.358244

www.winetrailsnw.com/wineries/cadaretta

Couvillion Winery 3

COUVILLION WINERY
opened: 2005
winemaker(s): Jill Noble
location: 86 Corkrum Road, Walla Walla, WA 99362
phone: 509-337-6133
web: www.couvillionwinery.com
e-mail: jill@couvillionwinery.com
fee: NA
hours: For special events 10 4
lat: 46.063304 **long:** -118.335067

www.winetrailsnw.com/wineries/couvillion_winery

Dumas Station Wines 4

DUMAS STATION WINES
winemaker(s): Jay and Doug
location: 36229 Highway 12, Dayton, WA 99362
phone: 509-382-8933
web: www.dumasstation.com
e-mail: info@dumasstation.com
fee: NA
hours: NA
lat: 46.287034 **long:** -118.059719

www.winetrailsnw.com/wineries/dumas_station_wines

Ensemble Cellars 5

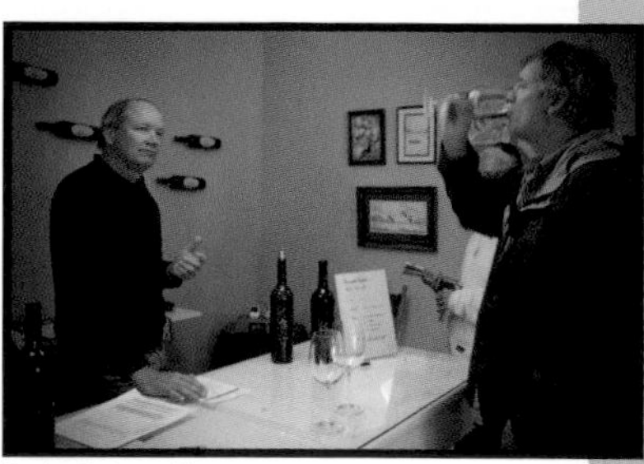
Craig Nelsen (l)

ENSEMBLE CELLARS
opened: 2005
winemaker(s): Craig Nelsen
location: 145 East Curtis Avenue, Walla Walla, WA 99362-0000
phone: 509-525-0231
web: www.ensemblecellars.com
e-mail: info@ensemblecellars.com
fee: NA
hours: For special events 10–4
lat: 46.091123 **long:** -118.276966

www.winetrailsnw.com/wineries/ensemble_cellars

Garrison Creek Cellars 6

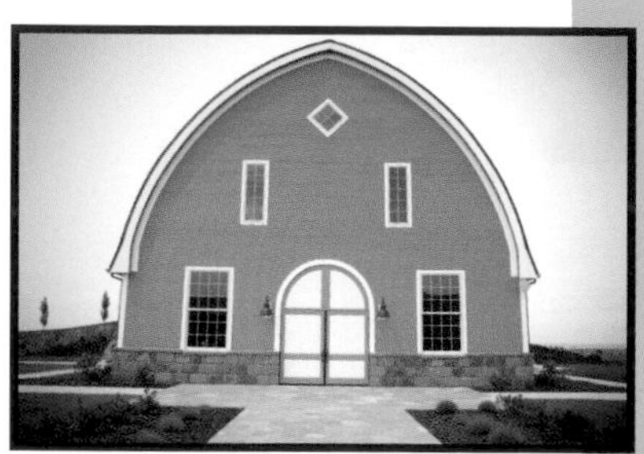

GARRISON CREEK CELLARS
winemaker(s): David March
location: 4153 Hood Road, Walla Walla, WA 99362-1860
phone: 509-386-4841
web: www.garrisoncreekcellars.com
e-mail: daystarpartners@gmail.com
picnic area: Yes
fee: NA
hours: NA
lat: 46.015209 **long:** -118.283572

www.winetrailsnw.com/wineries/garrison_creek_cellars

Gramercy Cellars 7

GRAMERCY CELLARS
opened: 2007
winemaker(s): Greg Harrington
location: 1825 JB George Road, Walla Walla, WA 99362
phone: 646-642-3138
web: www.gramercycellars.com
e-mail: greg@@gramercycellars.com
picnic area: Yes
fee: NA
hours: NA
lat: 46.005429 **long:** -118.374453

www.winetrailsnw.com/wineries/gramercy_cellars

Long Shadows Vintners 8

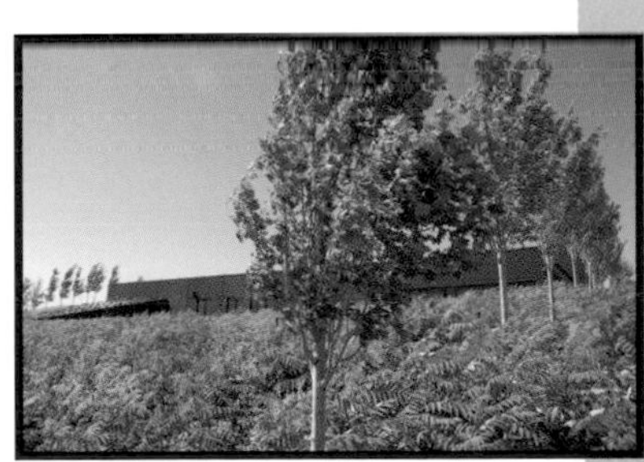

LONG SHADOWS VINTNERS
Poet's Leap, Chester Kidder, Sequel, Pirouette, Feather, Pedestal and Saggi
opened: 2002
winemaker(s): Allen Shoup et al
location: 1604 Frenchtown Road, Walla Walla, WA 99362
phone: 509-526-0905
web: www.longshadows.com
e-mail: info@longshadows.com
picnic area: Yes
tours: Yes
fee: NA
hours: NA
lat: 46.08715 **long:** -118.492539

www.winetrailsnw.com/wineries/long_shadows_vintners

Patrick M. Paul Vineyards 9

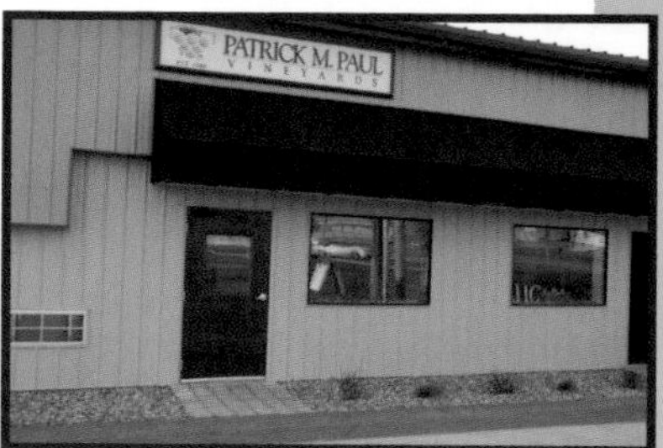

PATRICK M. PAUL VINEYARDS
opened: 1988
winemaker(s): Mike Paul
location: 124 West Boeing Avenue #3, Walla Walla, WA 99362
phone: 509-526-0676
e-mail: mike@pmpvineyards.com
tours: Yes
fee: Complimentary wine tasting
hours: Friday through Monday 11–4
lat: 46.090149 **long:** -118.279527

www.winetrailsnw.com/wineries/patrick_m_paul_vineyards

Revelry Vintners 10

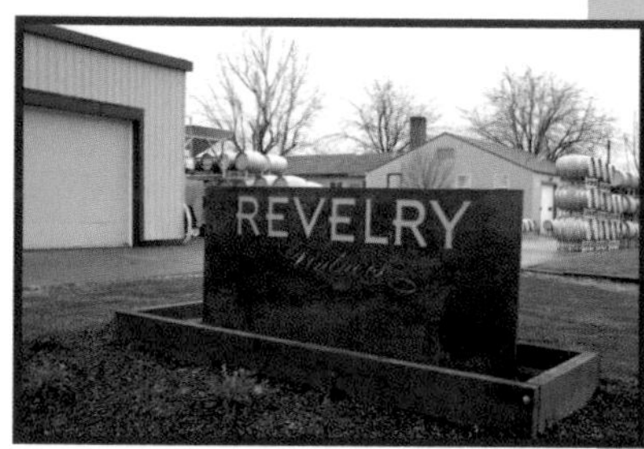

REVELRY VINTNERS
opened: 2005
winemaker(s): Jared Burns
location: 720 C Street, Walla Walla, WA 98362
phone: 509-414-6440
web: www.revelrywines.com
e-mail: info@revelrywines.com
wheelchair access: Yes
fee: TBD
hours: NA
lat: 46.052853 **long:** -118.377657

www.winetrailsnw.com/wineries/revelry_vintners

Robison Ranch Cellars 11

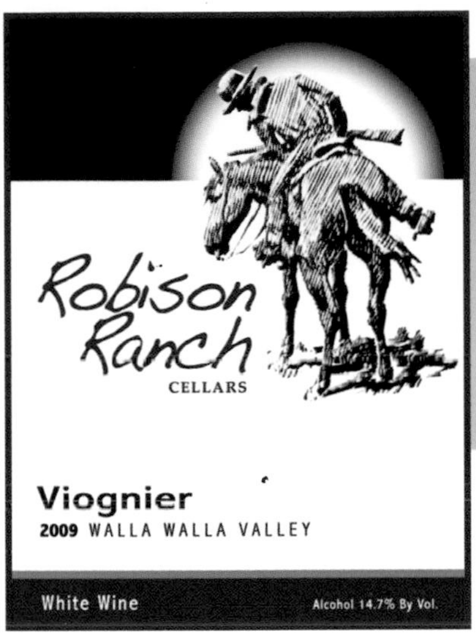

ROBISON RANCH CELLARS
opened: 2008
winemaker(s): Brad Riordan
location: 2839 Robison Ranch Road, Walla Walla, WA 99362
phone: 509-301-3480
web: www.robisonranchcellars.com
e-mail: robisonranchcellars@gmail.com
fee: NA
lat: 46.103694 **long:** -118.341379

www.winetrailsnw.com/wineries/robison_ranch_cellars

Tru Cellars 12

TRU CELLARS
opened: 2009
winemaker(s): Chad Diltz
location: 26 East Main Street, Walla Walla, WA 90362
phone: 509-876-2939
web: www.trucellars.com
e-mail: info@trucellars.com
gift shop: Yes
fee: Tasting fee applies
hours: NA
lat: 46.066847 **long:** -118.338166

www.winetrailsnw.com/wineries/tru_cellars

Tranche Cellars 13

By-Appointment-Only Wineries

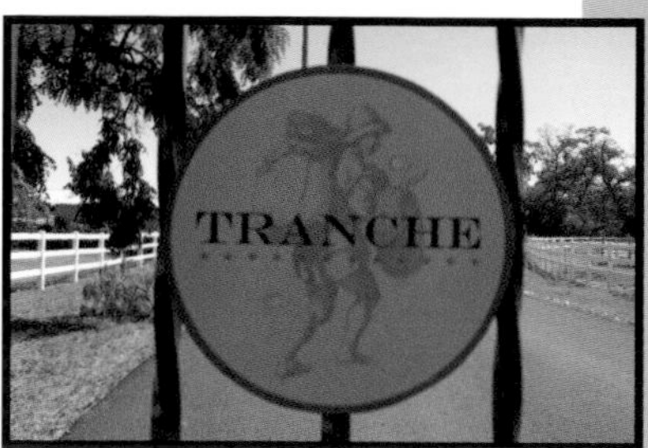

TRANCHE CELLARS
opened: 2009
winemaker(s): Kendall Mix
location: 705 Berney Drive, Walla Walla, WA 99362
phone: 509-526-3500
web: www.tranchecellars.com
e-mail: info@tranchecellars.com
fee: NA
hours: NA
lat: 46.063011 **long:** -118.284254

www.winetrailsnw.com/wineries/tranche_cellars

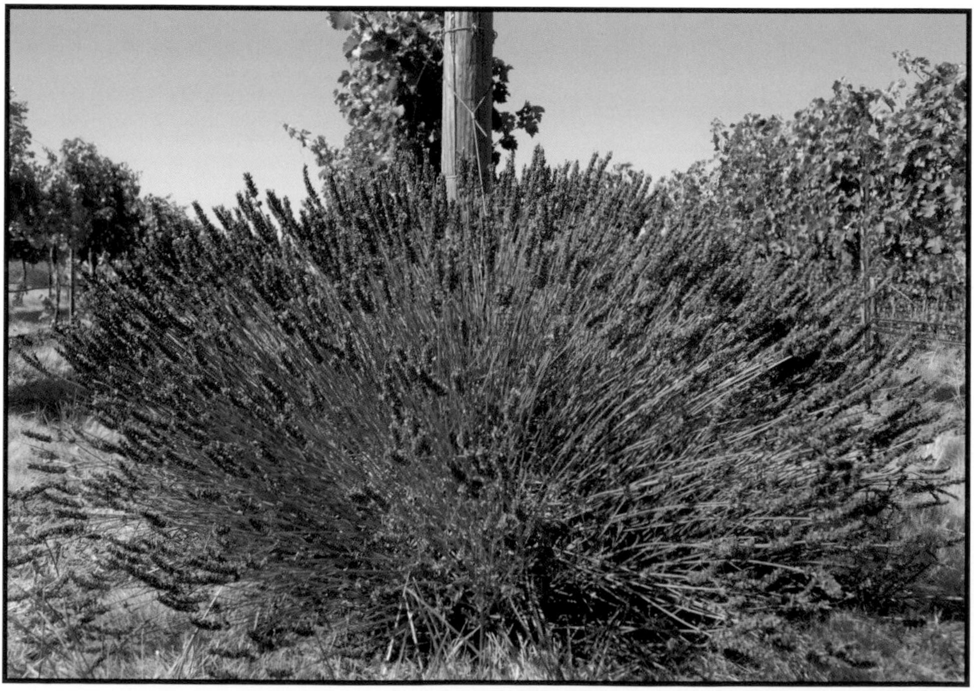

Wineries not Open to the Public

Cayuse Vineyards
www.cayusevineyards.com

Doubleback
www.doubleback.com

Dowsett Family Winery
www.dowsettwines.com

Gardena Creek Winery
www.gardenacreekwinery.com

KW Cellars

Lahar Winery

Leonetti Cellar
www.leonetticellar.com

NxNW Wine
www.nxnwwine.com

Rasa Vineyards
www.rasavineyards.com

Reynvaan Family Cellars
www.reynvaanfamilyvineyards.com

Sapphire Mountain Cellars
www.sapphiremountaincellars.com

Thirsty Pagans
www.thirstypagans.com

Vierra Vineyards Winery
www.vierravineyards.com

Wines of Substance
www.winesofsubstance.com

Wine Touring and Wheelchair Access

An increasing number of tasting rooms throughout the Pacific Northwest have become accessible by wheelchair. This accessibility is gained through designated special parking spaces for cars bearing wheelchair placards, the absence of stairs to impede access, wide doors, and restrooms meeting ADA standards.

Many Walla Walla wineries — particularly the newer ones that meet stiffer building codes — reflect a sensitivity to this issue and have been designed or redesigned to accommodate disabled travelers.

That said, even if the winery indicates that it is wheelchair accessible, we believe it's a good idea to call ahead if you have concerns. For example, if you have a van that is specially equipped for wheelchair loading and unloading, you may have questions about the winery's parking lot being large enough to accommodate the vehicle. Another possible problem for disabled visitors is access to areas outside designated-accessible spaces. Say you are attending a special event, such as a winemaker dinner or a wedding; you may have wheelchair access to the tasting room, but what about the rest of the winery, the bathroom facilities, and outdoors among the vineyards? Call or email the winery ahead of time to get the lowdown on the layout.

For general information to assist disabled travelers, check out these websites.

- Access-Able Travel Source (access-able.com).
- Global Access Disabled Travel Network (globalaccessnews.com).
- Mobility International (miusa.org).

Wine Touring with Pets

"Pets welcome" is a sign that you don't often see at wineries. In fact, quite the opposite. Wineries don't often welcome dogs into their tasting rooms. Too many things can go wrong, such as a counter-surfing dog snarfing crackers and cheese trays or scrapping with the winery cat.

That said, the wineries of Walla Walla deserve special mention for accommodating dogs. Many of them have gone out of their way to let visitors know that it is fine to bring their dogs. If you are planning a Walla Walla wine tour with your four-legged family member, check out each winery's website or call ahead. They may ask you to bring a leash, but including the family pet may be just fine.

Bing at Eleganté.

Ironically, a large percentage of wineries do have a winery dog, which has led to an explosion of coffee-table books featuring mug shots of winery pooches. However, even though the winery owners might be dog-friendly regarding their own pooch, introducing your own dog into the tasting room is bound to create territorial issues.

However, should Fido accompany you on your next wine tour, you will find a number of hotels and quaint country inns that welcome pets. Some may charge an additional fee, but it's typically a nominal amount.

If you do bring along your dog, pack doggy snacks and water, and allow for pit stops along the way. Always keep the window open and park in the shade, especially in hot weather, to avoid baking your dog. In the summertime, particularly in Walla Walla, it's downright dangerous to keep a dog in a car — even with windows open. Bottom line: Take your dog to the park, but not to the winery unless the winery notes they are dog friendly.

Wine Touring with Kids

As a general rule, wineries are not set up to handle little tykes — after all, these establishments are "no whining zones." The stacked bottles of wine and Riedel crystal are easy targets for a wandering 3-year-old. Few wineries offer a play area as part of the tasting room or a playground for kids to enjoy — although the former schoolhouse serving as the L'Ecole Nº 41 winery is a nice exception; check out its backyard playground. When play areas are included, they are often more a means of distracting the kids in order to allow parents to swirl, sip, and experience the wine. However, if you do have your children along and insist on checking out a winery or two, here are a few tips to make it a family-friendly experience.

First, make it informational and choose wineries that feature a wine tour. Treat it like a field trip and discover how wine is made. At harvest time, it is not unusual to see kids stomping grapes (talk about cheap labor). The smiles on their faces says it all.

Try to combine wine tasting with family activities, such as picnicking at the winery, checking out a hands-on museum (e.g., the Children's Museum of Walla Walla), or going on a nature hike. Involve the kids in the planning. Sure, you're picking up the tab, but if you cater to their needs, it's easier for them to accommodate you.

Don't attempt more than a couple of wineries in a day. Dragging kids to more than one or two wineries is a surefire way to ruin the day.

Finally, if your focus really is on wine tasting throughout the day, consider splitting up. Dad takes the kids the first day and enjoys kid-friendly activities, while mom checks out three or four must-see wineries. On day two, it's dad's turn to sample his favorite wineries, while mom entertains the kids. Divide and conquer!

There's plenty to do in Walla Walla wine country for families. However, to make it truly memorable, you need to plan ahead and create a win-win situation for both kids and parents.

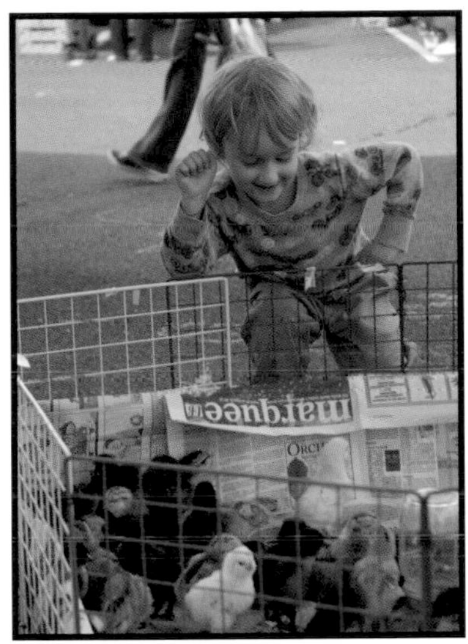

At the Farmer's Market.

Sip and Cycle

Choices abound in the Pacific Northwest for bicycling along lush vineyards and sampling amazing wines, and this is especially true in Walla Walla. What better way to work off some calories while taking in some much needed refreshment in the form of reds and whites. It's the ol' input and output equation — by the end of the day, you break even calorie-wise, but gain immeasurably in life's pleasures.

For cycling information related to Walla Walla, check out wwvalleycycling.com. This site provides all things cycling in the valley — local rides, maps, events, links, and more. For hundreds (no kidding) of Walla Walla bike routes, see mapmyride.com/, click "Find a Ride" and then search for Walla Walla. Look for regional bicycling, including regional tours, at bicyclepaper.com. On this site, "everything biking" abounds with respect to news and event information, including a number of rides that take you through the heart of wine country.

The State of Washington also kicks in with helpful information at the Department of Transportation's website at wsdot.wa.gov/Bike.

Now if you find yourself in Walla Walla sans bike or in need of equipment, such as a helmet, gloves, or jacket, you have two excellent bicycle retailers at your service. Just east of downtown Walla Walla, at 1503 E. Isaacs, is the Bicycle Barn (509-529-7860; open Monday-Saturday, 9 a.m.-6 p.m.). Or check out Allegro Cyclery, located downtown at 200 E. Main St. (509-525-4949), which offers a wide assortment of bicycle gear, bikes, and rentals. Open Monday through Saturday during normal business hours Allegro Cyclery is a key sponsor of the Tour of Walla Walla, held in mid-April each year (visit tofww.org).

A word of caution is in order here. Riding a bicycle is potentially dangerous. Accidents are often caused not by the cyclist's riding behavior, but by the car driver's inability to either see or exercise caution while negotiating around cyclists. Adding alcohol only compounds the danger. Riders need to have a tasting strategy: Either sip and spit with great frequency, or sample one or two wines at each winery and limit the number of tasting rooms you visit. Alternatively, plan your biking for the morning and leave the wine tasting for the afternoon. Drink responsibly, ride responsibly.

Weddings — Getting Married in Wine Country

"I do."

With those two words, you can finally relax knowing that all those months of planning are over. The flowers you chose, the colors selected for the dresses, and the vows you wrote (and rewrote) are behind you. Now you can undo your tie or shed those 4-inch heels and let lose — after all, you're in the heart of wine country and there is cabernet sauvignon awaiting your pleasure.

Getting hitched at a winery is gaining in popularity throughout the Northwest. Many wineries offer a quiet retreat for couples to share a special day with friends and family. What's more, an increasing number have become "destination wineries" for weddings, complete with creature comforts such as a spa for working out nuptial-day tension, overnight lodging with smelly soaps, ponds stocked with koi and, of course a cellar full of wines. The Walla Walla wineries that welcome weddings include Basel Cellars Estate Winery, Castillo de Feliciana Vineyard and Winery, Waterbrook Winery, Three Rivers Winery, and

Patit Creek Cellars. However, there are a number of other Walla Walla wineries that might consider accommodating your special day — Dunham Cellars, Walla Walla Vintners and College Cellars come to mind.

A word to the wise is in order if you wish to exchange vows in wine country: Once you have established your criteria (i.e., budget and size), nail down the winery setting as soon as possible - a year prior to the big day is key for booking popular wineries!

To reduce your risk of things going wrong, I offer this three-step process that guarantees success.

1. **Choose the location** — Wineries can accommodate wedding parties of varying sizes, from just two (can you say "elope"?) to several hundred well-wishers. It really depends on you, the couple. This is your day, and you get to choose what fits your personality, not to mention budget. For couples who are getting married the second time around or renewing their marriage vows, a big wedding may not be in the cards. When it comes to weddings, size matters. If you want a wedding that has a guest list approaching 250, most wineries can't accommodate an event of that size — they lack the parking facilities, the lawn space for chairs, or they have postage-stamp-size dance floors that are just too small for Uncle Willy's sprinkler dance steps. If you are looking at a destination winery, consider the number of out-of-town guests and whether or not the winery and nearby inns/resorts can accommodate them all.

The WineTrails Guy and new Bride (Kathleen) at Vista Hills Vineyard & Winery (Dayton, OR) 9/20/2009.

   Once you have selected potential wineries for your wedding, plan on visiting each one and speaking to its wedding/event coordinator. These folks have a wealth of information and can readily answer your questions concerning costs and availability for your ceremony. Imagine what the winery may look (or feel) like months away, during the morning or evening; think in terms of the chances of rain, sunlight for photography (best in the morning or early evening), and wind. You may decide to bag the idea of a "unity" candle for an outdoor event, being at the mercy of the wind. There's nothing like a candle that refuses to light or stay lit for a couple just starting out — an inauspicious beginning!

2. **Know thy wedding planner** — Many wineries have a person on staff responsible for planning weddings, or they can refer you to a preferred wedding planner if you need one. My advice — embrace their service. Bring your planner a latte and befriend that person. The fact is these people have tons of experience and know the pitfalls associated with putting on a wedding. They can suggest caterers, photographers, florists, transportation services, wedding officiants, and more. You don't have to use them, but through their experience, they have identified the most reliable and best-qualified companies in the area for these one-time services.

   Once you have met with a wedding planner, plan to reconnect several months in advance of the wedding to go through the myriad details associated with the event. By this time, you might have a special request that you didn't address the first time. For example, if you want champagne at each table for a toast, but the winery doesn't make sparkling wine, how do you handle that? Is the winery copasetic with the two of you exchanging vows while stomping grapes in a tub at harvest? This is your special day and it should reflect your personalities, but be sure you and the winery are on the same page.

   As the big day approaches, it is a good idea to visit the winery during the time of day you have reserved for your wedding. Note the light and wind conditions. Review the other "little things" that you didn't think about earlier, such as:

   - Does the bride's dressing room have full-length mirrors?
   - Will the musicians be located where they can be heard?
   - Does the area where the wedding will take place have wheelchair access?
   - Will non-wedding guests wander into the event *à la Wedding Crashers*?
   - What happens in the event of bad weather? Is the interior space large enough? Will you need to rent a tent as a backup?

3. **Day of the big event: Arrive early and expect the unexpected** — I understand that you think you have thought through all contingencies. But according to Murphy's Law, "Whatever can go wrong will go wrong," so be prepared for the unexpected. On the big day, emotions will be running rampant - acknowledge that. So if the caterer fails to deliver the ginger-peanut sauce for the fire-grilled spiced chicken skewers, don't freak out. Life will go on, and your guests will not mind. In fact, they may not even notice.

Plan to arrive early. Now is the time to review and, if necessary, change the setup. If Aunt Bertha forgot the special guest book, you can call your best friend and ask her to stop by the mall and pick one up. If the power cord isn't long enough to reach the AV equipment, there's time to dash to ACE Hardware for a new one. No worries! Just relax and recognize that these things will happen and may actually add to your special day. Friends of mine related that on their special day, the winery's linens were mixed up with those of a nearby hotel, and instead of regular tablecloths, they received form-fitting sheets for queen-size beds. After the bride's mother had a conniption, the groom and his friends draped the outdoor tables with the sheets, and after a few glasses of wine, the whole wedding party had a good laugh!

Now, one more piece of advice and it's perhaps the most important tip I can give: Have fun!

Wine Tasting 101

The key to tasting wine is to take it slow and concentrate. All that's required of you is to see, swirl, sniff, sip, and savor.

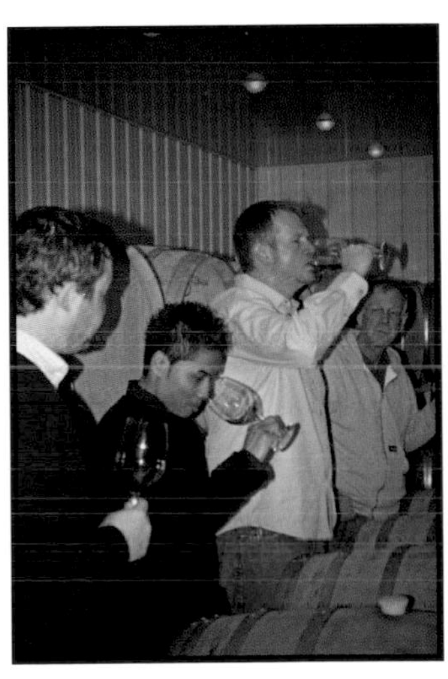

Seeing

A visual check of the wine informs you of the basic type of wine you are about to taste — red or white. Red wine ranges in color from purple to ruby red, deep red, red brown, and mahogany. White wine hues range from yellow green to straw, gold, yellow-brown, and amber brown. To judge the true color of a wine, hold your glass up to a white background (or wall or napkin). Where the wine falls in the color spectrum prepares your taste buds for what they are about to experience.

Once a wine has been poured, some folks like to tilt the wine glass and observe how the wine flows down the inside of the glass. However, there is no correlation between the "legs," or "tears," of wine on the inside of the glass and the taste of the wine itself.

Swirling

A wine just poured needs to stretch its legs and aerate. Swirling allows the wine to open up and release aromas. Up to this point in the wine's existence, oxygen has been a bad thing; now, oxygen is the wine's best friend. It allows the wine to create a bouquet. Most tasting rooms provide wine glasses roomy enough to swirl the wine without spillage. You need that space between the wine and your nose to smell the aroma. If you chance upon a winery that uses little plastic cups or tiny "orange juice glasses," you may want to consider shortening your visit and moving on to the next winery.

Smelling

The aroma given off by a wine is its "nose." Right after a vigorous swirl, quickly stick your nose as far down into the glass as possible and sniff. Concentrate and give your imagination free rein as you attempt to describe what you smell. In time, descriptions such as sweaty saddle, cat pee (no kidding), tar, kerosene, burnt match, and asparagus may enter your sniffing lexicon. Researchers say that flavor is 75 percent smell and 25 percent taste. (This explains why food tastes bland when you have a cold — you can't smell it.) Merlot, pinot noir, and cabernet sauvignon are known for their distinctive smells.

Sipping and Savoring

Most of us were taught in science class that the tongue has certain regions that taste salt, bitter, sweet, and sour. Have you ever seen those drawings of the tongue that depict which part of the tongue tastes what? But according to the latest research, all taste buds can taste salt, bitter, sweet, and sour to varying degrees. Taste buds cover the entire top of the tongue, front and back, which explains why you see sommeliers and wine connoisseurs vigorously swishing the wine around their mouth; they are getting the maximum exposure throughout their mouth to taste the wine. While you are swishing, your brain is also registering other sensations, such as heaviness, roundness, finish, and astringency from the tannins found in the wine. While the wine is in your mouth, focus on it for a few seconds. Swirl it around in your mouth and attempt to suck in a little air — without committing the faux pas of gagging — to pick up the full flavors of the wine.

Remember, take it slow and concentrate.

Tasting Room Etiquette

There are definite rules of the road when it comes to visiting tasting rooms, and most involve common sense. Moderation is a good thing. Those innocent little ounces add up. So have a strategy ahead of time and try to stick to it. Here's some WineTrail do's and don'ts:

Do:

- Drink responsibly — Designate a driver or hire a limo.
- Spit or dump as much as you want — That's what those buckets are for!

- Have patience with the wine pourer — Don't elbow your way forward with outstretched hand begging for another fill; they'll get to you.
- Have a tasting strategy — Choose which wines you would like to sample. If you are only interested in the reds, let your pourer know that.
- Ask questions — Tasting-room pourers are passionate about their wines and anxious to tell you why.
- Purchase wine if you want to — Assuming it is in your budget and you like it, spring for it.
- Be open to wines you believe you won't like — Reds, whites, port wines, late-harvest dessert wines, rosés — go on, try them! You might be surprised to learn how delicious, say, a dessert wine made from frozen grapes can taste. Open your mind when you open your mouth.
- Let them know if you like their wine — There's a reason the pourer is staring at you with an expectant look. If you like the wine, tell them. Winemakers live for such moments.

Don't:

- Generally, ask for a second helping — Unless you are contemplating purchasing a bottle or you need a second helping to clarify what you just tasted.
- Feel that you have to purchase a bottle of wine — The winery's primary goal is to give you a positive experience, so you tell your friends and family about it.
- Wear perfumes or colognes — Your nose needs to smell the wine.
- Attempt to engage the tasting-room staff in esoteric debates — Save the Hungarian vs. American oak debate for a conversation with the winemaker, not the poor pourer.
- Take anything — The wine glasses are theirs, not yours (unless the tasting fee includes a glass).
- Drink excessively — Keep your wits; spit/dump often and pace yourself.

Tertulia Cellars

The Walla Walla AVA

Established in 1984, the Walla Walla Valley American Viticultural Area, or AVA, comprises 300,000 acres stretching from the foothills of the Blue Mountains westward toward the Columbia River. (**WineTrail Trivia:** An acre is roughly the size of a football field minus its end zones.) The Walla Walla AVA is entirely contained within the much larger Columbia Valley AVA, which comprises more than 11 million acres, and is located in southeastern Washington and northeastern Oregon. The appellation lies at a latitude of 46 degrees north, approximately the same latitude as that of the world-renowned wine-growing region of Bordeaux, France.

People unfamiliar with the geography of Washington assume that Washington state is one big moss bed, given the prevalent images of rainy Seattle. However, the Cascade Mountains divide the state north to south, which gives rise to two distinct climatic regions. Whereas western Washington receives about 50 inches of rainfall annually, the precipitation in the Walla Walla Valley is only 15.5 inches per year, and the area enjoys a long growing season, between 190 and 220 days annually.

During Walla Walla's summer season, the plants get a healthy dose of sunshine with the long, hot days — and cool nights — associated with its northern latitude. To put this into perspective, during the summer, Walla Walla gets an average of 17.4 hours of sunlight per day, which is about two hours more per day than California's prime wine-growing region. The longer days allow the grapes to ripen fully, and the cool nights provide a higher natural acidity. Other than the occasional sunburned grape, the primary worry for Walla Walla grape growers is damaging frost, which can wreak havoc with the vines. In January 2004, an arctic blast destroyed much of the wine-grape crop and left winemakers scurrying to find growers whose crops had not been hit by the freeze. It was another hard lesson that, despite humans' best efforts, Mother Nature is the boss.

Between 12,000 and 15,000 years ago, the Walla Walla Valley was flooded by the Missoula floods, which carried millions of tons of rich sediments into the valley that settled on its basalt floor. Over time, wind-driven accumulations of silt, known as loess (pronounced as either "less" or "luss"), developed on the hillsides. The loess and flood sediments also contain layers of volcanic ash, from the result of explosive eruptions of Cascade Range volcanoes. Thus, geologists who study the area have determined that the appellation's soil doesn't come from the weathering of the underlying bedrock; floodwaters and wind transported the soil.

Its great soils and fantastic climate combine to make Walla Walla Valley an exceptional source for Bordeaux grape varietals, such as cabernet sauvignon and merlot. Chardonnay and syrah are also grown here, but this is "cab" country: About 41 percent of the grapes grown here are cabernet sauvignon. Other varieties grown include gewürztraminer, cabernet franc, sangiovese, grenache, Malbec, petit verdot, tempranillo, pinot gris, riesling, sauvignon blanc, semillon, and viognier. It's a smorgasbord of grape varieties, with reds dominating.

Decoding a Walla Walla Valley Wine Label

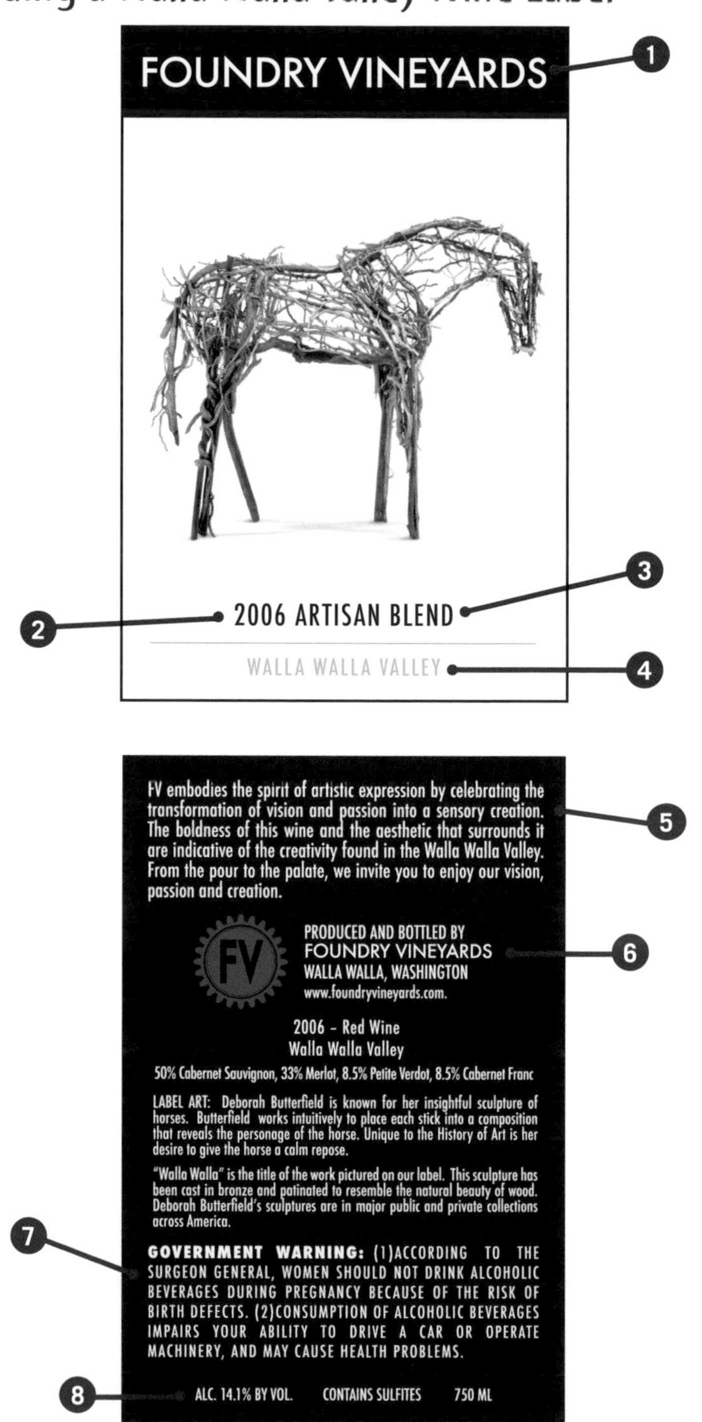

Front

1. **Winery Name**
2. **Vintage:** At least 95 percent of the grapes were harvested in the year shown on the label — if the fruit is from a designated viticultural area, such as the Walla Walla Valley AVA. The requirement lowers to 85 percent if the grapes come from a state or county appellation.
3. **Varietal:** At least 75 percent of the grapes come from a specific variety, such as cabernet franc, cabernet sauvignon, merlot, syrah, carménère, petite sirah, and chardonnay. In this case, "2006 Artisan Blend" means that there was no dominant grape variety used to produce this wine. The back of the label indicates that it is a Bordeaux blend of 50 percent cabernet sauvignon, 33 percent merlot, 8.5 percent petit verdot, and 8.5 percent cabernet franc.
4. **Appellation or American Viticultural Area:** Washington state law requires that any wine with a label claiming or implying that its contents are from "Washington" must contain at least 95 percent Washington-grown grapes. Thus, a label that specifies it is a "Walla Walla Valley" wine will have at least 95 percent of the grapes from the Walla Walla Valley AVA, even though, ironically, all the grapes may come from the Oregon side of the AVA.

Back

5. **Descriptive information:** Gives consumers additional information, albeit for marketing purposes.
6. **Produced and bottled by:** Denotes the winery that actually made and bottled the wine, and the winery's location.
7. **Government warning:** Cautions pregnant women that wine may cause health problems for their unborn babies; and that those driving a car or operating machinery may be impaired by drinking alcohol.
8. **Contents:** Indicates the presence of sulfites, volume (e.g., 750 ml), and alcohol content by volume. **Note:** Federal law requires wine bottles to be of specific sizes: 50 ml, 100 ml, 187 ml, 375 ml, 500 ml, 750 ml, 1 L, 1.5 L, or 3 L. Containers of more than 3 L must be whole liters in capacity. No other bottle sizes are permitted.

Additional Terms:

Vineyard designation: Identifies in which vineyard the grapes were grown. At least 95 percent of the wine must come from the designated vineyard.

Estate wine: Denotes that the winery and the vineyards are in the same appellation, the vineyards are controlled or owned by the winery, and the wine was created entirely at that winery.

Reserve wine: Implies the wine is of a higher quality than usual, or has been aged before sold, or both. Traditionally, winemakers would "reserve" some of their best wine rather than sell it immediately, hence the term.

"Growing green" designations (optional): Certifies wine is "organic" as designated by a seal of a USDA-accredited certifying agent placed on the label. Examples include Salmon Safe and LIVE (Low Input Viticulture and Enology) designations.

UPC/EAN Barcode (optional): Although not a regulatory requirement, a significant percentage of wineries place the UPC/EAN barcodes on back labels for retailer scanners.

Walla Walla Varieties - Whites

Chardonnay

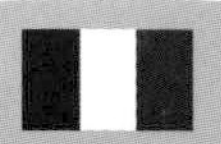

Burgundy origins, vigorous and adaptable to many soils. Cool climate grape. Typically aged in oak but trend toward un-oaked. Fruity with terms such as apple, peach, citrus and pineapple used to describe. Very food friendly.

Gewürztraminer

German-Alsatian grape variety reddish-brown thick skinned grape with typical spicy flavor. One of the earliest to mature. Prefers cool climate. Spicy, floral, fruity, lychee, honey and jasmine tea are terms often used to describe. Dry to sweet.

Pinot gris

Grayish-hue fruit (gris is French for gray) is called pinot grigio in Italy. Originating in Burgundy, the wine is very terroir dependent ranging in style from crisp, light and dry (Italy) to rich, fat, and honeyed (France's Alsace region and Western U.S.).

Riesling

German white grape originating in the Rhine River Valley. Very terroir expressive, rieslings balance on a fine line between acidity an delicacy. Flavor descriptors include peach, apple, quince and citrus. Riesling pairs wonderfully with grilled fish, chicken, Thai food and summer salads.

Walla Walla Valley AVA Profile

Location: Southeast Washington extending into northeastern Oregon. It is within Walla Walla County in Washington State and Umatilla County in Oregon and is part of the much larger Columbia Valley AVA.
Under Cultivation: 1,600 acres.
Weather: Growing season of 190 to 220 days, with annual rainfall averaging 15.5 inches (39 cm) per year.
Soil: Loess derived soils which are essentially unconsolidated, unstratified calcareous silt.
Topography: East of the Cascade Mountain Range, this area sits at the foot of the Blue Mountains, with vineyard elevations typically ranging from 650 feet to 1,500 feet.

Roussanne

Derived from the northern portion of France's Rhône region, often used for blending. The berries are russet colored when ripe — roux is French for the reddish brown color russet, the root for the variety's name. Full-bodied, with flavors of honey and pear.

Sauvignon Blanc

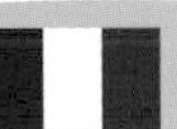

Green skinned grape originating in Bordeaux where it is often blended with semillon. Vigorous with tender skin, produces crisp, dry and refreshing wines. Fruity to grassy depending upon origin and viticulture methods.

Sémillon

Bordeaux derived grape vinified as a single variety or blended – often with sauvignon blanc. Vigorous, found world-wide. By itself, sémillon produces wines that are not well-rounded and very light in color. Blended with sauvignon blanc, the resulting wines can be extraordinary.

Viognier

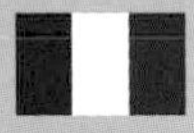

Golden colored wine with significant cultivation in the northern Rhône region of France. Often blended with other white grapes and syrah. Very fruity bouquet with pronounced floral notes.

Walla Walla Varieties - Reds

Barbera 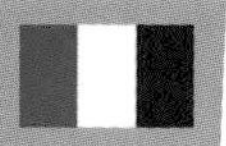

Italy's third most popular grape grown principally in the Piedmont area, vary significantly from medium body wines to powerful intense wines capable of cellaring. Deep ruby color, pink rim, noticeable levels of tannins and pronounced acidity.

Cabernet Franc 

Black-skinned Bordeaux grape often blended with cabernet sauvignon and merlot. Increasingly, it is vinified by itself. It prefers cooler climate relative to cabernet sauvignon. Aromas include raspberries, cassis, tobacco and floral.

Cabernet Sauvignon 

Blue-black berries with Bordeaux origins, cabernet sauvignon is the most important grape in the world. Vigorous, the grape prefers warm weather climates. Full-bodied, rich and tannic, it is often blended with merlot and cabernet franc to soften it.

Carménère 

Smooth, full, rich, dark fruits with good color. Once widely grown in Bordeaux but now principally grown in Chile where it was mistakenly thought to be merlot.

Cinsault 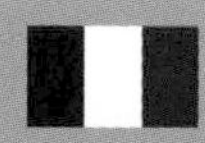

Robust, perfume, soft, fruity and flavorful, used to soften blends. Widely grown in southern France and used in Bandol, Cotes-du-Rhône, Chateaunuef-du-Pape and Tavel. In South Africa, crossed with pinot noir to create pinotage.

Couniose 

Notes of strawberries, violets, anise and pepper used primarily as a blending variety in southern France. One of the 13 permitted varieties in Chateauneuf-du-Pape.

Dolcetto 

Meaning "little sweet one" in Italian, this Piedmont deep colored variety has notes of almonds, plums and blackberries. Best drunk young.

Grenache 

Grenache grape does well in hot, dry regions and strong stalk makes it well suited for windy conditions. Grenache wines are sweet, fruity, and very low in tannins. Often exhibits high alcohol levels (15 to 16%). Widely planted in southern France with origins in Spain.

Malbec

Ink-dark with robust tannins, Malbec is a Bordeaux grape. It's put Argentina on the wine world map. Often blended with other Bordeaux grapes to produce clarets. Characterized by dark fruit notes and herbal aromas.

Merlot

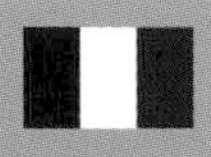

Popular Bordeaux grape often blended with cabernet sauvignon. Merlot is medium body ("fleshy") noble grape with hints of berry, plum and currant. Consistently described as smooth, it is lighter in color, acid and tannins than cabernet sauvignon.

Mourvèdre

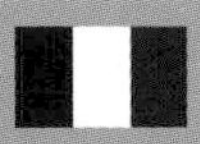

From southern France's Rhône region, mourvèdre grapes produce garnet-colored wines with spicy, peppery characteristics. Due to high tannins and alcohol levels, it is often blended with grenache. The grapes are thick-skinned exhibiting blue-black colors.

Nebbiolo

Considered Italy's most noble grape, Nebbiolo has notes of roses, cherries and tar. Grown widely throughout Piedmont, it is the variety in Barolo, Barbaresco, Gattinara, Ghemme and Langhe.

Petit Verdot

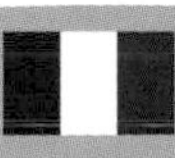

A high quality Bordeaux grape used primarily as a blending "seasoning" wine. Full-bodied, deep-colored with peppery, spicy flavor characteristics. High in tannins and alcohol. Increasing popularity as a standalone variety wine in new world.

Sangiovese

Considered by many to be Italy's "aristocratic" variety, sangiovese has notes of black cherries, spice, smoke, herbs and nuts. Chianti, Brunello di Montalcino, Super Tuscans and VinoNobile di Montalcino are all sangiovese-based wines.

Syrah

Vigorous and performs well in different soil types. Rhône derived variety, syrah is big-bodied and capable of aging for many years. Often blended with grenache and mouvrèdre in Rhône. In Australia, syrah is called shiraz.

Tempranillo

Spain's noble grape, tempranillo is a full-bodied wine ruby red in color. Aromas of berries, plum, tobacco, vanilla, leather and herb describe this wine. Tempranillo prefers mild to hot weather continental climate zones.

Zinfandel

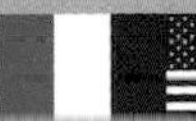

Identical with southern Italy's Primitivo grape, zinfandel is vinified in many styles including slightly sweet blush wine, red table wine, late harvest dessert wine, sparkling wine and port-style wines. Zinfandel is often characterized as hearty and spicy.

WHITES

WineTrail	Winery	Chardonnay	Gewürztraminer	Pinot gris	Riesling	Sauvignon blanc	Sémillon	Viognier	White Blends	Dessert Wines
	428								•	
	Abeja	•						•		
	Adamant Cellars								•	
	àMaurice Cellars	•						•	•	
	Amavi Cellars						•			•
	Ash Hollow Winery		•					•	•	
	Balboa Winery									
	Basel Cellars Estate Winery	•				•			•	
	Beresan Winery						•			
	Bergevin Lane Vineyards							•	•	
	Bunchgrass Winery									
	Buty Winery	•							•	
	Cadaretta	•				•	•		•	
	Canoe Ridge Vineyard	•	•		•					
	Castillo de Feliciana			•				•		
	CAVU Cellars					•				
	Cayuse Vineyards							•		
	Chateau Rollat Winery						•			
	College Cellars of Walla Walla				•		•			•
	Cougar Crest Estate Winery	•						•	•	•
	Couvillion Winery				•	•				
	DaMa Wines	•			•			•		
	Doubleback									
	Dowsett Family Winery		•							
	Dumas Station Wines									
	Dunham Cellars	•			•					
	Dusted Valley Vintners	•						•		
	El Corazon Winery									
	Eleganté Cellars		•							
	Ensemble Cellars									
	Five Star Cellars									
	Forgeron Cellars	•							•	•
	Fort Walla Walla Cellars									
	Foundry Vineyards	•							•	
	Gardena Creek Winery									
	Garrison Creek Cellars									
	Gifford Hirlinger Winery			•						

REDS

Barbera	Cabernet franc	Cabernet sauvignon	Carménère	Grenache	Malbec	Petit verdot	Red blends	Sangiovese	Syrah	Tempranillo	Rosé	Port-style wine	Pg #
							●						146
		●					●		●				222
		●					●		●		●		152
		●			●		●		●		●		168
		●							●		●		184
		●			●		●		●	●			156
							●		●				188
	●	●					●		●				178
	●	●	●		●		●		●				186
	●	●				●	●		●		●		110
		●			●		●		●				60
		●					●		●		●		144
		●					●		●				222
	●	●					●		●				116
							●			●			200
●		●			●		●				●		154
	●	●		●					●	●			229
		●					●				●		88
	●	●			●		●		●		●		164
	●	●		●			●		●		●		54
		●					●						223
		●					●		●				90
		●											229
							●						229
		●					●						223
	●	●					●		●				130
	●	●		●	●		●	●	●				202
	●		●		●		●		●		●		98
		●			●			●	●				134
		●					●						224
		●			●		●	●	●		●		136
●		●			●		●		●				104
		●					●		●				92
		●					●						112
		●											229
		●					●		●				224
		●			●	●				●			212

WineTrail	Winery	Chardonnay	Gewürztraminer	Pinot gris	Riesling	Sauvignon blanc	Sémillon	Viognier	White Blends	Dessert Wines
	Glencorrie									
	Gramercy Cellars									
	Isenhower Cellars									
	JLC Winery/Spofford Station						●	●		
	K Vintners	●			●			●		
	Kontos Cellars	●								
	L'Ecole Nº 41	●					●		●	●
	Le Chateau Winery	●				●			●	
	Leonetti Cellar									
	Locati Cellars			●						
	Lodmell Cellars	●				●	●			
	Long Shadows Vintners				●					
	Lowden Hills Winery				●			●		
	Mannina Cellars									
	Morrison Lane Winery							●		
	Nicholas Cole Cellars									
	Northstar Winery						●			
	Otis Kenyon Wine				●					
	Patit Creek Cellars	●			●					●
	Patrick M. Paul Vineyards									●
	Pepper Bridge Winery									
	Rasa Vineyards									
	Reininger Winery						●		●	
	Revelry Vintners	●								
	Reynvaan Family Cellars									
	Robison Ranch Cellars						●	●		
	Rôtie Cellars								●	
	Rulo Winery	●						●	●	
	Russell Creek Winery									
	Sapolil Cellars	●								
	Sapphire Mountain Cellars	●								
	Saviah Cellars	●				●	●		●	
	Seven Hills Winery			●	●			●		
	Skylite Cellars	●		●				●	●	●
	Sleight of Hand Cellars	●	●							
	Spring Valley Vineyard									
	Stephenson Cellars							●		

WHITES

REDS

Barbera	Cabernet franc	Cabernet sauvignon	Carménère	Grenache	Malbec	Petit verdot	Red blends	Sangiovese	Syrah	Tempranillo	Rosé	Port-style wine	Pg #
		●					●						52
									●	●			225
	●	●		●			●	●	●				204
		●	●		●	●	●		●	●	●		214
		●		●			●	●	●	●			166
	●	●			●	●	●		●				148
		●					●		●				48
	●				●		●	●					126
		●					●	●					229
●								●					70
							●		●		●		150
		●					●	●	●				225
		●					●		●				118
		●					●	●			●		138
●			●				●	●	●				108
	●	●				●	●		●				94
	●	●				●	●		●				196
		●	●		●		●		●				82
		●					●		●	●			132
	●	●					●						226
		●											198
							●		●				229
		●	●		●		●	●	●		●		56
		●					●						226
							●		●				229
						●			●		●		227
							●						86
		●					●		●		●		206
		●					●	●	●				128
							●		●				80
		●					●		●				229
	●	●			●		●		●				190
		●	●		●	●	●		●	●			72
		●			●		●		●		●		62
	●	●					●		●		●		76
	●	●			●	●	●		●				74
		●					●		●				100

WHITES

WineTrail	Winery	Chardonnay	Gewürztraminer	Pinot gris	Riesling	Sauvignon blanc	Sémillon	Viognier	White Blends	Dessert Wines
	Sweet Valley Wines							•		
	SYZYGY									
	Tamarack Cellars	•								
	Tertulia Cellars							•		•
	Thirsty Pagans									
	Three Rivers Winery	•	•		•	•				
	Tranche Cellars	•		•					•	
	Trio Vintners	•			•				•	
	Tru Cellars		•					•		
	Trust Cellars				•					
	Va Piano Vineyards					•	•			
	Walla Faces Wines									
	Walla Walla Village Winery	•	•		•					
	Walla Walla Vintners									
	Walla Walla Wine Works	•		•	•	•		•	•	•
	Waterbrook Winery	•		•	•	•			•	
	Watermill & Blue Mtn.					•		•		
	Waters Winery							•		
	Whitman Cellars				•			•		
	Woodward Canyon Winery	•			•	•				
	Zerba Cellars	•					•	•	•	•

REDS

Barbera	Cabernet franc	Cabernet sauvignon	Carménère	Grenache	Malbec	Petit verdot	Red blends	Sangiovese	Syrah	Tempranillo	Rosé	Port-style wine	Pg #
		●					●		●	●	●		78
		●					●		●				142
	●	●					●	●	●				140
		●	●		●		●		●	●	●		208
							●						229
	●	●		●	●		●		●	●	●		58
●		●					●		●				228
							●	●	●		●		102
													227
		●							●		●		210
		●					●		●				194
		●					●		●				96
	●	●					●		●				106
	●	●			●		●	●	●				170
	●	●		●		●	●	●	●	●	●		84
		●		●		●	●	●	●	●	●		50
		●					●		●				182
		●					●		●		●		192
		●					●		●			●	114
●		●					●		●				46
●	●	●			●		●	●	●	●	●		180

CAYUSE

CLOSED

CAYUSE

Get the Complete WineTrails Northwest Series!

WineTrails OF WASHINGTON

First Edition
Published December 2007
608-full color pages; 32 WineTrails; 228 wineries; 1 book
Only $19.95 plus S&H while the First Edition lasts!

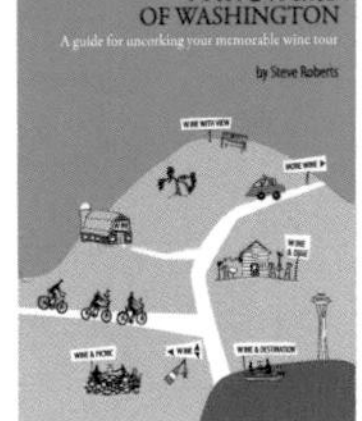

WineTrails OF OREGON

First Edition
Published 2009
Your guide to all things great about Oregon wine – travel, taste and experience.
Only $24.95 plus S&H!

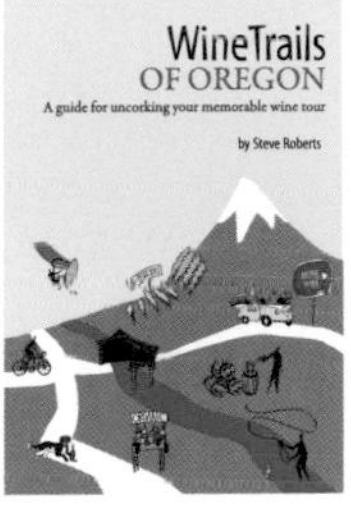

WineTrails OF IDAHO

First Edition
Published 2009
Sip and swirl through the Gem State and discover great wines!
Only $16.95 plus S&H!

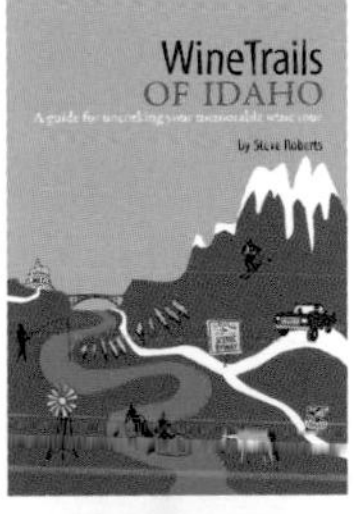

WineTrails OF WALLA WALLA

First Edition
Published 2010
Only $19.95 plus S&H!

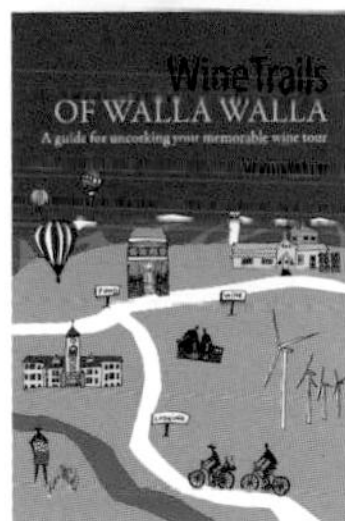

TO ORDER:
Call **800-533-6165** or order online at
www.winetrailsnw.com/shop

It's easy, it's convenient and the books are signed and personalized with your message. WineTrail guides are a great gift!

VISIT. TASTE. EXPERIENCE.

Garrison Creek Cellars

Index

The index covers locations, events, things to do, places to stay, restaurants and wineries. Cities and towns are listed in bold, while all non-winery information appears in italics. Unless otherwise indicated, wineries are located in Walla Walla and can be found individually in alphabetical order or under the city in which they belong.

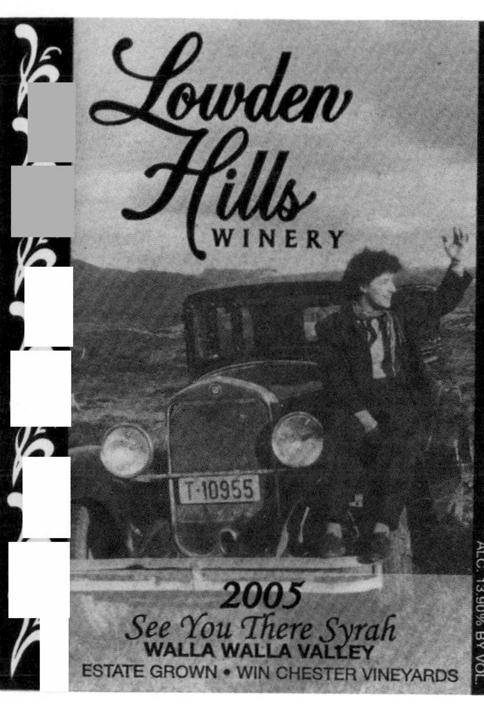

4²8

COLUMBIA VALLEY

2006

BOULEVARD

TABLE WINE

Alcohol 14.3% by volume

2007

55% GRENACHE | 35% SYRAH | 10% MOURVÈDRE

WASHINGTON STATE

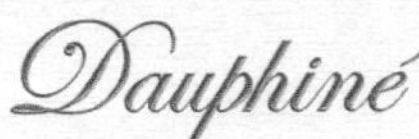

2006

WALLA WALLA VALLEY
ESTATE SYRAH

ALC. 15.4% BY VOL

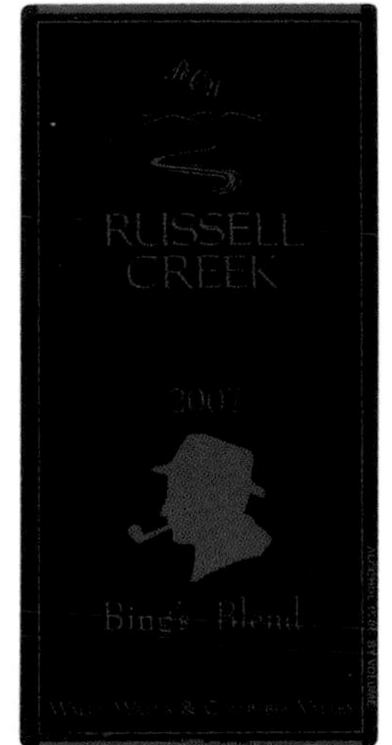

2006 Cabernet Sauvignon

Walla Walla Valley

ALCOHOL 14.2% BY VOLUME
CONTAINS SULFITES

LODMELL
CELLARS

MERLOT
Columbia Valley
2005

STEPHENSON
CELLARS

2006

WASHINGTON STATE SYRAH

ALC. 14.4% BY VOL.

2006

Edouard

de Rollat

The Finest Wine of Chateau Rollat Winery

Cabernet Sauvignon

Walla Walla Valley

14.4% ALC. BY VOL.

Tasting Notes

Tasting Notes

Caption